STAND UP
Speak Up

How Survivors Created a Movement to End Sexual Violence

TIM LENNON

Stand Up Speak Up
How Survivors Created a Movement to End Sexual Violence
By Timothy Lennon

Editor: M. Maeve Eagan
Cover and book design by Asya Blue Design

All rights reserved. No part of this publication may be reproduced, distributed, or transmitted in any form or by any means, including photocopying, recording, or other electronic or mechanical methods, without the prior written permission from the copyright owner. For permission requests, write to Tim Lennon, info@StandupSpeakup.org.

Disclaimer

The content in this book is provided for general informational and educational purposes only. It is not intended to replace professional medical, psychological, or legal advice. Readers should consult qualified professionals regarding their individual circumstances. The author and publisher assume no responsibility for any consequences arising from the use of the information contained herein. References to external sources are for informational purposes only and do not constitute endorsements. The availability of websites and contact details may change over time.

Artificial Intelligence (AI) was used to check the grammar and to obtain citations only. The text was written by the author, Timothy Lennon, without AI-generated alterations.

ISBN 979-8-9990395-0-7 Paperback
ISBN 979-8-9990395-1-4 Hardcover Dust Jacket
ISBN 979-8-9990395-3-8 Hardcover Case Laminate
ISBN 979-8-9990395-2-1 E-book

Copyright © 2025 by Timothy Lennon

Library of Congress Control Number: 2025916537

Printed in the United States of America

CONTENTS

Preface v
Chapter 1: Why Is God Doing This to Me? 1
Chapter 2: Victim to Advocate 16
Chapter 3: Survivors Step Up 26
Chapter 4: Scope of Abuse 40
Chapter 5: Why Survivors Don't Report 53
Chapter 6: Playbook of the Powerful 71
Chapter 7: Legacies of Oppression 95
Chapter 8: Privilege of Power and Power of Complicity 113
Chapter 9: Media Sounds the Alarm 128
Chapter 10: Social Media and #MeToo 147
Chapter 11: Power of Civil Society:
　　　　　　NGOs and Communities Engage 158
Chapter 12: Many Waves, One Ocean 170
Chapter 13: Coalitions, Associations, and Alliances Link Up 191
Chapter 14: Movement Engages in Politics 204
Chapter 15: Remedies & Calls to Action 226
Chapter 16: Celebrating the Future 238
Afterword 241
Endnotes 245
Acknowledgments 297
Index 303
About the Author 311

PREFACE

Survivors of sexual violence throw off the cloak of silence to challenge the cultures of subjugation and the institutions of power to build a new social movement powerful enough to change the world.

This book honors and celebrates the survivors who emerged from the shadows to create organizations and initiatives to fight back. Their activism became the foundation of the Survivors Movement.

I understand that a natural reaction to abuse may be to turn away from reading about its harsh reality; it is understandable. It's a tough topic, but this book celebrates the heroes and leaders, the survivors who are creating organizations that are changing the political and social culture of America. From cover to cover, this book celebrates the courage of leaders who stood up, fought back, and created a social and political force among thousands of activists and hundreds of organizations. This book empowers those who were harmed by arming them with analysis, historical challenges, victories, resources, and a call to action.

Survivors' activism and social media advocacy expose the scope of the previously hidden epidemic, where a fifth of the population suffers sexual abuse. Our Movement has won many battles yet continues to fight the bastions of resistance from backward social attitudes and powerful institutions.

As you turn the pages, you will see how courageous survivors have stood up, organized, and mobilized a new social movement since 2000, resulting in dramatic reforms in law, social relations, and culture. The ongoing collaboration between and among organizations follows similar social movements, such as the Women's and Civil Rights Movements. This book explores how survivors have transformed individual injury into a social and political force.

The growing influence emerged from courageous survivors who rose from past abuse to a movement where they are no longer alone, no longer victims, but advocates, leaders, and activists working for respect and dignity. Survivors have expanded political power by forming hundreds of organizations, reforming laws in dozens of states, initiating state investigations, and dominating the conversation in culture and politics.

Major exposés and scandals have hit all major institutions, as reflected in headlines nationwide, including the *Boston Globe's Spotlight* investigation, the Hollywood predators and Olympic gymnasts' scandals, the crimes of Jeffrey Epstein, and the #MeToo. Movement." Each revelation brings forward thousands of victims who were previously silent.

Survivor wins come from the tens of thousands advocating, organizing, writing, and supporting those harmed by sexual abuse, expanding our social, cultural, and political power. Survivor victories now dominate the media headlines and the message. Our decades of advocacy give us the credibility and authority to challenge any institution that relies on lies, deception, and coverups. Survivor organizations brought hope and solidarity to those harmed, signaling to those suffering in silence that we are not alone. Abuse will no longer be a topic hidden by shame and unspoken in society. Survivors are making history.

Although chapter 1 contains a caution with my story, which may cause distress to those sensitive to violence, it provides a brief background on my journey from victim at the age of twelve to world leader.

I want my book to change how we view and think of the world, leading to a transformation of society's social and political fabric. I want to empower the victim, challenge the powerful, and raise social awareness. I want to give voice to the millions of victims so that we can break free of past domination, take action, and create a world free of sexual abuse. I want to honor survivors and organizations that serve as the vanguard of this movement. We are winning the battle for justice and accountability.

PREFACE

"What I like about the idea of the movement is that when we come forward, we come forward as part of a movement, as opposed to 25–30 years ago when you came forward as an individual. Now, you can come forward as part of the movement with all that means politically and socially. And again, you're not alone." —Survivor of Michigan State University abuser, Dr. Nassar.

I'll extend to you an invitation: step forward, stand up, and speak up.

Tim Lennon
tim@standupspeakup.org

CHAPTER 1

WHY IS GOD DOING THIS TO ME?

Father Peter B. Murphy, an assistant priest at my parish, was a frequent visitor and welcomed guest in my parents' home. One evening, my father called me to join him and Murphy in my parents' bedroom. My mother was downstairs playing cards with friends. It was late, and I was already in my pajamas and ready for bed. The room was full of smoke, and both were drinking. Murphy asked my father if I could keep him company while my dad left to run an errand, maybe to buy cigarettes or more alcohol. As soon as my dad left, Murphy began to molest me. I froze. I was twelve years old.

I remained silent, bewildered, and afraid. Grabbing my hand, he guided it to fondle him, which soon led to him lying on top of me. I began to fight back and cry for help. To silence me, he smothered me with a pillow as I struggled. I couldn't breathe. My senses fled; I could no longer see, hear, or feel anything. I was mentally reeling and emotionally terrified, not understanding what was happening. I silently screamed, "Why is God doing this to me?" before I lost consciousness.

I could have died at that moment—I don't think he cared.

Fortunately, I returned to consciousness, standing in the bathroom as Father Murphy washed me down. Who knows how much later? I was in pain, hurt, confused, and disoriented. I cried all night. Even to this day, sixty years later, my younger brother Kevin, with whom I shared a bedroom, remembers me crying throughout the night, not knowing why.

Was the rape the first instance of abuse, the last, or just one of many instances? It would take fifty years before I remembered the months of molestation by Father Murphy; it would take another ten years before I remembered being raped. But to this day, the timeline of abuse remains unclear.

Father Murphy's molestations usually coincided with some activity—a trip to the movies, a neighborhood baseball game, or picnicking in the regional park. But sexual molestation was always part of the activity.

One evening, Murphy stopped by the house and chatted with my parents. He was inviting me to join him at a neighborhood softball game. As soon as I saw him at the door, I hid in the basement. I remember feeling dread and stomach-turning anxiety. Unfortunately, one of my younger brothers found my hiding place and was only too happy to announce my location. Abuse followed. Another time, he took another boy and me to the movies, alternately molesting both of us. I said nothing. I did nothing. I froze.

I was just a scared kid. I knew something was wrong, but I felt intimidated. The priest was God's representative on earth![1] He was a friend of the family—a frequent guest. I did not have the language or words to understand what was happening; I couldn't speak. My religious beliefs distorted my perception of what was happening. Permission and authority were given to the priests, not complaining children.

Corruption of Faith

On two different occasions, after molesting me, Father Murphy took me to two different priests for me to *confess* my sins while he waited. The first was another clergy pedophile, Father McFadden, a priest who I later learned had abused hundreds of children in Sioux City parishes.[2] They kept the lights dimmed as I made my confession. Father Murphy hovered at the door, just out of sight.

On the second instance of being sent to confess my sins, we had just returned from a park where Murphy had molested me. He sent me to knock on the rectory door, where an immigrant priest with few language skills answered. After I attempted to confess what happened to me (how can I confess if I don't know what I did wrong?), the priest got the gist of what I was saying and why I was there. I don't know if he was Ukrainian, Hungarian, or Russian and part of some Catholic Orthodox sect. He barely spoke English; I think that is why Murphy sent me to him. The priest sent me back to the car, where Father Murphy waited. He stood on the church steps yelling at Murphy in broken English with a marked East European accent, calling him a criminal and a coward, shaking his fist. Murphy cowered, not responding, waiting for me to get back in the car. I think in his drunken stupor, he was trying to *save my soul*. The corruption of his religious beliefs, combined with my abuse, led to the assumption that I had participated in the abuse and needed to confess. This corrupt thinking implied that my abuse was my fault—I was the sinner! There is no evidence that the two priests I confessed to reported to the bishop. If they did, the bishop did nothing.

I was a good Catholic boy, raised in a family of strong Catholic faith in an Irish neighborhood. Looking back, it's understandable that my devout faith connected the priest with God, equating Murphy as God's intermediary, acting on God's behalf. My associations with God and the priest reflected my religious training at home and in elementary school.

The months of my abuse stopped because Murphy got caught molesting another classmate from Blessed Sacrament. A parent reported to Bishop Mueller that Murphy was abusing his child, and the bishop quickly and quietly transferred Murphy out of town to another parish to escape public notice. The other priests of the parish and the nuns at the elementary school were silent, although rumors persisted amongst the school kids.

Even after the Diocese of Sioux City's Bishop Mueller transferred Murphy to another parish about two hours away, I still saw Murphy return to my neighborhood, hovering around, watching the kids, pushing me to hide, escape, and avoid any contact. The last time I saw Murphy, a few months after he was transferred, he was back in the neighborhood, sitting in his car watching a Little League baseball game in a nearby park—a predator searching for another victim. Describing child molesters as predators is accurate, as they study their prey like wild animals: hunt to find the weak, isolated, and forgotten. Seeing him made me physically sick and fearful. I made every attempt to slam an iron gate on the memories and feelings, locking them away.

Looking back, I see my emotional response involves other reactions, such as isolation and withdrawal from social life. At the time, I did not recognize how the abuse shaped my personality, and I can see how I became less confident, withdrawn, and isolated. Instead of stepping up to new adventures, I stepped back. My grades suffered.

Like many sexual predators, Father Murphy might have seen my large family of twelve children as a target, a fertile field for grooming children and potential victims. My parents were honored that a parish priest would visit our home, and my parents saw his attention to me as a special honor. Father Murphy arrived at our parish in 1959 when I was in the seventh or eighth grade at the parish elementary school, Blessed Sacrament. Murphy was an assistant at the church and an occasional teacher at the school.

When researching the circumstances of my abuse decades later, I found out that Murphy had been caught and removed from three parishes *previously* for abusing children. Bishop Mueller just *passed the trash* to my parish, part of the church hierarchy's long pattern of cover-ups. The church used a decades-long, maybe centuries-long, series of steps guiding the actions of bishops to cover up sexual abuse.[3] One such method was the transfer of abusive clergy to another parish or diocese to avoid accountability.

My hometown, Sioux City, Iowa, became known as *little Chicago* due to the large communities of Irish and Polish workers who migrated in the 1900s to work in the meat-packing plants. The after-war baby boom exploded in my Irish neighborhood: a children's playground, where families of six, eight, or ten children thrived. In the mid-fifties, children owned the streets. In the parish Catholic elementary grade school, I joined seventy other students. My musical tone-deafness freed me from the fifth-grade choir practices my classmates had to endure; however, I became an altar boy. I followed with four years of Catholic high school.

Years later, I learned that Murphy, when assigned to three parishes previously, abused boys and girls who were in their early to midteens. I found he moved on to younger children and boys each time after he got caught, possibly because younger victims were more accessible and easier to silence, and teenagers were more likely to fight back.

I remember at one of their national conferences that Phil Saviano, the leader of the Survivors Network of those Abused by Priests (SNAP), hosted a training session for leaders on how to research an abuser. One technique he suggested was to write and post short classified ads in local newspapers.[4] As part of my research on Murphy, I placed small personal ads in several local, small-town newspapers where he was assigned.[5] I simply stated, "Do you know the priest, Father Peter B. Murphy, at St. Patrick's parish from 1963 to 1965? Please contact me @ ___ email or P. O. Box_____. All information will be held in confidence." Although I did not mention abuse, I got five replies. I spoke with four victims who told similar stories of Murphy's abuse, church cover-ups, and his transfers to another parish to escape accountability. A volunteer church worker also contacted me from a small Iowa town to apologize, as she had participated in moving Murphy after the parish priest asked her to help Murphy pack and move when he was caught abusing a youth.

Buried Memories

At the time of my abuse in 1959, I remained silent. I did not say anything or tell anyone for three decades. I buried the memories, which surfaced in 1995 when I saw protesters from SNAP holding signs at the San Francisco Cathedral calling out a priest who sexually abused a child.

I was just returning to my home in the Mission District from Sunday breakfast in the North Beach area of San Francisco with my partner, Lisa. Curious, I stopped at the event and chatted with SNAP Leader Terri Light, who explained their protest against an accused priest at the Cathedral that the bishop refused to remove.

I was struck by the realization that I was sexually abused by a priest, too! That event evoked buried memories of the abuse I had suffered while I was growing up in Iowa thirty-six years earlier. I contacted Terri Light the following week, which became the first step and the start of my thirty-year commitment to participating in monthly SNAP peer support groups. Much like the support groups in Alcoholics Anonymous, which gain support and fellowship in meetings, SNAP peer support groups were, and are, crucial for my ongoing healing.

Abuse can force a victim to bury those memories as a form of self-protection, as I did for many decades. This mechanism is called dissociative amnesia, defined as "a psychological defense mechanism which, according to trauma therapists, enables people to split off painful events from conscious awareness for years."[6] Touching those painful memories is like grabbing a hot skillet without a hot pad, an event seared into your memory, forbidding any recall. Consciously and unconsciously, I buried the memories as too painful and made every attempt to forget the trauma. While burying memories can have short-term success, over time, it can rear its head and roar with suppressed emotions in vulnerable moments or when events trigger unwanted thoughts and emotions. These emotions, anger, depression, self-destruction, and grief, jump out in day-to-day events or with any related triggering stimuli. From the outside, an event, a conversation, or a news story can *trigger* a dramatic emotional response.

Challenge to the Church

Months later, after participating in SNAP support groups and public actions, I decided to *speak truth to power*. I had gained greater awareness of my abuse and the harm it created. I wrote a letter to the Diocese of Sioux City, dated February 8, 1996, about the abuse I suffered at the hands of Father Murphy. I explained that I knew he abused other children and, when caught, was sent to another parish and protected. I called him a vicious criminal.

My letter to the bishop of Sioux City described my experience.

> To Diocese of Sioux City,
>
> I was a member of Blessed Sacrament Parish and School when I was brutally assaulted and molested by Father Murphy. He was a priest at the parish and school. The molestation continued for several months. I know that he molested many other children, maybe a dozen or more. I was about ten years old or so, and probably in fifth grade—around 1957.[7]
>
> When he was discovered molesting another boy, he was transferred to another parish, and his behavior was covered up. Pity the poor parish he was transferred to—not knowing they were given a vicious criminal. After his re-assignment [to another parish in another Iowa town], I would notice him at Little League baseball games checking out the boys. How many other children did he assault and maim? How many assaults could have been avoided if the church had acted properly? Why wasn't he jailed? Why did the church cover it up? Is the preservation of the image of the institution of the church more important than the safety and well-being of children?
>
> Much of the original assault I still can't remember. What I do remember horrifies and terrorizes me. The abuse I suffered has crippled my life.
>
> I have many problems to deal with, which take time. It is

important for you to know of my experience. I also wanted you to know that your (Catholic Church) inactivity and coverup contributed to my injury and most likely placed dozens of other children at serious risk of injury. You need to do more to protect children.

You need to prosecute criminals, not hide and contribute to their continued criminal activities.

Two weeks later, the Diocese of Sioux City's chancellor acknowledged the grievous offense at the bishop's direction. He replied, in part,

Regrettably, the whole of our society for years chose to ignore the reality of this social ill. Such ignorance cannot be leveled against the church alone, for families and other social structures have experienced this pain as well, not only as structures wherein the victims of abuse exist, but the perpetrators also. . . . As to your allegation concerning Father Murphy, all I can offer to you is the information that Father Murphy died in 1980. Hence, it is impossible for us to address this matter with him. [my emphasis].

There was no apology or expressions of sympathy. There were no offers of support or messages of "How can we help?" Hammering home their disinterest, they said starkly that Father Murphy had died. The chancellor did not admit or explain the three previous transfers from parishes after accusations by other victims. My abuse stopped when he got caught abusing another child and was transferred the fourth time.

The church replied to my letter with evasion: "The whole of our society for years chose to ignore the reality" of sexual abuse. The church took no responsibility for transferring a child sexual predator to four parishes to hide sexual abuse from the police and the parishioners! They deflected accountability, suggesting that the families and society were equally responsible, not the church.

The abuse was, at best, ignored by bishops and brother priests. It suggests complicity on the part of some and avoidance on the part of others. Looking back on my abuse in 1960, I was alone, facing a predator revered as a holy person. I had no options or hope. When I wrote to Bishop Mueller of the Diocese of Sioux City in 1996, I wrote: "Much of the original assault I still can't remember." I knew frightening memories were buried.

Memories Emerge

New memories of my abuse were brought to the surface in 2008. My twin daughters were ten years old and moving from grade school to middle school. That event evoked previously suppressed memories of the violent rape from forty-eight years earlier. I was sixty-one.[8] All the terrifying memories of the rape that I had buried for fifty years emerged in a flood of anger and sadness that overwhelmed me. I was devastated.

The inspirational then-SNAP leader, David Clohessy, once said to me, "We come into painful buried memories when we have the strength to face them." It took me fifty years to gain the strength to face those painful memories. To this day, episodes of deep sadness sometimes overtake me as I understand how that abuse shattered many childhood dreams and caused long-term emotional and psychological harm. I continue to be challenged with low self-esteem, social anxiety, and depression.

Understanding and becoming conscious of the harm inflicted on me caused severe post-traumatic stress disorder (PTSD), which I call *the troubles*. I looked at my twin daughters growing up and was crushed. How could anyone harm a child? The memories destroyed my whole being, renewing the fear, horror, and anguish I felt when I was a child.

The new revelations reopened a wound. . . . I cried and cried. Social anxiety made it difficult to interact with others. I was barely able to function. I suffered months of depression, anxiety, nightmares, and a whole parcel of PTSD symptoms. I came to understand how the trauma had crippled me. I am fortunate to be here, as many victims of sexual violence do not survive. I survived—I am a survivor.

I received complete support from my wife and children throughout this time. They endured my bouts of crying, outbursts of anger, a swamp of social anxiety, and waves of depression. I would not be here without their support.

Challenging the Bishop

Two decades after my first letter to the bishop of Sioux City in 1996, I felt strong enough to write to the current bishop of the Diocese of Sioux City, Bishop Nickless, in 2016, requesting a meeting. I referenced the previous communication I wrote in 1996 and the deplorable reply I received from the previous bishop. A meeting was arranged, and I returned to Iowa to confront the bishop. My daughter Fiona accompanied me and acted as my supporter, witness, and advocate. She did not bear the burden I carried and continually challenged Bishop Nickless on the cover-ups by calling out his evasions and omissions and noting many previous church failures.

The bishop brought his lawyer, who defended him like a football tackle defends the quarterback. Any hesitation by the bishop was a signal for the attorney to jump in to divert from the topic and push away questions about the bishop's and the church's accountability. I benefited from the meeting as I spoke up to define my life after burying memories for decades. My meeting was a brave act; it was my *speaking truth to power* moment.

My daughter's advocacy during the meeting with the bishop gave me great support. She was not intimidated by his status and position. Days after that meeting in Iowa, my daughter wrote a long letter to the bishop detailing many conflicts and issues left unsaid.[9] Her last question addresses the safety of children:

> My last question to you is, how can you represent a religion that for centuries has lied to the very people who worship you and fail to protect the very children you call holy?

Bishop Nickless's reply was a note to me suggesting that my daughter no longer correspond with him! Evidently, he found my daughter's challenge troubling. Her question went unaddressed, a question that continues to be ignored by the hierarchy of the Catholic Church.

When I first contacted the previous bishop by mail twenty years earlier, I was just beginning my journey; I had little ability or experience in public speaking. By 2016, I had years of experience with SNAP events and press conferences. I had been active in organizing and participating in dozens of public events, outing clergy predators, and protesting the church's indifference.

The meeting with the bishop in 2016 was an opportunity to return home to Iowa to conduct media interviews and press events. I initiated a press conference and requested news interviews with media organizations in Sioux City, leading to several interviews and front-page coverage in the Sunday paper. I held press conferences and received media in the surrounding areas: Des Moines, Iowa; Sioux Falls, South Dakota; and Omaha, Nebraska.

When my story became public, I spoke with more classmates who shared stories of Murphy sneaking into homes uninvited and climbing into their beds. Fifty years after the abuse, there were fifty years of silence. As a result of the media coverage, I discovered Murphy also abused fifteen of my school classmates.[10]

Paths of Healing

I had carried the weight of the effects of PTSD for fifty years without being fully aware of its impact. I sought professional help, leading to my engagement with therapists. I found the most helpful therapy was eye movement desensitization and reprocessing (EMDR).[11] This therapy brought forward memories locked away for decades. Memories that continue to frighten me today. I had to relive the memories of the trauma and the overwhelming fear sparked by that trauma, abuse, and near-death. EMDR became a constant battle between dredging up dreadful memories and understanding how raising these memories helps me heal.

EMDR therapy brought memories to the surface to incorporate those violent incidents as part of my life. I had to muster every bit of my courage to bring memories forward. The object was to make those buried memories part of my whole self, my true self. As horrible and scary as they were, they are part of who I am. I could now move forward without having past tragedies emerge as triggers controlling my actions. I moved from victim to survivor, where I began to decide my future. I consider EMDR therapy the most courageous thing I have ever done.

My path of healing rests upon four elements:

- I have been blessed with the support of those closest to me: my twin daughters, Fiona and Maya, family, friends, and fellow advocates. Their support demonstrates I am not alone.
- Thirty years of monthly participation in SNAP peer support groups keep me on a path of healing. This ongoing peer support keeps me alive.
- Professional therapy enabled me to confront the past and control my future. I am fortunate that I had this resource, as not all survivors receive such support.
- Engaging in activism and fighting back through advocacy.

Taking action removes the burden of being a victim and enables me to fight back and control my life.

When talking with my daughter Maya, I mentioned that I had not come into my true self until I was sixty-three. Her reply was, "At least you got there!". True that.

Righteous Anger

What happened to me should not happen to another child. As I came to understand the harm I suffered, I also grew angrier that Bishop Mueller knew Murphy was a child abuser. That anger fueled my thirty years of activism and advocacy. I make no excuse for this powerful emotion as it helps me push forward even when faced with seemingly insurmountable obstacles, including legacies of oppression, institutions of power, and ideologies of influence.[12] I am fighting against institutions, ingrained cultures, and legacies that exploit victims.[13]

Misdirected anger can be self-destructive or cause harm to others. Many sexual violence victims carry a great deal of anger, leading some to a troubled life. Statistics show that 75 percent of male prisoners were victims of child abuse.[14]

Using anger in service to a righteous cause can serve to right the wrongs, hold predators accountable, and prevent future crimes. Like many (maybe all) survivors, I carry the burden of many symptoms of PTSD; anger is the emotion that helps me get up in the morning, face day-to-day challenges, and gives me the energy to battle back. As victims raised accusations, public protests were held in front of the churches to call out the accused clergy. These protests attracted the media, leading to other victims stepping forward and acknowledging abuse by the same accused clergy. Sometimes, civil lawsuits by victims against the church led to events expressing support and solidarity with the victims, which generated more support.

While SNAP was headquartered in Chicago, I also volunteered as a national online correspondent from 2010 to 2018. My principal responsibility was responding to the thousands of emails SNAP received nationwide. Over those eight years, I corresponded with thousands of survivors, connecting with dozens monthly via phone and email. I provided support and resources, often referring victims to 140 local and national SNAP leaders scattered across the nation. I embraced the volunteer work to fight back and focus my anger on positive actions.

I joined the SNAP Board of Directors in 2010 and served on the board until 2021. From 2018 to 2021, I served as president of the board of directors. One of the first actions I organized was an international event, *All Survivors Day*, to celebrate those who took action to heal, those working to hold predators accountable, and those advocating to prevent future abuse. Over thirty actions occurred in the USA and fourteen events in six nations overseas.

As president of SNAP, I made two trips to Rome to appeal to the Pope and the Vatican to call attention to the inaction of the Vatican in 2019 and 2021. Joining other survivors, we called on the Vatican to protect the vulnerable, hold predators accountable, help survivors, open the secret files on clergy predators, and heal the wounded. Both these visits coincided with the Pope's formation of a council that was supposed to address sexual violence in Catholic communities. In both cases, the Pope's council fell apart when civilian members stepped down due to the ineffectiveness of Vatican initiatives.

After stepping down as president of the SNAP board, I initiated a new project: a book on the emergence of the survivors' movement. The first step was to develop a website to anchor my ongoing advocacy and a resource for those harmed. In 2022, I created the website *StandupSpeakup.org* to provide information, resources, links, and helpful documentation for abuse survivors. My volunteer work with SNAP began a decades-long commitment to helping victims get help and support. Even though I stepped away from national leadership, I continued my role as a local SNAP leader in Tucson, Arizona, when I moved there in 2016. I joined Vickie Jahaske as coleader in a SNAP support group and as the leader of SNAP in Arizona. We sponsored monthly support groups, initiated local press events, and engaged in political advocacy on issues concerning survivors—and we still do.

Connecting Worldwide

My work introduced me to a worldwide network of survivor leaders engaged in educating, organizing, and mobilizing a new social movement of survivors. I was no longer alone. The following chapters highlight the leaders and organizations doing the work.

My journey as an activist began with support groups and local advocacy, which led to working as part of a national organization. I began to engage with the wider community of activists nationwide. I started to understand that my abuse was tied to a crisis that needed to be addressed worldwide, leading to more and more connections with other advocates, as we explore in the next chapter.

CHAPTER 2

VICTIM TO ADVOCATE

First Public Steps

My first public action as an advocate was holding a sign in front of a church in Santa Rosa, California, along with four other survivors from SNAP, to call attention to a priest in the parish accused of abusing a child. As we waited for the parishioners to finish Sunday mass, I felt uneasy, embarrassed, self-conscious, and awkward. On the other hand, I was buoyed by the presence of other survivors who bolstered my confidence.

By the end of the event, I felt like a burden had been lifted. I was fighting back, an action I could not do as a child. I also felt a sense of power and confidence, standing with other survivors, knowing I was not alone.

Typically, in the mid-1990s, during a protest in front of a church, we held simple signs naming the accused predator and calling for justice. Some of us held 5 x 7-inch photos of ourselves at the age of our abuse. We wanted to make a human connection and establish our credibility with the parishioners while warning them of an accused sexual predator serving in their parish.

Initially, as a victim, I was fearful of speaking up. I slowly shared bits and pieces of my story at support group meetings, and over time, I found courage and became more confident. After many months of participation in support groups, I was ready to share with my family and friends and eventually at public events. Each event bolstered my confidence and made telling my story in public easier. Speaking out about my abuse felt empowering. I moved from feeling like a victim . . . to a survivor who understood the abuse was not my fault . . . to an advocate who initiated events.

Typically, our local San Francisco Bay Area SNAP group held events protesting clergy abuse on the front steps of the San Francisco Cathedral, the Cathedral of Christ the Light—as well as churches in Oakland and Napa Valley, and nearby parishes in Silicon Valley. Due to the large urban population, there were many advocates and supporters to mobilize.

During those early days 1995, parishioners coming out of Sunday mass were in disbelief that their *nice, religious parish priest* was accused of abuse. It was not uncommon for parishioners to accuse us of being *Catholic haters* and *agents of Satan*, among other insults. Occasionally, it led to pushing and shoving as they passed. A parish priest appeared more than once, calling us out and shaking his fist. Times change. . . . By 2010, during an event after mass in San Francisco, parishioners passed without comment; by then, they knew of the widespread abuse in the church.

Looking back, I think those first public events were important for me to understand that I was a victim and not at fault for the abuse. For so long, I had buried the injuries I suffered: Shame, guilt, and low self-esteem were burdens that I carried for decades—a backpack of rocks would have been a lighter load. Telling my family and friends gave me the confidence to come forward. Each public event became a step in presenting myself as a survivor, leading to more confidence in sharing more of my story.

Volunteering to Support

After retiring from my job, I stepped up my engagement with SNAP to work full-time as a volunteer, acting as a correspondent for eight years and responding to emails sent to the national office.[15]

I communicated with dozens of survivors monthly via phone and email who were asking for support. Victims were often prompted to reach out after a local SNAP leader held a press conference. Victims stepped forward to say they were abused as well, a kind of *Me Too* moment before the 2017 *Me Too* tweet. When doing phone support, I got calls from a diversity of survivors—men and women of all ages. One time, I received a call from a survivor from North Dakota who shared his story of being abused by the parish priest when he was a child. He said he was eighty-four years old; notice of a nearby SNAP event prompted him to call. He thought he was the only one and had never shared his story previously.

Many victims think that they are the only ones; too many believe it is their fault. Abuse by a family member, priest, neighbor, or coach happens in secret. A victim sees and experiences the abuse as an action of an individual devoid of any social context. From the outside, we know, statistically, that most sexual predators abuse dozens of victims. It's easy to understand how victims think they are the only ones. When a predator is exposed, the cover of authority, prestige, and position is lifted, and victims come to understand that they are not the only ones.

As a volunteer, I passed comments and questions to national leadership and, in other cases, referred victims to one of the local SNAP leaders. Some wanted to share their story and be heard, leading to long phone conversations. Over time, I communicated with thousands of survivors, providing support and sharing resources, often referring victims to the hundreds of local and national leaders scattered across the nation.

I embraced volunteer work as a means to focus my anger on positive actions to fight back as an active agent. It enabled me to decide my own life and not let the past control my future. I volunteered in the national office from 2010 to 2018, was a member of the board of directors from 2010 to 2021, and served as president of the board from 2018 to 2021, briefly serving as temporary executive director from March to October 2018.

My journey as an advocate began slowly, but over the thirty years of sharing my story and explaining my history of abuse, it became easier to make public statements. Over time, I participated in over 200 media interviews, including interviews originating in seventeen countries.[16]

SNAP Origin

SNAP was founded in 1988 by Barbara Blaine to bring together survivors of abuse in the Catholic Church. Blaine grew up in a Catholic family and neighborhood in Toledo, Ohio, where she volunteered with other young girls at the church, caring for the altar and displays. In 1969, when Blaine was thirteen years old, a parish priest named Rev. Chet Warren began sexually abusing her and continued over the next four years. She did not report it to her parents, school, or therapist.[17]

Sixteen years later, in 1985, Blaine was living in Chicago when she read a series of articles in the *National Catholic Reporter* by Jason Berry, who exposed Rev. Gilbert Gauthe, a priest who abused dozens of children in Louisiana.[18] Blaine recognized she was not alone as a victim, reached out to others, and found many other victims of Catholic abuse and coverup. As a community organizer for Catholic Charities of the Archdiocese of Chicago, she had years of experience and transitioned to organizing survivors.

Blaine called on friends, coworkers, and community members to organize a community of mutual support. She and early organizers placed small, two-sentence announcements in local papers announcing support groups in cities around the United States. These initial steps of contacting local support groups soon expanded to a dozen support groups nationwide. This spontaneous success signaled a hidden population of survivors looking for help. Blaine spent the next thirty years building SNAP and advocating for clergy abuse survivors. This success set the stage for the creation of SNAP in 1988.

The *National Catholic Reporter* later quoted Blaine. "I didn't, at that point, understand that what had happened to me was really abuse. I just knew that whatever had happened between me and Warren was obviously causing this response . . . it was post-traumatic stress disorder."[19]

According to *the New York Times*, "Mr. Berry's articles helped her realize that the priest's actions had been a crime and that she (Blaine) was not at fault."[20]

Blaine wrote to her parish bishop, Bishop Hoffman, requesting acknowledgment, accountability, and action against the priest who abused her but received none. The church remained silent. Fueled by the church's ongoing refusal to respond, Blaine took action. Using her background as an advocate at the National Catholic Worker Movement, she reached out to other victims and began speaking out. Eventually, over a dozen more victims of Rev. Warren stepped forward.[21]

The support groups started by Blaine quickly grew into a national network of thousands of survivors. In an interview with the *Toledo City Paper*, Blaine spoke about SNAP's growth, which grew through small ads and word of mouth. "We'd spent so many years thinking we were the only ones—it was really affirming and consoling once we found other people."[22]

Only when Blaine was ready to name Father Warren on the *Oprah Winfrey Show* did the church hierarchy remove him from public ministry, keeping him from offering Catholic Mass in public, but Warren still served as a priest with all the privileges of a priest.[23] Eleven additional victims accused Warren of abuse, yet he was never defrocked or removed from the priesthood.[24]

Blaine inspired victims of the Catholic Church to begin the transformation into survivors, raise awareness, and compel action on a global scale to prevent future abuse. Her work extended SNAP's ability to reach clergy abuse victims. SNAP continues thirty-five years later as one of the most prominent survivor organizations in the world, with tens of thousands of members in the United States, Canada, and sixty other countries. About fifty support groups meet monthly, with over a hundred SNAP leaders in the USA and seven other countries.[25]

SNAP's executive director, David Clohessy, organized public actions for twenty years and fired up the media with impassioned press releases.

This brought forth more survivors who publicly shared their stories and served as a beacon for victims still in the dark. Heroes arose, morphing from victims to activists. Clohessy would train us at our annual leader meetings, having each of us practice mock media interviews. All of us were amateurs. The practice bolstered our confidence in initiating press events in dozens of cities nationwide.

Phil Saviano and *Spotlight*

Phil Saviano, a local SNAP leader from Boston, compiled a work history of Father David Holley, the priest who abused him. He discovered Holley's pattern of getting caught and transferred to escape accountability. Saviano also investigated and documented a dozen other Archdiocese of Boston priests who had been identified as predators. Similar to the numerous transfers of Fr. Holley, he saw the pattern of accused priests being transferred after getting caught for child abuse.

Saviano was 12 years old when Fr. Holley began sexually abusing him in 1964. "Like a good Catholic boy, I obeyed. And then I went to confession," he told an audience at a Voice of the Faithful Conference thirty-eight years later.[26] Like many survivors, Saviano tried to remain faithful to the Catholic Church.

As an adult, Saviano brought his complaint to the church, which rejected him. He publicly challenged the Catholic Archdiocese of Boston and Cardinal Bernard Francis Law in the media for ignoring his letters. In 1996, after a relentless pursuit of justice, Saviano received a financial settlement from the church but refused to stay silent. Until 2002, the practice of requiring nondisclosure agreements (NDA) was a common practice as a means of hiding clergy abuse.

"I became the first person that I know of to settle one of these sexual abuse lawsuits and maintain my ability to talk about the case," Saviano said.[27] He never received an apology from the church.

In one moment, Phil Saviano forged a path that would change the course of history. Mainstream media had little interest in his research of clergy sex abusers until he went to the *Boston Globe* with stacks of documentation and shared evidence of his abuser and others in the local church. The information stunned the reporters. Pulitzer Prize-winning reporter Mike Rezendes said that his four-hour conversation with Saviano was "a graduate-level seminar in clergy abuse." [28]

Saviano acknowledged the dramatic response by victims to the *Globe* newspaper series in a 2002 speech. "Just six months ago, I might have begun these remarks by saying that I am speaking on behalf of other victims of clergy sexual abuse. But I don't do that anymore. That's because, lately, victims have been speaking up for themselves."[29]

Cardinals, serving as the "Princes of the Church," are the global leaders of the church, the highest rank under the Pope.[30] The *Spotlight* investigation exposed Cardinal Law of the Archdiocese of Boston, who covered up the abuse of children by clergy for many years. Cardinal Law was subpoenaed to appear before a state grand jury but fled to the Vatican to escape accountability, where he received refuge.[31]

The Vatican acts as a government agency for the Catholic Church, running the day-to-day business of the largest institution in the world. It also functions as the ideological center, directing the faith and the faithful. The Vatican rewarded Cardinal Law with a powerful position in Rome until his death fifteen years later, providing a safe haven for a predator complicit in covering up the abuse of hundreds of children in the Boston area.[32]

No Longer Silent

Previously, survivors faced predators and institutions as individuals, thinking they were the only victims or that it was their fault. The imbalance of power and threats of intimidation hid the ocean of victims who remained silent.

The emergence of victims as activists and advocates signifies a shift in response to survivors coming forward. While there was just a seed of scattered survivor organizations at the turn of the century, a torrent of organizations, coalitions, associations, and social media initiatives multiplied over the following twenty-five years.

Media exposure reveals all that was previously hidden. Each revelation raised community awareness and social activism. For many parishioners, the exposure of church complicity in abuse in grand jury reports and media stories caused a rupture in faith and, as time passed, a dramatic reduction in church attendance. The public challenged the church, calling for an end to secrecy and silence. Yet today, cover-ups of sexual abuse by clergy continue.[33]

According to one accused child predator, Catholic Priest Lawrence Hecker: "It wasn't a big deal in those days [to abuse boys]. [. . .] Asked if archdiocesan officials were aware, Hecker said: 'Yeah, they knew.'"[34] A 2011 memo written by a nun serving as Aymond's abuse Victims Assistance Coordinator informed the archbishop that Hecker "was known among . . . boys as a predator."[35]

Louisiana state authorities suspected a larger problem of trafficking due to extensive complaints, investigating whether the church operated a child trafficking ring responsible for "widespread sexual abuse of minors dating back decades" that was "covered up and not reported to law enforcement."[36]

In 2018, still reeling from #MeToo's tidal wave of solidarity, new accusations against the church exposed dramatic abuse at hundreds of parishes in Pennsylvania. The Pennsylvania Grand Jury report investigated six dioceses in 2018, exposing widespread abuse by clergy and further documenting complicity, cover-ups, and payoff schemes. The report revealed the actions of the hierarchy and bishop of the Diocese of Altoona-Johnston, especially their scheme to pay off victims for silence.[37] Reaching a nationwide audience, it led many parishioners to leave the church.

The church, the largest institution in the world, with its tremendous power, could not stop the bleeding from the *Spotlight* investigation, the Altoona-Johnston Grand Jury report, and media investigations.[38] *CNN* reported on a Gallup survey that showed by 2019, a third of parishioners questioned their faith in the Catholic Church due to this exposure of clergy sexual abuse.[39]

The Catholic Church, as an institution, stood at the forefront of its documented history of complicity in covering up sexual abuse. This institution protected its power and prestige at the expense of victims. While the church highlights its moral authority, at the same time, it goes to great efforts to hide the stain of widespread clergy abuse. Similar efforts of denial and coverup are made in all sectors of society, most notably in those revered institutions of high public esteem, such as the Boy Scouts, universities, entertainment industries, government, medical practices, team sports, and the Olympic Committee.

Predators gravitate to those institutions that provide access to potential victims. Dominant institutions also create conditions of vulnerability to exploit opportunities, as in the following cases: unequal power differences (bosses, coaches, doctors, etc.), revered authority (parents, teachers, priests, ministers, etc.), and social power (money, Hollywood, status). They may present themselves as a moral authority due to their position and high social status. We see sexual abuse across the spectrum of revered American institutions.

Public awareness fueled social and political action, cascading with the formation of a survivors' movement. This movement was bolstered by hundreds of survivor organizations, thousands of initiatives, dozens of diverse coalitions, and a host of spirited political interventions. The movement challenged legacies and institutions imprisoned by old ideas and practices. Millions of social media posts and blogs added to the social foundation of the movement by addressing all sectors of society with programs to prevent, advocate, politically intervene, embrace healing, raise social awareness, and create resources for survivors. Survivors of sexual abuse have emerged from silence and exploitation to build a powerful new social movement through these organizations, initiatives, coalitions, and political interventions.

Courageous survivors have organized to direct conversations, determine agendas, and formulate strategies. They no longer remain in the background, waiting for others to act. The formation of each new survivor organization becomes a rallying point that prompts others to join. Encouraging solidarity, connection, and social action between and among survivors enables us to step out of the darkness to name the crimes and the criminals. Our collective strength challenges the powers of privilege and exploitation in all sectors of society: political, cultural, and social.

Leaders continue to emerge, working to end sexual violence in all sectors of society. Some of these leaders, who stepped up, organized, and created survivor organizations, share their journey in the following chapter.

CHAPTER 3

SURVIVORS STEP UP

"The answer is simple: I believe truth is a moral force in the universe. By speaking truth out loud, we refuse complicity with falsity, injustice, and oppression. By speaking the truth out loud, we affirm the human dignity of those who have been abused within this faith group—abused not only by the sexual violence of pastors but also by the gaslighting, coverups, duplicity, and disparagement of so many others in SBC leadership."[40]

Christa Brown, a survivor of sexual abuse, described her passion for speaking the truth as she addressed clergy abuse in the Southern Baptist Convention (SBC) community.[41] She was quoted in a December 3, 2023, post by the Baptist advocacy group Together We Heal.

Brown founded the organization Stop Baptist Predators website in 2006, the first effort to address clergy abuse in the Baptist community. Brown is also the author of *Baptistland: A Memoir of Abuse, Betrayal, and Transformation*, a memoir sharing her life and experience of sexual abuse in a Southern Baptist church in Texas. Brown stood up and spoke out, becoming a leader in the community, calling out predators and complicit churches who covered for them.[42]

After writing an op-ed for the *Dallas Morning News*, Brown said survivors flooded her inbox with similar stories. "That's when I knew that my story was, tragically, quite common."[43]

In my correspondence with Brown, she provided context and background: "Immediately after that 2006 *Dallas Morning News* op-ed was when I began keeping an online list of convicted and credibly accused Baptist clergy sex abusers, with names drawn from public documents. In six years' time, I gathered the names of 170 Southern Baptist pastors in my database. [. . .] Meanwhile I worked at documenting the extent of the problem, deciding that if the southern Baptist convention wouldn't keep a database on their abusive clergy, then I would keep one for them—to at least show it could be done and to get past the incessant reflections of those who insisted that Baptist cases were 'just isolated incidents.'[44] It was also important because it laid a foundation for the *Houston Chronicle*'s 'Abuse of Faith' exposé in 2019, in which they put together a database of 380 abusive Baptist pastors over 20 years, which included most of the names on my prior list."[45]

A 2019 landmark investigation by the *Houston Chronicle* and *San Antonio Express-News* into sexual abuse in Southern Baptist churches displayed headshots and mugshots of ministers and religious leaders who'd been accused of abusing 700 victims over twenty years.[46] The series provided an unprecedented look at sexual misconduct across the denomination, detailing allegations against 380 church leaders in twenty states.

Courage, Secrecy, and Power

Andrea Constand didn't know that actor and comedian Bill Cosby had sexually assaulted other women when she went to the police in 2005. Constand suffered severe PTSD symptoms, including a deep sense of isolation, after Cosby drugged and raped her. Yet she was not the first or last to be drugged by Cosby. The drugging of victims to facilitate rape became so common it created a new word, *roofie*, which is a slang term that describes the secret drugging of an unsuspecting victim to facilitate rape.[47]

Cosby was still known as *America's Dad* when he was Constand's mentor at Temple University. She came forward publicly after sharing her experience with her family because she felt "believed" and "it was the right thing to do."[48]

When I interviewed Constand in January 2022, she felt she had "no choice" in stepping forward as an activist. She shared two driving forces for her advocacy: turning the negative into a positive and channeling "all the pain, all the trauma, all the tragedy, and discomforts to help someone else."[49] Many survivors consider her the *Joan of Arc* in the case against Bill Cosby for her courage in taking on a powerful Hollywood actor.

Constand's signing an NDA was part of the settlement in her civil case against Cosby, which she filed after Montgomery County DA Bruce Castor dropped her criminal case in 2005 for "lack of evidence."[50]

In her book, *The Moment: Standing Up to Bill Cosby, Speaking Up for Women*, she shared her journey from victim to survivor.[51] Constand wrote, "When I filed suit against him in civil court, I thought I would be heard and empowered by that honesty. But the NDA meant that I returned home with an even bigger secret than the one I had left Philadelphia in the first place. If I said even a single word to anyone about the most defining moment in my life, I could be sued."[52]

That experience left Constand feeling guarded, "having to watch what I said and shared—left me feeling profoundly alone."[53]

Nonetheless, the attention raised by Constand's case prompted other victims to step forward. "I think about the Jane Does who came out in 2004 and 2005 and what those women meant to me. Those women were a survivors' movement. Then, in 2014, another 20 to 40 women came out of the woodwork, which eventually led to 'Me Too'; that's when I felt the Movement. You could feel the momentum of people saying, 'It didn't only happen to Andrea, but it happened to me too.'"[54]

In our interview, Constand focused on her healing journey from victim to survivor. "My passion, enthusiasm, and inspiration are about becoming whole again and what that means—to go from being a victim to a survivor."[55] She believes that healing is the most important element of her journey. "When something is taken away from you as a victim, you were whole before, but then you're fractured. We all want to be whole."[56]

An Army of Survivors

A new storm of accusations against public figures hit when gymnast Rachael Denhollander stepped forward in 2016, accusing Michigan State University (MSU) and U.S. Olympic team coach Dr. Larry Nassar of sexual abuse in an interview with the *Indianapolis Star* newspaper.[57] The CBS program "60 Minutes" followed the story, gaining a broader audience. Denhollander spoke about the university's evasion of many previous accusations, which prompted her to contact the media. "And the reason everyone who heard about Nassar's abuse did not believe it is because they did not listen. They did not listen in 1997, 1998, 1999, 2000, 2004, or 2014. No one knew, according to your definition of knowing, because no one handled the reports of abuse properly."[58]

Despite multiple accusations of abuse against Nassar as early as 1994, MSU officials dismissed victims, ignored complaints, failed to notify police, and instead *filed them away* as hearsay to protect the prominent athletic physician. The police declined to charge Nassar. Instead, in 2012, he was inducted into the USA Gymnastics Hall of Fame and officially cleared by an MSU investigation in 2014.

Criminal charges were eventually brought against Nassar for his abuse of Denhollander in July 2017.[59] Her courage helped break the silence around Nassar, empowering over 500 more victims to step forward.[60]

Years later, Denhollander spoke at Nassar's sentencing hearing, calling out the complicity of the institutions that protected him, including MSU, the federation, and the Olympic Committee. Her victim impact statement, asking, "How much is a little girl worth?" became a call to action for other survivors. "I was wrong in my third belief—that surely if someone had been made aware of what Larry was doing, they would report it, and ensure it was legitimate before ever allowing him near another child."[61]

Several institutions, including Michigan State administrators, Olympic Committee leaders, and government agencies, failed to act. The FBI received reports of abuse but falsified documents to sidetrack the investigation. In a 2024 *Associated Press* article, Attorney John Manly, who represented over two dozen of Nassar's victims, commented on a U.S. Justice Department audit report of the FBI's handling of child sex offenses. "This report makes clear that the FBI is simply not doing its job when it comes to protecting our children from the monsters among us who stalk them."[62]

Olympic Gymnast McKayla Maroney emphasized the problem in a 2024 interview with *USA Today*. "After telling my entire story of abuse to the FBI in the summer of 2015, not only did the FBI not report my abuse, but when they eventually documented my report 17 months later, they made entirely false claims about what I said."[63]

In 2018, Denhollander joined other gymnasts and athletes to establish The Army of Survivors. This nonprofit advocacy organization brings "awareness, accountability, and transparency to sexual violence against athletes at all levels."[64] Their programs include advocacy in the legislative sphere to reform laws, develop programs that raise community awareness of team sports, and institute best practices and policies to safeguard athletes. The Army of Survivors establishes training and curricula to ensure safeguarding within athletics, uniting athletes across a national network to foster mutual support and collaboration.

Dr. Larry Nassar was an athletic doctor at MSU State University and the team doctor for the USA Olympic Gymnastics from 1986 until 2016. He used many mechanisms similar to the "playbook" used by the church, preying on hundreds of young women and girls and gaining national notoriety as a prolific sexual predator.[65]

Brave Gymnasts Who Stepped Forward

Sarah Klein was a gymnast at MSU when Nassar abused her, initially testifying anonymously at his trial and providing a victim statement as Jane Doe #125.[66]

Later, Olympian teammates asked Klein to accept the Arthur Ashe Award for Courage at the Excellence in Sports Performance Yearly

(EPSY) Awards, given to recognize individual and team athletic achievement, on behalf of two hundred athletes. "Make no mistake," Klein said. "We are here on this stage to present an image for the world to see, a portrait of survival, a new vision of courage . . . telling our stories of abuse over and over and over again in graphic detail is not easy. We're sacrificing privacy, being judged and scrutinized, and it's grueling and painful, but it is time."[67]

Klein suggested a course of action. "We must start caring about children's safety more than we care about adults' reputations."[68] Klein said she was initially reluctant to accept this honor due to her previous anonymity.[69] However, she realized she was not receiving the award as a victim, but rather because she was brave. In 2022, I had the opportunity to interview her, and she described coming forward publicly as "a moment in time where nothing is ever going to be the same after."[70] But she was inspired to be an advocate for survivors. "When I did that speech, it was like, not only do I have a voice for myself, but I have a voice for everyone if I choose to use it now. I've been gifted that again and again. And when I realized I can't just go back to hiding after this, I realized I could do it well, and it was almost like it all made sense."[71]

Klein recalled her experience at the ESPY Awards. "I thought, I can do this. Because I am still standing, and I did survive. And I did survive for some reason, unbeknownst to me, and I still can't tell you how I got through a lot because I shouldn't still be standing and educated as a lawyer with two beautiful kids. Everything went wrong. But somehow, it went so right."[72]

She emphasized the profound impact of her advocacy by "giving meaning to that suffering and giving meaning to what happened to me and what was taken from me."[73]

In January 2018, a judge sentenced Nassar to 40 to 175 years in prison.[74] Subsequent lawsuits against MSU demanded accountability for ignoring many years of reports of Nassar's abuse. Like the church, the university hierarchy was more concerned about status, power, and prestige than Nassar's victims.[75]

In our conversation, Klein reflected on her recovery and advocacy work. "It's always been a couple of steps forward and ten steps back, just something I got used to."[76] She started a podcast addressing social justice issues with leaders, advocates, and activists.[77] Klein refers to her podcast, "Our Fights" [Apple Podcasts], as an effort to make sure we all recognize that we're in this together despite the various circumstances where our age, genders, and where we grew up are all different. Despite the disparity of backgrounds, our circumstances are "really, really similar."

As an attorney, she now fights for survivors in court and points to the limitations in achieving justice due to insufficient evidence or evasions of accountability. Klein explained that advocacy revolves around the law and making sure the law gives every survivor a chance. She celebrates the courage of survivors who stepped forward to share their stories and help other victims. Klein feels like "it's a badge of honor because you went through something you never deserved, and you're still standing."[78]

Klein emphasized the growing power of solidarity and building a new social movement of survivors that created amazing change through public disclosure. Simply talking about topics never discussed publicly has been powerful. "I'm really proud to be part of it."[79]

Nomi Abadi—A Musician Shares Her Story

In February 2022, I interviewed composer, pianist, and singer Nomi Abadi, the founder and president of the Female Composer Safety League, an organization supporting women in the music and film industry.[80] Abadi's experience includes composing music for companies like Apple, Bose, and NASA, as well as for films and games.

Abadi started her career as a child prodigy in classical piano. When not performing world tours, she was isolated and homeschooled, an experience she likened to being raised in a cult. At home, she survived her father's physical, sexual, and verbal abuse yet showed courage early on. "I would push him back all the time. I was proudly disrespectful of my dad. I remember feeling almost proud of myself if I had to push him off or elbow him, even though it would be met with major consequences."[81] Abadi legally divorced her dad when she was twelve. "The victim-to-survivor journey is never linear. It never just goes, 'Oh, I'm out. I did it. I'm free.' What happens is peaks and valleys like [how] I got rid of my dad. That was really great."[82]

After a mentor and teacher later abused her, she came to realize how her early abuse enabled others to groom her. "[It was] this bizarre, familial kind of abuse that almost, I don't want to say, it was comforting but very familiar to me. You may or may not end up facing that monster over and over again in your life."[83]

Her *big journey* surfaced as she connected to her body. "My body should always be comfortable, and if my body isn't comfortable around someone, I've learned that it has gone in lockstep with the abusive environments that I've been in. So somatic therapy (for me) is important."[84]

Abadi also connected with other survivors through her advocacy, describing the network as "incredible." "I can't believe how many survivors I've met from so many different walks of life, and we have the same story."[85]

When survivors share their stories, it has a ripple effect that helps other victims understand their abuse and creates a sense of solidarity, Abadi explained. "I think the ripple effect is when we share a story; the effect becomes: one person comes forward, then another person. At the end of the day, it doesn't matter if we share that abuser or if we share these circumstances at all. I think we can all relate."[86]

The Female Composer Safety League

Abadi stepped forward to work with her community and empower female composers to fight against sexual exploitation in their field through her organization, the Female Composer Safety League.

In 2018, accusations plagued the music industry. *Digital Music News* documented twenty musicians and industry leaders who were accused of sexual abuse in just one year.[87] Vice Media reported on the industry's culture of abuse in a February 2024 article, "The Dollars and Desperation Silencing #MeToo in Music: Sexual misconduct is built into the foundation of the music industry."[88] The article stated: "The music world continues to project expectations that women are valued primarily as objects, not human beings: Hit music videos still feature women as little more than sexual accoutrements for their male stars, and female artists' appearances remain a disproportionate focus of critical essays and reviews."[89]

The article described the "power brokers who actually control the industry" as still "overwhelmingly a boys' club."[90] Survivors and activists fought back when they published the 233-page report and investigation of sexual abuse within the music industry, "Sound Off: Make Music Safe Report. This Comprehensive Report Chronicles The Scathing History and Financial Impact of Decades of Sexual Abuse and Coverups, from the 1950s to the Present." Dated February 27, 2024, the report combined advocacy organizations' efforts by Lift Our Voices, The Female Composer Safety League, The Punk Rock Therapist, and The Representation Project to document and expose sexual abuse and identify accused predators within the music industry. Well-known artists were outed: Prince, Elvis, Jerry Lee Lewis, Nikki Sixx, Sting, and other world-class musicians racked up dozens of accusations. Victims stepped forward to provide victim statements and accusations.[91]

R. Kelly Exposed

One of the most widely known accused predators was Robert Sylvester Kelly, better known as R. Kelly. Raised in Southside Chicago, Kelly became famous as an R&B producer, composer, and performer—winning three Grammys and selling seventy-five million records.[92] Numerous accusations by young girls and women of sexual and physical abuse spanned decades, from 1991 to 2018, though he was not convicted of a crime until 2021, followed by another conviction in 2022.[93]

I interviewed Lizzette Martinez in March 2022 about her decision to report R. Kelly to the police five years after her abuse ended in 2017. Martinez was a seventeen-year-old with dreams of establishing a musical career when she met Kelly at a shopping mall in 1995, leading to several years of physical and sexual violence.

At first, Martinez believed her hopes of becoming a professional singer were about to come true, but the mentorship quickly turned into sexual grooming. After struggling to free herself of the relationship and rebuild her life and musical career, allegations against Kelly surfaced. The first allegation was made by fifteen-year-old Tiffany Hawkins in 1991. Yet in 1994, at twenty-seven years old, R. Kelly married 15-year-old aspiring singer Aaliyah [Aaliyah Dana Haughton], who died in a mysterious plane crash in 2001.[94]

Accounts by several previous victims led Martinez to come forward with her own story to BuzzFeed and then Lifetime for a documentary about Kelly's abuse. In 2022, he was sentenced to thirty years in prison by a New York City judge after being convicted of eight counts of sex trafficking and one of racketeering. Later that year, he was convicted of child sexual abuse in a second federal trial in Chicago, receiving a thirty-year sentence.[95]

Martinez shared that she began to heal by writing her memoir and forming a nonprofit that helps survivors of sexual abuse.[96] Her journey from victim to advocate took many years to reach the point where she felt she could step forward and speak for other survivors. Despite the bumpy road, she is still going. "You gotta be strong enough for other women to lean on you; I think I'm at that point."[97]

When One Steps Forward, Another Follows

"I hadn't even breathed a word of it for decades."[98]

Michelle Francis-Smith, a Canada-based women's pelvic health expert, massage therapist, perinatal sexuality counselor, and intimacy coach, spoke with me in 2022 about how she minimized the abuse she experienced as a teenager. "I somehow blamed myself . . . I'd convinced myself that no matter what I was told, this was all my fault." Francis-Smith met Andrea Constand while working as a massage therapist and professor in Toronto, Canada. Inspired by Constand's story and courage, Francis-Smith realized she had her own story to tell. In our interview, she explained that her transition from victim to survivor happened organically through twenty years as a massage therapist, learning to help survivors regain ownership of their bodies through somatic healing. Hearing stories similar to her own helped her identify as a survivor. "It took me so long to realize this through other peoples' stories, similar occurrences or different experiences of rape, sexual assault, and violence, that I had experienced the same thing."[99]

Francis-Smith struggled to "even understand and accept that something was done to me, that something was taken from me when I was 15."[100] She questioned her understanding of her abuse. "How could it possibly have been sexual assault when it was another black person, in a low-income area, close to where I lived, who also played basketball in the neighborhood that I did and had their struggles? I identified so much with my victimizer that I couldn't see myself as worthy or needing any support or advocacy or anything. And many other women who look just like me have had these experiences and are going through life believing their voices don't matter."

It wasn't until she met Constand that she spoke of the rape again. Constand then invited her into the world of advocacy, empowering her to begin her healing journey. "Her support gave me a platform to be a face and a voice for survivors." Constand's encouragement inspired Francis-Smith's confidence. "She told me, I didn't know about your experience, but you knew what I was going through, and you were there for me as my educator to keep me grounded and [help me] do what I was there to do. How do you not see how powerful you are? You have a voice in this space."

While connecting with survivors, Francis-Smith connected with her mission of fighting for herself and other victims. "I would see survivors as clients, and they would talk about being disconnected from their bodies, not liking parts of their bodies and connecting it to some of their experiences. I didn't reveal my experiences to them, yet I was using language like: 'Are you getting support? Are you reaching into the community and learning about resources?' That became my mission. I didn't realize it then, and it's only come to my awareness in the last ten years, but I was fighting for myself behind the scenes. I was fighting for that little girl."[101]

During the COVID-19 pandemic of 2020, Constand asked Francis-Smith for help to facilitate virtual Healing Circles—a safe, supportive environment created by survivors for survivors where Francis-Smith began to embrace her power as an advocate for others, especially Black women. "That validation has [helped] my healing and definitely opened me up to the advocacy role," Francis-Smith said. She later became a facilitator in support groups through Constand's nonprofit, Hope, Healing, and Transformation, where she found her power as an advocate.

Incest: The Hidden Plague

Incest is a horrific crime that society rarely addresses, insufficiently investigates, and seldom prosecutes; it is a hidden scourge of society. Many children carry the burden of self-blame, shame, and paralysis arising from incest. The emotional power of betrayal undercuts the foundation of a secure and healthy childhood. Incest escapes society's notice as a hidden sin, leading to insufficient societal efforts to address it.

An incest survivor explained, "I just didn't want to share that with anyone. I felt the shame and just didn't want to re-live it. I was miserable and anxious and suicidal at a time in my late teens and early twenties, and not sure if I was gonna make it."[102]

She worked with a rape crisis center and as a volunteer with the Rape, Abuse, Incest National Network's (RAINN) Speakers' Bureau, explaining that the more she told her story, the more she wanted to do. She explains, "I began to see myself as an advocate and a survivor leader."[103] This anonymous victim described her transition from victim to advocate. "When you are a child, you really don't think about changing your circumstances; you think about surviving. But when you become older and independent, you realize this is different. Now, I have the power to step in and do something. So I did." This anonymous interviewee hoped to connect with other advocates through social media. She worked with a small support group of incest survivors that quickly grew on nearly every continent.

As the interviewee continued, she explained her path. "Inside, I kept feeling like my survivor experience had been hidden. But I kept feeling the strong sense inside that I had a story to tell. If I told it, other people might learn something from it, get some value, and maybe even be compelled to do something right. I was really hoping that I will be part of the change."[104]

Government agencies and parents alike treated children as of little value until the rise of children's rights in the mid-1950s. Lingering legacies of parent domination and religious conviction holding children as secondary enabled harm and tragedy, leading to an environment in which children are silenced.

A leader in the incest community, Suzanne Isaza, founder of Incest AWARE, wrote on the organization's website, "No one wants to talk about it. Incest is called a taboo for a good reason: it is one of the most hidden forms of sexual assault and one that was not addressed during the #MeToo movement. Our society's anxiety about family abuse and the belief that 'what happens behind closed doors is a private matter' creates a cloud of secrecy that feels impossible to break."[105] The actual numbers are difficult to quantify the familial connection between the predator and victim, where reporting is low.[106] Discovering the true scope of the problem demands and requires more investigation and research.

Rebels Step Forward

The stain of violence throughout all sectors of society created the rebels who stood up and fought back. The challenges facing newly formed organizations are monumental, given that they face entrenched ideologies, institutions, and social dynamics. The first step is to understand the scope of sexual violence in society, which we examine in the next chapter.

An essay in the anthology edited by Jaclyn Friedman and Jessica Valenti *Yes Means Yes, Visions of Female Sexual Power & a World Without Rape*, cited the unity of a Durham, North Carolina group, UBUNTU, led by women of color and survivors who expressed solidarity and made a call to action. "We are not waiting for leaders—we are each of us leaders, and we are stepping up to build a world without sexual violence."[107]

Brown, Constand, Denhollander, Klein, Abadi, and others courageously came forward, inspiring hundreds more to tell their stories. These women, along with many others, became known as the Silence Breakers. They joined actors speaking out about powerful figures in the entertainment industry, athletes, artists, farmworkers, newscasters, students, and survivors of all faiths, genders, sexualities, and backgrounds from all industries and walks of life. They connected through attorneys, social media, and support groups, forming friendships, networks, and organizations to form the #MeToo and survivors' movements.

Each of them once believed they were alone in their experience, blaming themselves for the abuse they endured. Whether they were the first or last to come forward, they became integral to the healing survivors experienced due to the supportive communities formed through the movement. Being heard and believed and learning that their abuse was part of a larger pattern fostered healing whether their perpetrators were held accountable or not. Even for those survivors who never got justice, the solidarity they found through the movement proved incredibly healing. They forged a path on which survivors can walk together as they move past a legacy of pain and isolation toward a brighter future.

In the following chapters, the book introduces leaders, organizations, associations, coalitions, and initiatives that are indeed stepping up. The task ahead demands attention from all to address the ubiquity of sexual abuse in society, as we see in chapter 4 on the "Scope of Abuse."

CHAPTER 4

SCOPE OF ABUSE

The Scope of Abuse

The scope of sexual abuse in society is hidden.

It's impossible to pinpoint when sexual abuse in human society began since it shows up in the earliest historical texts of every civilization. We do know that it did not begin this decade, this century, or this millennium. Tragically, such violence continues in modern society, where twenty-five million Americans have been raped, sexually assaulted, or harassed.[108] All of us suffer.

Many critics question the statistics that show high rates of abuse in hopes of denying its corruption. Yet numerous surveys and statistical investigations confirm it's a problem of epidemic proportions. Some even think the percentage of those harmed by sexual violence is higher.[109] The biggest question is, why isn't the scope of these crimes more widely known? The curse of sexual violence raises the following question by Mia Fontaine in her article, "America Has an Incest Problem," in the *Atlantic* magazine:

> How can the United States possibly realize its full potential when close to a third of the population has experienced psychic and/or physical trauma during the years they're

developing neurologically and emotionally, forming their very identity, beliefs, and social patterns?[110]

RAINN is the largest organization addressing sexual abuse in the United States. Founded in 1994, it was created to support survivors, raise awareness, and compel law reforms. In 2013, RAINN documented that 600,000 people, including children, are sexually assaulted each year.[111] Studies show that one out of every six women and one out of thirty-three men have been victims of attempted or completed rape. That's 20 percent of our population (66 million people). These statistics do not include other forms of sexual abuse and harassment.[112] Research shows that 74 percent of victims of sexual abuse know their abusers.[113]

Broad Scale of Abuse

The result of a large-scale study commissioned in 2018 by Stop Street Harassment, a volunteer-run nonprofit organization, exposed a broader scale of abuse:

- 81 percent of women and 43 percent of men reported experiencing sexual harassment or assault in their lifetime;
- More than 3 in 4 women (77 percent) and 1 in 3 men (34 percent) experienced verbal sexual harassment;
- 1 in 2 women (51 percent) and 1 in 6 men (17 percent) were sexually touched in an unwelcome way;
- Around 4 in 10 women (41 percent) and 1 in 4 men (22 percent) experienced cyber sexual harassment.[114]

There continues to be a battle between prosecutors and politicians to step out of settled, routine politics with the ideology of patriarchy to prosecute these crimes. Sexual abuse is an indelible characteristic of our society, a crime where many have evaded accountability.

Imagine a society where 96 percent of rapists are imprisoned; then erase that thought. Look at reality: Today, "out of every 1,000 sexual assaults, 975 perpetrators will walk free."[115]

Blame and Shame

It would be easy to point to weak and cowardly politicians for not enacting tough laws. We can blame the toothless laws that deny justice to victims. We can blame the government for its lack of leadership and vision. We can blame the education system for failing to teach each generation about sexual violence. We can blame society as a whole for failing to look.

While it's rare that any sexual abuser, child molester, or rapist will go to jail, victims of child sex abuse comprise a considerable percentage of those in jail.[116] This tragic fact besetting survivors is they are more likely to suffer drug addiction, alcoholism, crippling emotional damage, and suicide. Many, too many, are incarcerated due to the galaxy of troubles of PTSD. So, victims of sexual abuse become victims of the effects of that abuse.

Rape and sexual abuse were previously hidden from social view, reduced to a crime of deviant men or *loose* women. Victim shaming (what she wore, how late it was, how much she drank, etc.) deflected the crime as a failure of the victim, not the social attitudes and institutions complicit in the abuse. A scattering of articles pointed to a few cases of sexual abuse in the 1950s and 1960s. While knowledge of sexual violence and harassment remained a topic of episodic interest, the rise of women's liberation, the second wave in the 1970s, propelled the awareness of sexual abuse into broad social consciousness. The work of Susan Brownmiller's influential book, *Against Our Will: Men, Women and Rape*, in 1975 ignited public consciousness.[117] "Rape had been cloaked in stigma and silence for much of American history. Prior to the women's movement of the 1970s, it was understood to be a rare occurrence, as few survivors came forward."[118]

Piling on to the tragedy of sexual violence and harassment is the enormous economic burden placed on the victim and society as a result of sexual violence in society.[119] Abuse can be a lifelong burden of pain and suffering. The road to healing is a lifelong journey.

Victims bear the brunt of healthcare costs for their injuries caused by sexual abuse. Healing from psychological and emotional damage requires years, and for some, a lifetime of therapy. High costs include lost jobs, healthcare (medical and psychological), alternative education, and training costs. Some survivors can barely function in society due to the grievous injury inflicted upon them, making it nearly impossible to work at a job or study at school. Society pays for the crimes of a few.

Emotional and Social Costs

Sexual abuse affects a victim's emotional well-being and social functioning, causing catastrophic injury that leads many to suicide; over a third of women rape survivors have contemplated suicide at some point after their assault, and 13 percent had attempted suicide, according to "Rape in America: A Report to the Nation," 1992.[120] We are called survivors as we continue to survive and face a myriad of challenges, including anxiety, insomnia, nightmares, flashbacks, depression, inability to trust, low self-esteem, fear, guilt, shame, and a plethora of related somatic diseases. [121]

Every day, I carry the burden of fighting back against depression and burning anger sixty years after the abuse. The plague of problems continues to be expressed in low self-esteem, depression, and diminished social engagement many decades later.[122]

RAINN lists some of the ramifications of sexual violence on their website:

- 94 percent of women who are raped experience symptoms of PTSD during the two weeks following the rape.
- 30 percent of women report symptoms of PTSD nine months after the rape.

- 33 percent of women who are raped contemplate suicide.
- 13 percent of women who are raped attempt suicide.
- Approximately 70 percent of rape or sexual assault victims experience moderate to severe distress, a larger percentage than any other violent crime.[123]

Child Abuse

Darkness to Light is a nonprofit formed twenty-five years ago, and it's their vision to empower "adults to prevent, recognize, and react responsibly to child sexual abuse through awareness, education, and the reduction of stigma. We believe protecting children is an adult's responsibility, and that education and training are key to empowering action." As one of the largest survivor organizations, they developed child safety education and prevention programs in a dozen countries worldwide and assessed the harmful effects of child abuse guided by the vision of a world "free from child sexual abuse."[124]

> There are many social costs as a result of child sexual abuse. Delinquency and crime, often stemming from substance abuse, are more prevalent in adolescents with a history of child sexual abuse. Adult survivors are also more likely to become involved in crime, both as perpetrators and as victims. Other social costs include:

- Academic problems
- Teen pregnancy
- Sexual behavior and over-sexualized behavior problems

There are many health-related costs to survivors of sexual abuse. Generally, adult victims have higher rates of healthcare utilization and report significantly more health complaints when compared to adults without a history of child sexual abuse. Some health-related issues include:

- Emotional and mental health problems are often the first consequence and sign of child sexual abuse.
- Substance abuse problems are common, often beginning in childhood or adolescence and lasting into adulthood.
- Obesity and eating disorders are more common in women who have a history of child sexual abuse. The resulting health issues as a result of obesity include diabetes and heart disease.[125]

Darkness to Light shares the thoughts of Johnson County Children's Advocacy Center: "The impact of child sexual abuse is devastating for survivors but also affects those close to them, as well as the surrounding community. It is the root cause of many social and health issues and touches all of us in one way or another."[126]

One study titled Adverse Effects of Child Sex Abuse, "The Economic Burden of Child Maltreatment in the United States, 2015," points to damages from $210,012 to $830,928 per child abuse victim in a lifetime![127]

Johnson County Children's Advocacy Center gives further evidence of the economic impact of child sex abuse in our communities:

> The health and social impacts of child sexual abuse on a survivor last a lifetime and affect us all socially and financially. The average lifetime cost per victim of child abuse is $210,012, costing the US billions annually. These expenses are largely paid for by the public sector—the taxpayer:
>
> - Healthcare costs
> - Criminal justice costs
> - Child welfare costs
> - Special education costs
> - Productivity losses[128]

Vulnerable Communities

Marginalized communities, such as immigrants and people of color, are diminished and condemned to increased vulnerability.[129] Approximately 80 percent of Latina farmworkers surveyed for a study published in 2015 by Oxfam stated they experienced sexual violence on the job. In comparison, roughly 25–50 percent of all women in the workforce have experienced at least one incident of sexual violence.[130]

Racism and other biases affect our understanding of the actual scope of abuse. The survivor advocacy and support nonprofit, Incest AWARE, points to a startling statistic when examining abuse in people of color and LGBTQ+ communities.

> People of color and the LGBTQ+ community experience sexual assault/incest at shocking rates. For example, the American Psychological Association reports that one in five black women is a survivor of rape, 35 percent of black women are the targets of some form of sexual violence during their lifetime, and up to 60% of black women experience coercive sexual contact by the age of 18—yet for every black woman who reports rape, at least 15 others do not.[131]

The Human Rights Campaign once provided a succinct description [now quoted by Care Campus Resources & Education UC Merced] of why some communities experience higher rates of abuse and exploitation. "As a community, LGBTQ people face higher rates of poverty, stigma, and marginalization, which put us at greater risk for sexual assault. We also face higher rates of hate-motivated violence, which can often take the form of sexual assault."[132]

Incest often remains unspoken.[133] The social costs of sexual abuse are immense, as highlighted in a 2013 *Atlantic* article "America Has an Incest Problem" by Mia Fontaine, and she states, "Incest is the single biggest commonality between drug and alcohol addiction, mental illness, teenage and adult prostitution, criminal activity, and eating disorders."[134]

Some Over, Some Under

Male chauvinism and supremacy create an environment that overwhelms survivors' independence and agency over their own lives. Unequal gender relations, male supremacist ideology, and institutional arrogance maintained and reproduced this system of oppression for centuries. Society and complicit institutions sustained their authority with economic domination, intimidation, power, and control of popular ideology, such as newspapers, social media, TV, and radio, which are programmed to reproduce the status quo.

As examined in later chapters, several mechanisms—institutional inertia, complicit indifference (can't fight city hall), and naked power protected the institutions of power and muzzled the fightback. The biases against women and children as second-class citizens burden society with lower income, decreased life expectancy, and social dependency. In addition, economic disparity can lead to subservience, where survivors lack the agency and power to challenge their role in society. Social disinterest and institutional cover-ups aid silence. All of these processes limit awareness of the scope of sexual abuse and violence in society.[135]

Sectors of Subjugation

Sexual violence corrupts the social fabric of America, as every sector of society is affected. The full scope requires individual study of dozens of sectors, hopefully written by future advocates and researchers. These areas demand and require further investigations and reporting. Many of these sectors are examined throughout this book, such as predators from religious institutions, Hollywood, and schools. Here, we will briefly look at three sectors: colleges, the military, and men as victims to broaden the examination into the scope of sexual violence.

Below, we shall provide a brief introduction to a few of the sectors to highlight how each is affected. While each is worthy of a complete book investigation, a short review is provided here.

Colleges

Colleges may be one of the first steps toward independence for young people leaving home. These students may not have the social skills or awareness to ward off predation by teachers or fellow students. The status of youth adds to other intersections of vulnerability, including race, gender, income status, sexual orientation, and ability. The harm inflicted on students, from the cradle of childhood to adulthood, from dependence to independence, sexual abuse thrives on college campuses like wild weeds. One survey found evidence of widespread violence at thirty-three universities, as pointed out in a 2021 *The Washington Post* story, despite the government's effort fifty-six years earlier with the passage of Title IV, designed to ensure the safety of women in college.[136] The U.S. Department of Education, through the Higher Education Act of 1965, authorized the attorney general (AG) to address sexual harassment and discrimination.[137] It failed to be effective.

According to the survey, college presidents and officials were complicit in covering up abuse when notified. One example included the failures of Michigan State in response to the abuse of gymnasts.[138]

The Association of American Universities, in a large study, found that 13 percent of all students experienced a form of sexual assault, and 61 percent experienced sexual harassment.[139] Grooming and power over students hide and color the nature of consent. If a professor can define the future academic success of a student, then it raises the question of power and consent.[140] The low number of students reporting compounds this problem. According to a study by the Association of American Universities, "Overall rates of reporting to campus officials and law enforcement or others were low, ranging from five percent to 28 percent, depending on the specific type of behavior."[141]

These low reporting rates add to the American Association of University Women's study, which showed 89 percent of colleges don't report rapes.[142] The low reporting by victims and the absence of reporting by universities hide the true scope of sexual abuse on campus. The failure of universities to report is systematic and pervasive, as we have seen in the cases of coach Jerry Sandusky, Dr. Larry Nassar, gynecologist Dr. George Tyndall and athletic team doctor Richard Strauss.[143] Universities are not reporting or are uninterested in gathering information, with the statistics showing an unhealthy student environment.

The Campus Sexual Assault Study described alarming statistics. Their executive summary provided a devastating view of the scope of sexual violence:

> Being a victim of sexual assault is one of the most violating experiences anyone can endure and can cause immediate, as well as long-term, physical and mental health consequences. Of rape victims, 25% to 45% suffer from nongenital trauma; 19% to 22% suffer from genital trauma; up to 40% get sexually transmitted diseases (STDs); and 1% to 5% become pregnant, resulting in an estimated 32,000 rape-related pregnancies in the United States annually. Four out of five rape victims subsequently suffer from chronic physical or psychological conditions, and rape victims are 13 times more likely to attempt suicide. Overall, rape is believed to carry the highest annual victim cost of any crime. The annual victim costs are $127 billion, followed by assault at $93 billion per year, murder at $61 billion per year, and child abuse at $56 billion per year.[144]

The Clery Act of 1990 compelled reporting of crimes by "colleges and universities to report campus crime data, support victims of violence, and publicly outline the policies and procedures they have put into place to improve campus safety."[145] Yet, as we see in the statistics above, this act had little impact decades later either from insufficient enforcement by Secretaries of Education or absence of Clergy Act protections for students.

Military

The history of sexual assault and rape in the military is long, but the accountability history is very brief.[146] According to advocates outside the military, attorneys Hill and Ponton highlight a crucial element in how the military addressed sexual assault and rape. "Military rape law did not begin until the late 1980s."[147] Even when reporting sexual assault and rape, victims typically become subject to further harassment and abuse.

According to widely accepted statistics, one out of four women and one out of six men are abused; however, the statistics are significantly higher in the military.[148] Those statistics belie the immense pressure of rank, privilege (male), authority, legacy, and hierarchy placed upon those serving.[149] Men are abused as well. There is no reason or evidence to believe that military services and academies better protect victims than society. That in itself is tragic. Instead of having a formidable hierarchical structure to protect service members, it has been a path to assert dominance and abuse.

Military officer and researcher James Griffith studied the effects of sexual harassment in the military and found extensive harm. "[the] survey data from soldiers (12,567 soldiers in 180 company-sized units) who completed the Unit Risk Inventory administered during calendar year 2010 were analyzed using hierarchical linear modeling. At the individual level, sexual harassment was associated with a fivefold increase for risk of suicide."[150]

While laws codifying sexual abuse were on the books in the late 1980s, it wasn't until after 2012 that the Pentagon took the issue seriously. Survivors and advocates inside and outside the military forced the issue. The vast majority of victims, 75 percent or more, never reported their abuse.[151]

Only recently has it been *safe* for victims to come forward. In 2019, U.S. Senator Martha McSally reported her rape by a superior officer in the military. Her status as a U.S. senator gave credence and a platform to the issue of abuse in the military, pointing to a long history of silence about abuse in the military services.[152]

Thankfully, military survivor organizations have formed in the last decade, including Never Alone: Military Trauma Healing, Glass Soldier, Protect Our Defenders Foundation, and Servicewomen Action Network. Despite their efforts, sexual harassment, abuse, and violence remain crucial issues for service members.

Male Victims

A 2005 U.S. Centers for Disease Control study on San Diego Kaiser Permanente HMO members reported that "one in six boys are sexually abused by age 18."[153] Male victims are also underreported due to the stigma of being male survivors. According to the organization 1 in 6, the scope of sexual abuse of men is significant. "Men who've had such experiences are at much greater risk than those who haven't for serious mental health problems, including symptoms of post-traumatic stress disorder and depression, alcoholism and drug abuse, suicidal thoughts, and suicide attempts, problems in intimate relationships, and underachievement at school and work."[154]

While women suffer a high percentage of abuse, male college students are also sexually assaulted. A well-known example is Jerry Sandusky, a coach at Pennsylvania State, who used his position and authority to abuse ten male athletes.[155] He also formed a youth charity to expand and increase his circle of possible targets.

Women as Predators

The vast majority, 86 percent, of all victims of sexual abuse are women. And 96 percent of all perpetrators are men.[156] Yet, there is a growing awareness of female perpetrators.[157]

Researcher and writer Lara Stemple, who works with the Health and Human Rights Project at UCLA, points to the scope of this abuse. She concluded that we need to "completely rethink our assumptions about sexual victimization, and especially our fallback model that men are always the perpetrators and women the victims."[158]

This topic demands further investigation and analysis as it contradicts common beliefs in society. The above studies clash with other, well-known studies that do not find the same level of abuse by women.

All of Us Are the Last Casualty

The last casualty is American society. The curse of sexual violence harms millions of victims, causing tremendous trauma to every community. The *scope of the problem* reaches all ages, genders, races, and communities and has been widely hidden and covered up, until recently.

Society has hidden the scope of sexual violence under a fog of silence, shame, and powerlessness. Misogyny, male supremacy, and the arrogance of unequal power had a vested interest in denying the scope of abuse. There were no compelling forces to oppose sexual violence. Ignorance, fear, intimidation, and the ideology of oppression kept the lid on social awareness. The outcries for justice were quickly dismissed as outliers.

To combat abuse, we must know and understand the scope of the problem, the statistics, the emotional and psychological impact, and the economic burden. Sometimes, we tune out the *noise* in the background. We consume news stories, exposés, and documentaries as onetime events, ignoring and overlooking the overwhelming prevalence of sexual violence in society. We look away at uncomfortable truths, homelessness, trash in the streets—we walk by. Sexual violence, abuse, and harassment directly harm a third of the population. The other two-thirds are affected by indirect and secondary means via social or personal relations, yet fail to recognize the effects and harm as a society. Learning the scope of the problem enables us to fight the problem.

CHAPTER 5

WHY SURVIVORS DON'T REPORT

Legacy of Position, Power, and Status

Millions of viewers watched the televised Senate confirmation hearings when Professor Christine Blasey Ford gave riveting testimony about being sexually assaulted by Supreme Court nominee Brett Kavanaugh at a party in the 1980s.

These hearings were a cruel reminder of how the Senate treated Anita Hill during her testimony about sexual harassment by the then-Supreme Court nominee Clarence Thomas in 1991. The all-male majority of eleven Republican members engaged female prosecutor Rachel Mitchell to question Blasey Ford *to give them cover and deflect from the all-male optics.*[159] The questions reflected the style of a prosecutor looking for contradictions, errors, lacunae, and misstatements—it gave the appearance that Blasey Ford was the subject of prosecution, not a witness testifying about abuse.

Partisan Senate members condoned Kavanaugh's behavior through dismissal of Blasey Ford's testimony and refusal to seek corroborating testimony; altogether, the event exposed the power of patriarchy. They highlighted the privilege of the Senate's *old boys' club*, an institution marred by two hundred years of history of male supremacy. Ford initially came forward anonymously, later explaining to *The Washington Post*, "Why suffer through the annihilation if it's not going to matter?"[160] She later revealed her identity after it was leaked and faced a storm of comments. However, many opinion writers and a few rogue senators identified the hearings as a backlash to #MeToo activism. The hearings demonstrated misogynistic values and how easy it was to reject and devalue the testimony of a woman.

In support of Kavanaugh, even then President Trump chimed in, commenting that if the attack were "as bad as she says," she or her parents would've reported it to authorities when it happened more than thirty years ago.[161] Trump's tone-deaf comments dismissed any understanding of trauma, and the barriers victims feel when coming forward.

Trump's attack sparked renewed outrage on social media. Following the popularity of #MeToo, a new hashtag, #WhyIDidntReport, arrived and exploded on social media. Within a few hours, 38,000 Tweets shared personal stories of why survivors didn't report, raging across the internet like a brushfire.[162]

By the end of the year, over 720,000 tweets contained the hashtag #WhyIDidntReport, flooding social media with stories similar to Ford's.[163] Across the world, millions of women detailed the consequences of reporting abuse, illustrating the daily challenges victims face. The outpouring of emotion revealed the fear, anger, and shame experienced by many survivors of sexual violence.

The Guardian assembled a collection of responses from the hundreds of letters they received, reflecting the outrage in an article titled "You Are Not Alone: Your Reaction to Christine Blasey Ford's Testimony."[164] Survivors shared their experiences in a *Vox* article: "The Ford-Kavanaugh Sexual Assault Hearings, Explained," Ezra Klein, the founder of *Vox* and former editor-at-large, pointed to the over-reaching influence of male supremacy. "We ended the day in much the same place we started: his word against hers. But even as everyone agreed Ford's word was credible, it didn't matter. There was still Kavanaugh's word." Klein succinctly defined male supremacy: "She was 100 percent sure, and he was 100 percent sure, but it was his 100 percent sure that mattered."[165]

Facts and Statistics Carry Little Weight

The FBI established a hotline to follow up on Ford's accusations, requesting corroborating witnesses and supporting information. They received over 4,500 tips, which they passed on to Trump's White House, which took no further action and squashed further investigation.[166] The tragedy of Ms. Ford's treatment by the highest levels of the government caused significant damage to survivors and has had a chilling effect on the willingness of victims to report. The burial of the tips signaled to all women, to all victims, that sexual violence was not worthy of action by authorities.

An article in *USA Today*, in November 2013, cited a study by the National Research Council, "Study: Sexual Assaults Greatly Underreported," documents that 80 percent of sexual assaults are not reported to law enforcement![167] The study "recommends ways the U.S. Department of Justice's Bureau of Justice Statistics can improve its surveys of sexual assault cases." They also examined "how a half-dozen other methods of counting sexual assaults compare," showing that "some 80 percent of sexual assaults go unreported to law enforcement." They recommend the National Crime Victimization Survey "adopt new approaches" to correctly document the scope of sexual abuse, suggesting the survey had "undercounted sexual assaults for years."[168]

An article, "#WhyIDidntReport: Women Speak Out About Sexual Assault on Twitter," published in the *Journal of Forensic Nursing*, analyzed the details behind the hashtag posts. "Overall, 68.7% of posts mentioned a specific reason for not reporting; of these, 24.1% referred to the perpetrator being in a position of power, 36.3% feared not being believed, 20.6% mentioned that others invalidated the assault, 47.6% mentioned a specific form of violence."[169]

Institutional Failures Silence Justice

The criminal justice system's historic indifference to sexual violence is a mechanism to diminish victims' ability to voice accusations. Attorney John Manly called out the power and privilege of the Catholic hierarchy when he represented hundreds of victims at the hands of Catholic clergy. His advocacy enabled hundreds of clergy survivors to win a $660 million case against the Archdiocese of Los Angeles in July 2007. Manly pointed to the political forces silencing victims in an interview with the *New York Times* on July 16, 2007. "I think the question people need to ask themselves is, how can (Cardinal) Roger Mahony pay three-quarters of a billion for criminal acts and essentially walk free? Especially since it's other people's money, he has clearly been given special treatment by law enforcement and the power structure in LA. When will there be some accountability, and if not, why?".[170]

Manly expressed frustration that victims have few options for justice, describing how survivors have "been forced to use the civil courts to expose sexual predators and call church officials to account because the criminal justice system had failed."[171] Survivors have few resources, little knowledge, and a guide to make a report. Even if they have options, how can they challenge billion-dollar corporations and institutions?

No Justice

Our justice system's tradition of leniency in sexual assault cases greatly deters reporting. Santa Clara Judge Michael Persky gave Stanford University student Brock Turner a minimal sentence of six months after he was found guilty of sexually assaulting fellow student, Chanel Miller, after she passed out on her way home from a party. The victim began the trial as "Emily Doe" and later stepped forward publicly as an anti-rape activist. She wrote a 7,000-words-plus witness statement, downloaded from BuzzFeed "shared by millions, even read aloud on the floor of Congress."[172] The judge and apologists downplayed the attempted rape because Turner came from a *good family*, exposing the privilege afforded to affluent White families. Despite allegations of race, gender, and class bias by Judge Persky for his lenient sentencing of Turner, the California Commission on Judicial Performance found no wrongdoing in their investigation. Outraged citizens exacted justice; Judge Persky was recalled by voters on June 5, 2018, during the California primary elections.[173]

Another example is the sentencing of billionaire financier Jeffrey Epstein, whose rich and powerful friends enabled him to escape accountability for decades. He pleaded guilty in 2008 to procuring a child for prostitution and soliciting a prostitute in Florida after investigations into the sexual abuse of a fourteen-year-old. Epstein served less than thirteen months with extensive work release privileges as part of a controversial plea deal even though federal officials had identified thirty-six girls, some as young as fourteen years old, whom Epstein had allegedly sexually abused.[174]

Within Epstein's circle were other powerful men: England's Prince Andrew, former presidents Bill Clinton and Donald Trump, and dozens of notable actors, politicians, and financial titans, many of whom were complicit in the sexual abuse of minors. Most victims lack the resources and standing to challenge the world's wealthiest and most powerful men.[175] When Epstein was arrested in July 2019 on federal charges of trafficking in Florida and New York, the prosecutor gave Epstein a light sentence.[176]

Epidemic

An academic study in the *Journal of Marital and Family Therapy* reported the effect of the hashtag #WhyIDidntReport, demonstrating its tremendous social impact. They point to sexual assault as a worldwide epidemic "affecting individuals from all backgrounds in all cultures."[177] The reluctance to report can be attributed to several limitations, including intimidation, fear, potential workplace dismissal, social network isolation, and a lack of support.

RAINN's research highlights a tragic fact in its report, "The Vast Majority of Perpetrators Will Not Go to Jail or Prison." Their research illustrates the tragedy that out of 1,000 sexual assaults, only 25 perpetrators will be incarcerated.[178]

The Maryland Coalition Against Sexual Assault published data from the same study showing that "African American girls and women 12 years old and older experienced higher rates of rape and sexual assault than white, Asian, and Latina girls and women from 2005–2010."[179] This finding is supported by a Department of Justice (DOJ) survey and published by the National Center on Violence Against Women in the Black Community: "For every Black woman who reports rape, at least 15 Black women do not report."[180]

RAINN's website provides eight reasons why victims of sexual violence never report.

Of the sexual violence crimes not reported to police from 2005 to 2010, the victims gave the following reasons for not reporting.

- 20% feared retaliation
- 13% believed the police would not do anything to help
- 13% believed it was a personal matter
- 8% reported to a different official
- 8% believed it was not important enough to report
- 7% did not want to get the perpetrator in trouble
- 2% believed the police could not do anything to help
- 30% gave another reason or did not cite one reason[181]

A *Huffington Post* article dated January 31, 2023, "When The Criminal Legal System Doesn't Believe 'Imperfect Victims,'" raised challenges to the justice system.[182] Leigh Goodmark, a University of Maryland law professor, argued that "the criminal legal system—law enforcement, prosecutors, judges, the prison industrial complex—doesn't protect survivors. Instead, it retraumatizes and penalizes them for the violence they endured, particularly if they are not white or wealthy." Goodman commented, "I have yet to meet a woman in prison who has not experienced some form of gender-based trauma."[183] While victims of sexual violence may not know the official statistics for reporting abuse, they do recognize that the legal/justice system does not lean in favor of the victim. Why should a victim report when they might end up being charged?

Legal Silencing by Other Means—NDAs

Powerful individuals, organizations, and companies go to incredible lengths to silence future accusations using NDAs, which, broadly speaking, exchange a pile of money for silence. We saw the use of NDAs with Weinstein, Epstein, the Catholic Church, Bill O'Reilly, and other famous predators. This NDA mechanism allows the powerful to escape accountability. It is a formidable obstacle to reporting, as it both silences the victim, hides the ubiquity of abuse, and allows a predator to continue to abuse. As a result, the scope of abuse is hidden, and other victims feel that they're the only ones.

The *Boston Globe's Spotlight* investigation in 2002 on abuse in the Catholic Church revealed how the church offered financial settlements to parents in exchange for keeping quiet using NDAs.[184] At all costs, the church hierarchy worked to hide the extent of abuse from parishioners and to protect their authority and prestige, as we will see in the next chapter.

On one hand, the church was an overwhelming power in a society that used its social and economic power to overwhelm any complainant coming forward individually with accusations of clergy abuse. This institution also used a bevy of attorneys to block accusations or legally intimidate victims. On the other hand, victims came forward as individuals, facing the largest institution in the world. They did not know the possible dozens of other victims by the same clergy predator that the church was aware of but kept hidden. Lastly, the social power of the church influenced the prosecution of crimes, relying on its hierarchy to handle the *problem* in-house. Prosecutors were more likely to *bend the knee* and acquiesce to the request of church officials due to the church's political power. Victims had few options but to sign an NDA and accept compensation.[185]

In 2022, President Joe Biden signed the Speak Out Act, which bars the use of NDAs in sexual harassment cases as a condition of employment.[186]

Beliefs, Popular Culture, and Ideology

Blaming and shaming the victim can be powerful methods of imposing silence. They shift accountability from the perpetrator to the victim and intimidate victims into maintaining silence. These actions, by design, keep victims quiet. Those with power, position, and prestige hold the superior position of authority, thereby maintaining the status quo of unequal power.

Too often, the media serves as an echo chamber for the powerful who accuse victims of lying. Victims can be accused of promiscuity, alcohol consumption, or style of dress to diminish their credibility. One narrative suggests that women must protect themselves: *It is their fault, besides boys will be boys.*

An academic article titled "Trauma, Social Media, and #WhyIDidntReport: An Analysis of Twitter Posts About Reluctance to Report Sexual Assault" analyzed posts about the reluctance to report sexual assault. The article concludes several common myths obscuring the severity and scope of sexual violence, "husbands cannot rape their wives, men cannot be raped, women enjoy or ask to be raped (by dressing in certain ways or acting provocatively), and women lie about being raped."[187]

After being blamed and shamed, victims often internalize these feelings, condemning themselves for things like drinking, inviting a rapist into their home, or not fighting back—as a result, they don't report. They may regret their actions and feel guilt, shame, and humiliation.

Tragically, these cases of perceived self-responsibility connect to the psychology of inferiority and vulnerability. The victim may fear the social stigma as a burden too heavy to bear, leading to social isolation and severe depression.

Survivors suffer a tremendous emotional toll, often attempting to ignore it to spare themselves from traumatic emotions, even hiding the abuse from family and friends. Yet burying the memories resolves nothing; it merely provides a temporary respite before exploding in conscious awareness through *triggers*, like a place, event, image, or even a scent, leading to unexpected eruptions of traumatic responses and PTSD.

Some people dismiss rape as falling into a *gray area*. This destructive transition shifts blame from the predator to the victim. Lisa Jervis, in the anthology *Yes Means Yes*, describes the terminology of "a gray area" as "gray rape."[188] This reframing serves to "shift responsibility from rapists to victims." She condemns this categorizing of rape as "a disgusting, destructive, victim-blaming cultural construct that encourages women to hate ourselves, doubt ourselves, blame ourselves, take responsibility for other people's criminal behavior, fear our desires, and distrust our own instincts."[189]

One of her contributors explains, "I thought it was my fault. I felt humiliated and ashamed, and I was too ashamed and confused to tell anyone what had happened. I tried to forget about it."[190]

Law professor Cass Sunstein was direct when he quoted Timur Kuran in a 2021 anthology of the #MeToo Movement: "Victims have silenced themselves."[191] Self-blame may originate when victim blaming and ridicule are inflicted from the outside. In my many years of advocacy working with survivors of sexual violence, I communicated with men who shared that they feared their father's response if they shared about their abuse as children. Robert, who waited decades to disclose his abuse, said, "I was afraid my father would kill the priest." Another man waited until his father passed away before making his abuse public for the same reason.

The burden carried by abused children embodies two weights: the abuse and the fear of the parental response. Too often, parents refuse to believe their children and discourage disclosure, as in the case of Barry, who was beaten with a belt after telling his parents about being abused by a priest. Mary told me about how her mom washed her mouth out with soap for daring to accuse a priest of abuse, explaining, "He would never do that; he's such a good priest."

Due to my conservative Irish Catholic upbringing, I had no foundation for understanding my rape. I didn't understand the assault and did not have the language to describe it. At the time, I thought, "Why is God doing this to me?" Knowledge and discussions of sex, genitals, and touching were taboo topics in a conservative Catholic family. Survivor advocacy organizations document thousands of similar stories.

Misplaced Loyalty

Misplaced loyalty to the perpetrator deforms victims' understanding of their abuse; the perpetrator may be a family member, religious leader, coach, friend of the family, teacher, relative, or government leader. The position, status, and authority of the abuser provide a platform to exploit. The Stockholm Syndrome describes the *bonding* that happens when a victim attempts to cope with the abuse. Researcher Ashley Olivine explains: "The abuser uses rewards and punishments within the cycles of abuse to maintain an emotional attachment to the abused person."[192]

Children are vulnerable due to their limited life experiences and immaturity, leading to isolation and bonding with the predator. Poverty, racism, and a harmful home environment can exacerbate vulnerability. This, in turn, can lead to a coping mechanism of attachment and bonding to endure and survive life-threatening situations. Coping may lead to denial, selective memory, dependence, minimization of abuse, and empathy for the abuser. Olivine clarifies the circumstances: "It is more likely to occur when there is a perceived threat to a person's physical and psychological survival."[193] The syndrome cultivates bonding to lead victims to believe they are special. When they learn of others, it provides context for their abuse, and they might later realize it was not a *relationship*, but this awareness may take years or decades to surface.

It's important to note that victims see rapists go free every day through the media, so why report? RAINN points to less than 3 percent of perpetrators incarcerated and 97 percent who escape accountability.[194] A victim may question reporting their abuse, knowing that the social, political, and economic power of the abuser can diminish the authority and credibility of the victim.

Adding to hopelessness is the lack of definition and awareness of consent. "I truly thought that fearfully giving up after saying no twenty times counted as consent," Cara Kulwicki wrote in her essay, "Real Sex Education," for the 2008 anthology *Yes Means Yes, Visions of Female Sexual Power & a World Without Rape.* [195] Kulwicki stressed the importance of awareness: "I just didn't realize that what was being done to me was rape. For that reason, it took me years to realize why I felt so traumatized."[196] The ideology of rape culture undermined her understanding of rape.

Manipulation

A practiced and skilled manipulator can use their power, prestige, and authority to manipulate a victim using psychological methods to make them question their sanity. The vast power differential between the perpetrator and the victim enables those holding power to cause the victim to question their judgment.

Dismissals of abuse accusations that appear in public discourse include "Get over it," "It happened a long time ago," "Forget it," "It just happened once," "Are you sure you weren't leading him along?" "He would never do that," and "He has a family—you don't want to ruin that do you?" Powerful institutions can swat away complaints and reduce any accusation to *she said, he said*, thereby enforcing silence through denial and intimidation, which are forms of gaslighting. Society has a responsibility to address these issues. Sadly, there is a long thread of sexual violence that is excused and justified.

In her book, *Believing: Our Thirty-Year Journey to End Gender Violence*, Anita Hill reflects on whether Senator Arlen Specter was gaslighting or mansplaining during her televised cross-examination during the 1991 Senate Hearings for Justice Clarence Thomas's nomination to the Supreme Court. Professor Hill concluded that it was both. "Mansplaining was the technique, and gaslighting was the goal. Both are for denial employed to discount the claims of abuse; they deserve to be called out because they prevent women from being heard and believed when they testify about abuse."[197] Both mansplaining and gaslighting tactics "foster self-doubt, coaxing victims into thinking that coming forward is pointless, that no one will care."

Vulnerability and Social Status

Lisa Brunner, a victim growing up on the White Earth Reservation [White Earth Nation] in Minnesota, shared her story with *The Guardian*: "When she was raped at 15 and then again at 16, she didn't bother calling the police"[198] as the police failed to protect her mother from assaults. "I knew that law enforcement wouldn't do anything because I watched how they did nothing to the beatings that this man—coward, I should say—did to my mother," [199] said Brunner. *The Guardian* article shared Brunner's story of her daughter who was raped at seventeen by a White man about five blocks from their home on the reservation. Still, ten years later, she "hasn't heard anything from law enforcement officials."[200]

Subjugating the disenfranchised imposes ongoing vulnerability on whole classes of people. Backward views cause increased instances of sexual violence and abuse against LGBTQ+ communities. Reduced social standing keeps these communities oppressed, which points to the power differential of the dominant society. Reporting abuse may lead to gender orientation outings, intimidation, job discrimination, social isolation, and ostracization.

The National Sexual Violence Resource Center, NSVRC, addresses several issues of marginalized groups and reasons for not reporting. The more victims are dominated, the more likely they will be intimidated.

Individuals who are members of groups that have historically been devalued continue to face higher rates of sexual harassment, assault, and abuse.

- People with intellectual disabilities are sexually assaulted at a rate more than seven times higher than people with no disabilities.
- Nearly 50% of transgender people have experienced sexual violence at some point in their lives. These rates are even higher for trans people of color and those who have done sex work, been homeless, or have (or had) a disability.
- Black non-Hispanic women (44%) and multiracial non-Hispanic women (54%) are significantly more likely to have experienced rape, physical violence, or stalking by an intimate in their lifetime, compared to White non-Hispanic women (35%).
- 1 in 3 Native American/Alaskan Indian (NA/AI) women will be raped or sexually assaulted in her lifetime, making the average annual rate of rape and sexual assault among American Indians 3.5 times higher than for all other races.

These statistics serve as a reminder that sexual violence is rooted in inequality and disparities of power. It also serves as a reminder that discrimination and oppression are ongoing issues. For example, ongoing racism and oppression faced by women of color put them at a greater risk of experiencing sexual assault.[201]

The dominant patriarchal system nurtures the corruption of vulnerable communities, which, in turn, reproduces and bolsters male domination and control. The power of male supremacy reigns.

Economic Intimidation and Barriers

If you complain of abuse, you are at risk at home, at the workplace, and with your social network. Economic intimidation impedes a victim's ability to achieve accountability; for example, reporting sexual harassment can threaten promotion, further isolating the accuser. The victim is then reduced to an outsider, a complainer. Another penalty is the diminishment of status and authority; a victim is *frozen out* of workplace dynamics. This action automatically sets up a threat to their job security and future.

The most common form of intimidation is the direct threat of a victim losing their job and other penalties, such as endangering security, promotion, or status within the organization. Loss of income can be devastating to those dependent on their jobs, and these motivators often deter victims from reporting abuse. Every organization has a company culture and *climate* that foretells whether supervisors will address sexual harassment. The culture informs victims when considering reporting abuse in the workplace.

Incest—The Forbidden Topic

Incest by a family member ignites pressure and intimidation that evoke strong emotional prohibitions against reporting. The profound emotional burden engendered by familiar ties discourages reporting and prohibits disclosure. Author Shirley Davis, in her online article titled "Incest: The Secret No One Should Keep," provides the truth: "Secrecy is a sexual predator's best friend. Because incestuous sexual abuse is so heinous, the adults who perpetrate the trauma always use secrecy to hide their crimes. Perpetrators of incest often use tactics to keep their victims in line, such as threatening them or shaming them into silence."[202]

Grooming, love, and emotional connection bind the victim to silence, a link that evokes self-blame and doubt. Other elements that discourage incest survivors from reporting include the risk of breaking up the family, potential incarceration of family members, losing security, shunning, and losing their homes. Some victims don't want their family members imprisoned. Others fear being tossed out of their home if they report.

The emotional cost of incest is enormous. Victims endure great psychological stress due to familial connections. Victims may be so discouraged and overwhelmed that they cannot report.

Grooming—A Tool in the Bag of Tricks

One tool predators use to gain access to the vulnerable is to go to great lengths to be charming, personable, friendly, and the life of the party. A significant part of grooming is emotional manipulation. A predator cultivates a victim to establish trust and exploit vulnerability. Fr. Murphy, the priest who abused me, charmed the whole parish with his jovial facade, using a bonhomie persona as a mask to gain access to victims and, equally importantly, groom the community around them. This enabled Murphy to violate boundaries and gain access because "He was such a nice priest." They embed themselves within the lives of families and communities.

Henry, a survivor of years-long abuse by a priest, told me his story over many conversations. He told me of his need for attention due to his absent father and a mother unable to care for four children due to alcoholism and emotional instability. Lacking parental love, guidance, and emotional connection, he carried this burden for several decades. During that time, he experienced several bouts of homelessness in Southern California. His need for connection went unfulfilled until he met the parish priest. Growing up in a dysfunctional household, a kind word, special favor, or reward from an authority figure can open the door to the grooming process.

When the priest came into Henry's life, he provided an avenue of escape through attention, a rare event. The mother's friendship with the priest was likely no accident, which involved the abuse of all four of her children: three boys and a girl. The children became easy prey in an insecure, chaotic household without attention and little love. Throughout this book, we see instances of misplaced loyalty, especially with children such as Henry, a twelve-year-old from a broken home with a missing father and alcoholic mother. The predator *rescued* Henry from a family marked by dysfunction, turmoil, and trauma; the priest took him on cross-country trips, camping, and holiday events, which led to years of sexual exploitation and rape. Abuse accompanied this connection for over a decade, resulting in bonding with the predator.

Children—The Most Vulnerable Rarely Report

Child victims may never report or take decades to report sexual abuse. There are many reasons, but two factors stand out. According to the advocacy organization CHILD USA, the average age of a child victim coming forward from childhood sexual abuse is fifty-two years old.[203] And according to two major organizations: RAINN and Darkness to Light, most child abuse victims never come forward.[204]

There are several areas where the abuse of children is unique and worthy of deeper examination. A 2010 study by the National Institute of Health, "Suicide and Fatal Drug Overdose in Child Sexual Abuse Victims," illustrated the increased risk of suicide and overdose.[205] The journal of the AMA, *JAMA Network*, provided a stark finding in a similar study: "Sexual abuse was associated with 3.5-fold increased odds for suicide attempts."[206] The national education and advocacy organization Darkness to Light (D2L) also highlights the increased risk: "Children who are sexually abused are at significantly greater risk for later post-traumatic stress and other anxiety symptoms, depression, and suicide attempts."[207]

An article posted on the LACASA Center advocacy website examined the effects of Penn State football coach Jerry Sandusky's abuse and sheds light on the complexity of silence. They list several issues limiting reporting, such as self-blame, shame, fear, and other factors. "The reasons many survivors remain silent are not black and white. They are complex."[208]

A blog post by a survivor named Toni Tails, titled "This Is Why I Kept Sexual Abuse a Secret for 20 Years: Ten Reasons Children Don't Reveal

Sex Abuse," provides an insightful analysis of why children stay silent.

1. They didn't know it was abuse.
2. They don't remember the abuse.
3. They think the abuse is their fault.
4. They are afraid to tell anyone about the abuse.
5. They are ashamed of the abuse.
6. They don't trust anyone with their secret.
7. They don't want to hurt their loved ones.
8. They think they deserve it.
9. They don't have the terminology to tell.
10. They think no one will believe them.[209]

In addition, Darkness to Light reports that 62 percent of victims of child sexual abuse never report their abuse. In a similar CHILD USA study, they report: "The process of disclosure often takes decades, and the "ideal" timing of disclosure should be up to the victim. Over 70% of victims do not disclose within five years of their experience of abuse. Approximately 1 in 5 victims of CSA never disclose their experiences of abuse."[210]

Academics analyzed the "#WhyIDidntReport" phenomenon to understand better why " victims of sexual violence don't disclose or report." In their study, "Disclosure, Twitter, and the Power of #WhyIDidntReport: Applying French and Raven's Bases of Power to Tweets from Victims of Sexual Violence," the authors concluded with this thought: "Careful analysis of #WhyIDidntReport posts reveals that perceptions of power are influential in the process of not disclosing or reporting sexual violence."[211]

Silence and Silence

Institutional legacy, ideological conformity, and political powerlessness enforce and reinforce silence in all spheres of society. Outside forces compel silence through intimidation, threats, subjugation, and payoffs. Trauma can emotionally damage a victim, so often, the only recourse is to bury the memory or attempt to do so. Memories can be so painful that any trigger may bring forth a galaxy of PTSD symptoms. Avoiding memories is one course of action for survivors; it explains why they don't disclose their abuse. Internal mechanisms of fear, emotional distress, economic vulnerability, and loyalty to familial abusers can silence victims. None of these mechanisms is natural. None provides justice.

Even in the best cases, many victims are beaten down, emotionally damaged, and economically disenfranchised by reporting and find silence to be a temporary respite from the trauma. Raising community awareness is essential for victims to heal and demand justice. The next chapter examines political and social pressure used by institutions to silence, hide, and cover up using a strategy called the *playbook*, a series of plays used to deny justice for victims.

CHAPTER 6

PLAYBOOK OF THE POWERFUL

The Plays

After I first reported partial memories of abuse by the parish priest, I discovered the church hierarchy used a *playbook* to cover up the crimes. Despite Father Murphy getting caught four times in four different parishes, no one notified the community of his serial abuses.[212] The church kept moving him along to new parishes each time he was caught. One play was secrecy as secrecy is paramount for the church.

Although Murphy was caught multiple times, the church never named him as a predator until after I met with Bishop Nickless in 2016 and demanded he be listed on the known clergy predators list established by the watchdog nonprofit, BishopAccountability.[213] Until then, the church continued to promote Murphy through church assignments and parish newsletters.

Two plays, gaslighting and coverup, were used to con the parishioners and deflect attention. A book published by the Diocese of Sioux City called *Living Stones: Priests in the Diocese of Sioux City: 1856–2004* described Murphy as "probably most resembles Jesus, the eternal high priest in his frustrations. Jesus was so misunderstood by many of the people he loved so dearly."[214] The Sioux City bishop and church hierarchy knew he was a predator, yet he was referred to as "most resembles Jesus."

The Playbook Is Revealed

The first mention of a *playbook* came when the Pennsylvania Grand Jury issued a report in August 2018 about the actions of the Catholic Church hierarchy in covering up abuse.[215] After a two-year investigation, the report described numerous actions taken by the church that the grand jury called the playbook, describing specific actions used systematically by the Catholic Church to hide its complicity. The FBI's National Center for the Analysis of Violent Crime commented on the report and also concluded the material revealed something akin to "a playbook for concealing the truth."[216]

Bishops embraced this playbook as a practical template for responses to accusations of clergy abuse and have used it for decades, if not centuries, to cover up, deter, prevent, obfuscate, and eliminate accusations of abuse.

Other institutions, including corporations, Hollywood studios, universities, Boy Scouts, the military, families, and other offending institutions, developed a similar pattern to deal with violence. Each creates its unique playbook, using the lessons practiced by the Catholic Church, to create an environment to discourage reporting.

The Pennsylvania Grand Jury described the church's *playbook* as a set of seven procedures: using euphemisms, not investigating, creating phony excuses, continuing to support the accused, transferring to a new parish, hiding reasons for transfer, and not contacting the police.[217]

- First, make sure to use euphemisms rather than real words to describe the sexual assaults in diocese documents. Never say "rape"; say "inappropriate contact" or "boundary issues."

- Second, don't conduct genuine investigations with properly trained personnel. Instead, assign fellow clergy members to ask inadequate questions and then make credibility determinations about the colleagues with whom they live and work.
- Third, for an appearance of integrity, send priests for "evaluation" at church-run psychiatric treatment centers. Allow these experts to "diagnose" whether the priest was a pedophile, based largely on the priest's "self-reports," regardless of whether the priest had actually engaged in sexual contact with a child.
- Fourth, when a priest does have to be removed, don't say why. Tell his parishioners that he is on "sick leave," or suffering from "nervous exhaustion." Or say nothing at all.
- Fifth, even if a priest is raping children, keep providing him housing and living expenses, although he may be using these resources to facilitate more sexual assaults.
- Sixth, if a predator's conduct becomes known to the community, don't remove him from the priesthood to ensure that no more children will be victimized. Instead, transfer him to a new location where no one will know he is a child abuser.
- Finally and above all, don't tell the police. Child sexual abuse, even short of actual penetration, is and has, for all relevant times, been a crime. But don't treat it that way; handle it like a personnel matter, "in-house."[218]

The grand juries and investigatory commissions, media investigations, and survivor stories uncovered hidden crimes, demonstrating elements of similar playbooks implemented by many institutions.[219] The implementation of these strategies is a discrete campaign designed to address each unique circumstance. But make no mistake, corporations, schools, churches, and social institutions use variations of the playbook.

Below I define the five *plays* I believe best describe the *playbook* used in all sectors of society, based on more than thirty years of advocacy and national leadership.

Five Plays of the Playbook

Like Watergate, the coverup can equal the crime in severity. Failure to report to the police and allowing a predator to continue to abuse, without consequences, can cause a significant ongoing threat to any community. Implementing any part of the playbook by institutions depends on power dynamics, social and economic status, and situation. The principal elements essential to any playbook are

1. Maintaining secrecy and cover-ups,
2. Gaslighting,
3. Intimidation, shame, and blame,
4. Legal escapes, NDAs, SOL laws,
5. Power differential (power, prestige, or authority).

All plays are designed to avoid accountability for offenders and justice for the victims. Various combinations are made to meet the unique needs and circumstances of each social sector. So, we may find a *mix-and-match* combination of plays for each situation.

1. Secrecy and Cover-Ups

At all costs, predators and institutions that defend them demand that abuse must be kept secret.[220] For years, the bishops of the Diocese of Sioux City hid the alleged crimes of Fr. Coyle, a high school teacher at my Catholic high school in Iowa. After he was publicly exposed, Coyle admitted to the bishop that he abused over fifty boys. The Diocese of Sioux City's diocese spokeswoman Susan O'Brien admitted, "His total number of victims could be higher than 50 because the diocese remains 'uncertain of an accurate number.'"[221] The church sidesteps the number as something indefinite, but they did know of his prolific abuse of boys for thirty years without notifying the public to allow protection of the children.[222] How many children would have benefited if the church had notified the parents, enabling support and healing for the children? The bishops transferred him nine times, a clear sign of coverup.

The diocese never reported to the police, contacted victims, or offered support or counseling to those harmed. Instead, Coyle was moved on to another parish, a form of *passing the trash*.

At a SNAP conference in 2011, Charles, a survivor of childhood abuse, told me of his parent's experience reporting his abuse to the Colorado bishop. The bishop called in the offending priest to have him confess his sins; by doing so, the bishop used the *seal of confession*, absolving the predator's crimes and hiding the offense from parishioners. It also enabled the bishop to keep the crime secret, effectively hiding it from both the police and parishioners.[223] There was no accountability, just silence and coverup. The only action taken was to transfer the priest, removing him from public accountability, and causing a threat to the parishioners of another parish.

Whistleblower Siobhan O'Connor, during an interview, October 2018, on the TV program "60 Minutes," exposed how the Bishop of Buffalo, New York, hid clergy predators.[224] She revealed that Bishop Malone had records of 119 abusers yet only publicly acknowledged forty-two.[225] Four years later, BishopAccountability, the organization that tracks Catholic sexual predators, publicly identified 209 clergy predators in the Diocese of Buffalo from 1972 to 2022.[226] Bishop Malone was not the first bishop to embrace the religious values of holiness, justice, and morality while endangering the church community. One more example of a bishop protecting the institution over the community.

Another *play* in the coverup is the destruction of documents. In 2019, *Vox Media* quoted German Cardinal Reinhard Marx of the Catholic

Church: "Files that could have documented the terrible deeds and named those responsible were destroyed, or not even created." This is one of the practices that survivors have documented for years, but church officials have long kept secret. "Instead of the perpetrators, the victims were regulated and silence imposed on them. The stipulated procedures and processes for the prosecution of offenses were deliberately not complied with, but instead canceled or overridden."[227]

The Pennsylvania Grand Jury report investigated six dioceses in Pennsylvania, which followed previous grand jury investigations in the Archdiocese of Philadelphia in 2005 and 2011 and the Diocese of Altoona-Johnston in 2016.[228] The Altoona-Johnston (Pennsylvania) Grand Jury report of 2018 exposed over 300 accused clergy predators and pointed to over a thousand victims.[229] The report recounted the testimony of FBI agents. "While each church district had its idiosyncrasies, the pattern was pretty much the same. The main thing was not to help children but to avoid 'scandal.'"[230]

The report revealed the destruction of documents by the church hierarchy to conceal the wrongdoing of priests.[231] A newspaper article called for the community to read the report, pointing out the coverup of abuse for decades.[232]

The grand jury showed an example of a 1994 memo by Cardinal Bevilacqua from the Archdiocese of Philadelphia and Bishop Cullen of the Diocese of Allentown that "ordered the shredding of a list of 35 priests suspected of sexually abusing children."[233] The church hierarchy has a long practice of promoting those who abuse and cover up, such as in the case of Fr. Doerfler of Green Bay, Wisconsin, who admitted in court that he destroyed all documents accusing the clergy of abuse in 2011. Two years later, Doerfler was promoted to Bishop of Marquette, Michigan diocese.[234]

There are so many reports of the destruction of records by clergy that the Justice Department wrote to all American Catholic bishops, saying, "Don't destroy evidence."[235] This begs the question: Does telling criminals not to commit a crime stop them from doing so? The headline from the

York Daily Record in 2018 says it all. "Feds put Catholic churches across the nation on notice: Don't destroy any evidence of abuse."[236] Truly an exceptional command given that the church presents itself as a moral authority—ironically, they have to be commanded to do the right thing.[237]

2. Gaslighting

Fr. Murphy took me to two local priests in other parishes to *confess my sins*, where I confessed the instances of abuse by Murphy, yet neither of them reported my abuse to the police or even, evidently, the bishop.[238] This silence suggested a message that the abuse I suffered was no big deal or my fault.

Gaslighting is a form of psychological abuse that compounds violence. David W. Wahl, PhD, a psychologist and sex researcher, defines gaslighting as a manipulative tool used by predators. "Sexual gaslighting, therefore, is the psychological and abusive manipulation of another person to get them to question their reality around a sexual situation."[239] Dr. Wahl emphasizes that gaslighting is "about power. It's about controlling the narrative and the sexuality of the person being victimized." The primary goal is for the gaslighter to get their victim to doubt their reality. This is often accomplished by reshaping reality—"This is what you wanted, not me."[240]

A *Washington Post* article in 2023 describes the harmful impact of gaslighting: "When it comes to gaslighting, perpetrators use jabs of shame, criticism, and conversation pivots to belittle the victim and reinstate their own sense of power and quest for control."[241]

Predators have an arsenal of weapons to use against those who challenge their actions and behaviors. An article from Benson & Associates compiled common responses used by predators as a means to gaslight victims. I included my analysis in italics following the bullet points to describe some effects.[242]

- **Outright Lying**: "Stating blatant untruths in an accusatory manner. This may also look like the abuser denying things they have said, done, or promised":

    "She's making it up."
    "I've never even met that child."
    "I know what you did."
    "She loved it."
    "I never assaulted you."
    "I never went to that bar."

    The predator works to deceive and redirect responsibility away from themselves and onto the victim, lying or reconstructing a memory to absolve the predator and blame the victim.

- **Withholding**: Refusing to listen or pretending to not understand the victim, even when their meaning is clear.

    "Your account is really confusing."
    "I don't even think you know what you are talking about."
    "I know what you did and I'm waiting for you to tell me the truth."
    "Wow, I truly have no clue how you could even say these things."

- **Countering**: Questioning the memory or experiences of the victim, even though the victim is correct (and the abuser knows this):

    "Are you sure it even happened?"
    "Are you sure you didn't like it a little bit?"
    "I was just trying to help you."
    "No, I think you're mistaken (about the assault)."
    "We both know what really happened. I don't know why you would lie."

    Argumentative efforts to redefine the perception of reality.

- **Blocking or Diverting**: Changing the conversation from subject matter to questioning the motives of the victim to take back control:

    > "You just want to hurt me because you're jealous."
    > "How could you say things like that?"
    > "Why do you always play the victim?"
    > "You should be ashamed."
    > "After everything I did for you, this is how you act?"

    Belittling the victim to reduce their agency and control the narrative, and project the abuser's own negative actions and faults onto the victim.

- **Trivializing**: Minimizing or refusing to acknowledge the feelings, thoughts, or experiences of the victim. This may also look like shaming or embarrassing the victim for their normal, valid, human emotions:

    > "You need to lighten up."
    > "You know I was just joking around."
    > "You don't even know what real abuse is."
    > "You are way too sensitive."
    > "You don't even have a degree, you're far from an expert."

    Challenging the mental stability of the victim. Various forms of challenges and denials are used to manipulate emotions, controlling the narrative by oscillating between anger and love.

During my decade-long volunteer work as a SNAP correspondent, I engaged with hundreds of survivors through phone conversations and email communication, many of whom mentioned sharing their abuse in confession with other priests, where the victim felt ignored, dismissed, and ultimately responsible for their own abuse. During several conversations with women, they related stories of their abuse as children, being told by priests that they were equally responsible, by suggesting they *enticed* the priest.

Frank, a survivor from Colorado, reported that the second in command in the Archdiocese of Denver, the Vicar General, disparaged the victim when he shared his experience as an altar boy. The Vicar General minimized the horrific crime by saying the harm the victim suffered "was nothing compared to the suffering of Jesus on the cross."[243]

Accused predators have a common theme of denial: "It never happened," as we saw with Tara Reade's accusation against President Joe Biden and the accusation by Christine Blasey Ford against Supreme Court Judge Brett Kavanaugh. The overwhelming power of established notables smothers the voice of the victim. Lying also takes the form of gaslighting, a form of psychological abuse where a person or group makes someone question their sanity, perception of reality, or memories.[244]

Minimizing abuse and harassment, another form of gaslighting, becomes a defensive response by predators in their attempt to place responsibility on the victim. Predators use their social standing to reinforce their power over the victim and compel compliance through social dominance and intimidation. Predators may use the dynamic of unequal power to force compliance with their demands and deflect the burden of guilt. At every point, predators seek ways to excuse bad behavior.

In about 2010, while working as a volunteer for SNAP, I received a call from Patty, who lived in the Northwest part of the country and was abused in San Francisco. I asked how I could help. At first, her voice was faint, and her words were hesitant. Sensing her anxiety, I tried to sound pleasant and gave her space to tell her story. Over several phone conversations that followed, Patty's story of childhood abuse surfaced. She was eleven years old when the abuse started. A well-known and socially popular priest, Fr. Miles O'Brien Riley, frequently took her out of class at the nearby Catholic elementary school to the San Francisco Cathedral choir loft and raped her many times over several months.[245]

Fr. Riley was a popular media presence in San Francisco on radio and TV shows, and over the years, several other minors accused Riley of abuse. One accusation by a sixteen-year-old girl led to his retirement in 2003. He was not removed from the priesthood; he simply lost his public ability to act as a priest. Neither Fr. Riley nor Archbishop Levada provided a reason for his retirement, allowing Fr. Riley to skirt the limits of his retirement by continuing to celebrate marriages and baptize babies in the years following. The muddled and dishonest actions by the archbishop of not publicly revealing Riley's serial abuse gave the impression that he was still a priest in good standing despite the promises of the National Council of Bishops in their Dallas Charter to remove offending clergy, and post their names in parish bulletins.

As a result of the abuse, Patty suffered from depression, anxiety, and low self-esteem. Manipulation, deception, and lies by the diocese added to her PTSD symptoms by introducing doubt and self-blame. She initially sought help from the church by contacting the Archdiocese of San Francisco and spoke with the diocesan Victim Assistant Coordinator, who told her she had no legal or civil options due to the SOL laws.[246] Patty was offered and then accepted meager financial assistance for therapy that she continued for several years.

Unknown to Patty, the church's Victim Assistant lied; during her first contact, she had the opportunity, if she had known, to report to the police and file a criminal complaint or sue the church through civil legal action. Because of the delay, Patty lost any ability to hold the church accountable. When she learned of her rights, the SOL's criminal and civil options had run out. Stringing Patty along with deception and manipulation until the SOL expired enabled the church to avoid accountability and ruined her ability to take legal action. Once the SOL timed out, the church ended the support for the little therapy they did supply.

A large institution can overwhelm any public discussion with the overwhelming power of PR, insurance companies, and pulpit-preaching priests, all coming from the fountain of power.

An article by Psychology Today gives an in-depth explanation of gaslighting:

> The term gaslighting comes from a 1938 play, Gas Light, and its film adaptation. Gaslighting can occur in personal or professional relationships, and victims are targeted at the core of their being: their sense of identity and self-worth. Manipulative people who engage in gaslighting do so to attain power over their victims, either because they simply derive warped enjoyment from the act or because they wish to emotionally, physically, or financially control their victim.
>
> A relationship with a gaslighter may initially seem to be going quite well. They may praise the victim on a first date and immediately confide in them. Such disclosure, before any intimacy has been established, establishes trust quickly; it's part of a tactic known as love bombing. The more quickly a victim becomes enamored, the more quickly the next phase of manipulation can begin.
>
> A gaslighter will initially lie about simple things, but the volume of misinformation soon grows, and the gaslighter may accuse the victim of lying if he or she questions the narrative. They typically deploy occasional positive reinforcement to confuse the victim, but at the same time, they may attempt to turn [sic] others against the victim, even their own friends and family, by telling them that the victim is lying or delusional.[247]

These tactics apply to institutions, too, which use their power and authority to achieve their means of avoiding accountability and justice. In cases of systematic abuse, the offending institution will make every effort to deflect, defer, and deny abuse. They may attempt to mollify parents or the victim. Offending institutions like the church will declare they will take action, telling the victims, "We'll take care of it." Deception is a major play in the gaslighter's toolkit. In some workplace conditions, they transfer the victim, not the offender. In all cases, the institution needs to maintain control of the situation.

3. Intimidation—Shame and Blame, Threats, Defamation, Vilification

A common practice used to isolate and silence victims is to use manipulative practices that feel like an attack. The harmful set of practices is known by its acronym, DARVO, which means to "deny, attack, reverse victim-offender."[248] The offender places the blame on the victim to erase accountability; it is the highest form of victim manipulation. DARVO is related to gaslighting but aggressively attacks the victim as another tool to silence them.

Shaming and blaming accomplish two actions: They become powerful tools for predators to silence victims, allowing the criminal to escape/avoid accountability.

When using DARVO, the perpetrator wraps themselves in the victim's role—they want to appear as victims, evade accountability, and undermine the seriousness of the crime. DARVO's common theme is to blame victims for the abuse. An abuser uses the inequality of the power dynamic between aggressor and victim, which works when the abuser is more socially connected than the victim, such as employer/employee, priest/penitent, teacher/student, statesman/subservient, and therapist/patient. They also use these higher social standings to dismiss and blame the victim.

Predators and the institutions covering for them often use the *stick* to maintain silence, including physical threats and intimidation. In the Catholic community, many victims have been condemned to hell and damnation if they tell of their abuse.

Social threats can also happen in social settings among family, friends, neighbors, community members, or within social organizations (Rotary

Club, neighborhood association, athletic club, etc.). Threats can include excluding, shunning, isolating, and banning victims. In the workplace, offending bosses routinely use firing, freezing future pay and promotions, transfers, and demotions.

Sometimes, the threat can be subtle when the victim finds that they are excluded from meetings or decision-making actions. While not directly penalizing pay or position, it tends to isolate and *send a message* to assert dominance over the victim. Even when not actively threatening, the message emphasizes the power imbalance.

Reports of abuse by Hollywood producers, such as Harvey Weinstein, highlighted the practice of blacklisting those who would not submit to "casting couch" demands.[249] At Weinstein's trial, these demands were revealed. Dawn Dunning was an aspiring actor when Weinstein invited her to a hotel suite for a screen test. "While his employees were frantically working in the main room, Dunning testified, she was ushered into an adjacent bedroom where she found the producer sitting on a bed."[250] Dunning said Weinstein screamed when she laughed at his proposal that she join him in a threesome with his assistant. Weinstein then assaulted Ms. Dunning. Her voice quivering, she told the jury, "I stood up, and I was in shock" as Weinstein shouted at her, "You'll never make it in this business! That's how this industry works!"[251]

Many powerful people in the entertainment industry used variations of these threats as part of the playbook.[252] Since 2000, an emerging wave of survivors have stepped forward publicly to name the crime and the criminal. No longer can the powerful individual, company, or institution stand above the challenge of survivors. The outing of Weinstein as a predator demonstrates the rising power of survivors.[253]

Judgment and deception are powerful themes in the playbook. The Catholic hierarchy admits that some clergy predators are within their midst, using a category for clergy members who've been accused when they find specific accusations *credible*. The arbitrary designation varies from parish to parish, diocese to diocese. Who decides whether it's credible? It's another play in the playbook that uses phony categories to hide accountability. Each diocese has its review board: the bishop, a diocesan functionary, the diocese attorney, and a few notable parishioners.

There are significant problems with this scheme: 1.) Who decides what information is presented to the review board? Answer: the bishop.[254] 2.) Who decides to take action when a priest is accused? Answer: the bishop. 3.) The bishop can reframe the accusation from molestation to *inappropriate* attention to a student. 4.) The bishop appoints the review board and has the final say in determining the course of future action.

4. Nondisclosure Agreements, SOL, Settlements, and Awards

Nondisclosure agreements are also an important part of the playbook, as they act as a legal contract to ensure silence. Many influential people have used NDAs to compel silence, including Hollywood producer Harvey Weinstein, actor Bill Cosby, talk radio host Bill O'Reilly, and high-profile corporate executives. As we saw in the payout chart in the previous chapter, the church would pay according to their definitions of the severity of violence suffered by children. The Pennsylvania Grand Jury investigation exposed a chart of suggested payments for various cases of abuse.[255]

LEVEL OF ABUSE	RANGE OF PAYMENT
1. Above clothing, genital fondling	$10,000–$25,000
2. Fondling under clothes; masturbation	$15,000–$40,000
3. Oral sex	$25,000–$75,000
4. Sodomy; Intercourse	$50,000–$175,000

How do you place a dollar amount on a traumatic assault? How can you place a dollar amount on a lifetime of depression, low self-esteem, sadness, iron-hot anger, and other PTSD symptoms? As a victim, I see how the offer of even one dollar acknowledges the crime and responsibility. At the same time, no amount of money will make it better.

On the other hand, I used the chart to gain compensation. When I returned to Iowa to speak with Bishop Nickless, I wanted the bishop and the church to know the harm that I suffered and to advocate for myself and other victims. I also appealed for the abuser's name to be publicly disclosed and compensation for therapy. After the meeting, the bishop and I corresponded. While I did not mention it directly, I did pursue redress. Bishop Nickless replied to one email that I "was asking more than what other victims had requested." I replied: "If you are going to compare me to other victims I will compare you to other bishops." I included the grand jury payout chart above. As a result, the next email notified me that the Diocese of Sioux City would award me $100,000 in 2016. I did not have to sign an NDA in exchange due to the public exposure of the *Boston Globe* investigation of 2002. Parishioner outrage pushed the church to stop forcing victims to sign NDAs and make some changes.[256]

Previously, the Catholic Church used NDAs frequently, but widespread objection forced the church hierarchy to take action to ban NDAs in 2002.[257] In addition, the Catholic Church developed significant reforms and accountability in the church. The United States Conference of Catholic Bishops developed the "Charter for the Protection of Children and Young People" soon after the Boston scandal.[258] The national conference of hundreds of bishops recognized the severity of the crisis in their preamble.

> Preamble: The church in the United States is experiencing a crisis without precedent in our times. The abuse of children and young people by some priests and bishops, and the ways in which we bishops addressed these crimes and sins, have caused enormous pain, anger, and confusion. Innocent victims

and their families have suffered terribly. In the past, secrecy has created an atmosphere that has inhibited the healing process and, in some cases, enabled sexually abusive behavior to be repeated.[259]

One major reform included in this charter prohibited future use of NDAs to silence victims. At the same time, we need to recognize that most victims don't report to civil authorities, the church, or their families. Victims act as individuals facing a powerful institution without the means or ability to make an allegation. The charter was created to codify the church's response to abuse while not compelling the church to report all violence within their dioceses.

Catholics, Baptists, and Nondisclosure Agreements

On September 26, 2006, an open letter to the Southern Baptist Conference, SBC, by Christa Brown, and three SNAP leaders called for reform of NDAs that they describe as a means to "extract a secrecy agreement in exchange for minimal assistance with counseling costs."[260] "This tactic further exploits those who have already been dreadfully wounded and are in desperate need of counseling. It robs victims of their voice and of the liberty to eventually speak of their trauma if they choose. Such contractualized secrecy leaves others at risk for new harm and undermines the safety of Baptist churches. We would also suggest that it is a tactic that resists the movement of God's spirit, who works for healing and justice. Therefore, we ask the SBC Executive Committee to publicize the SBC's disapproval of such secrecy contracts by urging state conventions and churches that such contracts should not be enforced against victims who might now choose to break a contract for secrecy." The letter continues to ask that the SBC leadership demonstrate a "commitment to supporting those who reveal such abuse rather than the churches that strive to keep it secret."[261]

A February 20, 2006, SNAP press statement asked some questions about SBC using secrecy to hide abuse and threaten future victims. "How many abusive ministers' names are in that file and how many kids have they hurt? Why aren't the parents of Baptist kids entitled to know which ministers' names are in that file? If you learned that your own kid had been raped by a Baptist minister, would you be content to have the minister's name simply sitting in a confidential file, while the minister himself was still working in another church?" The statement continues with a plea for full disclosure: "We call upon the Baptist General Convention of Texas to disclose the names in that file so that parents can be warned and kids can be protected."[262]

Yet almost two decades later, the SBC fails to act or protect its parishioners. Brown described the issue in 2025:

The SBC Executive Committee president Jeff Iorg announced that there had been 674 abuse reports made to the hotline, 59 percent involving alleged abuse of minors and 41 percent involving alleged abuse of adults. Yet we know near-nothing about who those reported pastors are, about whether congregants have been informed, or about whether independent investigations were done. How do those reports, just sitting there, make anyone else safer? And how do they provide any healing validation to the survivors, who often want desperately for the truth to be acknowledged about their pastor-perpetrators? What we do know is that not a single name of any reported pastor has been added to any SBC database, and they won't be anytime soon because the database has been sidelined.[263]

The newsletter, "Good Faith Media," described the simple truth of NDAs: "Predators are known to seek out positions that provide access and power over the young, and the ministry is one such position. Yet the Southern Baptist SBC's free-wheeling style of local-church autonomy has only minimal safeguards outside the local church."[264]

Ministry Watch, an advocacy website that promotes accountability and integrity for Christian and Baptist ministries, provides insight by citing examples of NDAs across religious communities, including Catholic and Mormon churches. Ministry Watch ties together the common practices of Weinstein, Reilly, Cosby, the Catholic Church, and Donald Trump. "If you're famous, powerful, and wealthy, NDAs can cover up your dirty deeds. Harvey Weinstein, Bill O'Reilly, Bill Cosby, The Catholic Church, and Donald Trump, have used nondisclosure agreements to hide abuse, helping them abuse again."[265]

As widespread awareness grew about the ubiquity of violence and the use of NDAs to cover up crimes, the Speak Out Act was passed in 2022. "The law will allow employees to talk about their experiences with harassment or assault at work by invalidating nondisclosure agreements (NDAs) that force workers to remain silent in these cases."[266]

The evangelical community resisted the elimination of NDAs outright, but the "overwhelming majority of evangelical leaders (93 percent) believe pre-existing NDAs should be waived when a leader faces credible allegations of abuse."[267]

Attorney John Manly of California has represented thousands of victims of violence and bluntly laid out the condition of NDAs and silence. "Sexual molestation and assault are crimes that occur in secret, and abusers thrive in a culture of silence."[268] He continued with the choices every victim and attorney faces.[269] "Non-disclosure agreements place victims and their attorneys in an untenable position. They are given the choice between giving victims the ability to pay for therapy and other medical treatment to help them recover from their abuse or face years of protracted litigation with uncertain results." Manly continued to show the impact of NDAs on victims. "Healing does not occur when victims are forced to remain silent about their abuse, and the public cannot be protected from abusers when law enforcement does not learn their identities."[270]

As mentioned in the previous chapter, there are numerous other methods to keep victims from reporting. Bill O'Reilly, a mainstay of *Fox News*, paid a dozen payoffs in millions of dollars, one reaching $32 million.[271] The settlements for one victim, Ms. Wiehl, were a direct quid pro quo. Ms. Wiehl, a longtime network analyst with *Fox News*, alleged that she suffered "repeated harassment, a nonconsensual relationship, and received pornography and other sexually explicit materials."[272] The settlement demanded in return "all photos, text messages, and other communications between the two would be destroyed."[273]

In corporate America, there are tangible benefits to victims who remain silent; if the victim *plays ball*, there is a prospect of a future benefit or opportunity; these benefits may include work promotions, extended vacations, therapy, or medical care.[274]

5. No Accountability—Power, Economic, Political, and Social

Many victims of abuse and harassment take years to recognize that such actions were abusive. Too many felt it was their fault. Power dynamics, class oppression, and social subservience can overwhelm them. As we saw in the sections above, predators exploit vulnerability, insecurity, and fear. Those in control of a company or institution can use that power due to privilege, statute, authority, and position. These vultures use patriarchal memes and structures to pressure against reporting.

There is a direct correlation that women suffer the vast majority of abuse at the hands of men and that men overwhelmingly control society through roles such as elected officials, police, judges, prosecutors, and other governors of social interaction. Male supremacy and misogyny reign as dominant ideologies throughout society; we see too many instances of the failure of prosecutors to prosecute predators and enforce laws. Too often, politicians bow to the pressure of insurance companies and the social and economic power of institutions, such as the Catholic Church.

Victims with low social standing have limited resources to challenge an opposition of great wealth and power. Tragically, many victims may be dependent upon the workplace or institution, such as when they are employees and have limited options for other employment. The *system* is so rigged against victims that many are discouraged from reporting altogether.[275]

When institutions have power dominance, they control the message, the process, and the independent investigations, if done at all. Other institutions follow the model practiced by the Catholic hierarchy where *internal* investigations are little more than shams. Failure to even interview the victim reduces the process to a meaningless "he said, she said" situation, or that a complaint is merely an administrative task to be filed away.

When a bishop . . . or a corporate . . . or university president can overrule any decision of an inquiry that a review board makes, there is little justice.[276] Remember that even this skewed procedure is further tainted as the bishop selects appointees for the review board, which is all the better to enforce secrecy and silence.

Baptists Use the Playbook

To protect their power and prestige, other offending institutions took similar actions of the playbook. A *Washington Post* article from 2022 covered the SBC's database of alleged abusers and their response to violence titled, "Southern Baptist Leaders Covered Up Sex Abuse, Kept Secret Database."[277] The SBC, the largest Baptist organization in the world, has covered up abuse for decades, moving predators and failing to notify new parishes, just like the Catholic Church.[278] The SBC used secrecy and denial to keep the scope of abuse hidden, a powerful play in the playbook.[279] Like the Catholic Church, the SBC hid the fact that it kept a database of accused ministers, not disclosing to the National Assembly its existence or warning parishioners of an accused predator minister coming to their community.[280]

Faced with mounting pressure from forces outside the SBC leadership, namely survivor advocates and media investigations, the national SBC acknowledged the database's existence and promised its release. After repeated attempts to report, activists were met "with resistance, stonewalling, and even outright hostility from some within the EC (Executive Committee of the SBC)."[281] Vice News reporter, Sarah Stankorb reported in 2023, "Paige Patterson, a former SBC president, characterized SNAP advocates, which would include Brown, SNAP's Baptist director, as 'evil-doers who have slandered others,' and 'just as reprehensible as sex criminals.'"[282]

In a six-part *Houston Chronicle* series, featuring an interview with Terry Gross, host of the *NPR* radio program "Fresh Air," reporter Robert Downen described how the hierarchy of the SBC vilified and threatened survivor advocate Christa Brown, who took up the fight against abuse within the Baptist community.[283] Downen reports that the SBC hierarchy called advocate Christa Brown "an evil doer to a satanic distraction from evangelism," She was called as "reprehensible as a sex criminal by a top leader of the Southern Baptist Convention." Comments went unchallenged in the SBC. [284] Brown created the Stop Baptist Predators website, which provides a wealth of information on abuse in the SBC and Baptist community, and she published a book, *Baptistland*, 2024, recounting her healing.[285]

After years of prodding from Brown and other activists, the SBC posted the report in its entirety in May 2022.[286] The report created an "Offender Information System" and listed 703 alleged abusers with some redactions.[287] The Sarah Stankorb article cited the cost: "Up and down SBC's once-secret list were accounts of abuse, battery, and rape. Some ministers were later charged and pleaded guilty; others were hired as preachers while already registered sex offenders. Reams of gruesome abuses were known, documented, and neatly organized in spreadsheet boxes."[288]

Earlier, the SBC acknowledged an FBI investigation that warned SBC leadership because of their "mishandling of abuse cases."[289] An outside force, the nonprofit BaptistAccountability Project, documented the abuse within the Baptist community. The project, based on the template of the Catholic database, BishopAccountability, arose in response to the *Boston Globe Spotlight* investigation in Boston, Massachusetts.[290]

Brown expressed the relief many survivors felt when the SBC's report was revealed.[291] "This means so much to us survivors," she said. "It's a reflection of how cruel it was to stonewall any kind of validation for decades. For survivors to heal, this kind of validation is an acknowledgment of the truth of the horror of what was done to us."[292]

The *Houston Chronicle* headline, "Offend, Then Repeat," referred to the SBC's practice of moving ministers around after being caught sexually abusing their parishioners.[293] The exposure was just part two of a six-part investigation of abuse and cover-ups in the Baptist community. The Baptist's response and practice were similar to the Catholic Church's *play* for moving predators around when caught.[294] In a desire to maintain power and control, the SBC used the actions of the playbook to keep secrets, maintain silence, transfer accused predators, and avoid accountability, which, in turn, compelled the formulation of its own version of the playbook.[295]

A 2024 headline from the *Religion News Service* highlighted how SBC leadership waved the white flag and surrendered. "SBC Abuse Reform Task Force Ends Its Work With No Names on Database And No Long-term Plan."[296] The article reported that the task force "will end its work next week without a single name published on a database of abusers." This was the second time that a proposed database of accused pastors was delayed due to "denominational apathy, legal worries and a desire to protect donations to the Southern Baptist Convention's mission programs."[297]

In a 2025 opinion piece in the Baptist News Global by Christa Brown, David Clohessy, Dave Pittman, and Chellee Taylor, they wrote "Please, no more hollow words on sexual abuse reform," and called out the SBC for the "long documented history of stonewalling survivors and turning a blind eye to abusers, talk of incrementalism seems as yet another form of complicity. While we wait for a tiny incremental step to materialize, more kids and congregants will be sexually violated by abusive pastors and betrayed by church officials who turn their backs."[298]

Boy Scouts

Other institutions took similar steps. The Boy Scouts kept secret files of predators going back to 1919, compiling tens of thousands of files in what they called the "Perversion Files."[299] The Boy Scouts joined the insurance industry, the Catholic Church, public schools, and nonprofit organizations to block legislation and lobby against child abuse statutes as part of their playbook.[300] These special interest groups opposed an opening to allow more victims to receive justice in court. And when "legislation has been introduced, equally coordinated opposition has followed from the groups that stand to lose the most."[301]

Eventually, the outrage of survivors and advocacy by their attorneys forced the secret Boy Scout files open. In other cases, when the community challenges institutions to take action, they can respond, "We are investigating," yet no investigations are undertaken; instead, they kick the can down the road. Statements of diversion falsely assure the parishioners that the authorities are taking action yet fail to do so.

The Powerful Are Challenged

Knowledge is power. Making informed decisions based on an understanding of power dynamics gives victims power; understanding the playbook changes the dynamic and will help defeat its manipulations and intimidations. The playbook has been effective in silencing victims and protecting the predator. Keep in mind that 70 percent of victims never step forward publicly.

However, if we know the methods, we can fight back. Even so, obstacles remain in civil society where institutions act through legacy social practices and beliefs to maintain and reproduce a monolith, as we see in the next chapter.

CHAPTER 7

LEGACIES OF OPPRESSION

Anita Hill Faces the Boys of the Senate

"Not so bad."

In three words, Wyoming Senator Alan Simpson attempted to dismiss Anita Hill's Senate Hearing testimony on the candidacy of Supreme Court Nominee Clarence Thomas, referring to Hill's testimony of harassment as "not so bad." Senator Simpson followed with a contemptuous comment that her testimony was "sexual harassment crap," demeaning Hill and every woman who has been harassed by a boss and attempted to obtain justice and accountability.[302]

Anita Hill's 1991 testimony, first before U.S. Congress and then to the Senate, and the resulting backlash demonstrated how politicians (and society in general) exhibit patriarchal and misogynistic views.[303] Professor Hill exemplified courage when giving explosive testimony that sparked a national debate about the prevalence of harassment in the workplace. Then Senator Joe Biden led a panel of fourteen male senators who interrogated Professor Hill about the abuse she suffered at the hands of Thomas, eventually leading to an arbitrary dismissal of her accusations. Professor Hill's dignified testimony starkly contrasted with the dismissive questions and responses from the committee. She brought the issue of harassment to the front page of every newspaper.

In her book *Believing: Our Thirty-year Journey to End Gender Violence*, Hill criticized these outlooks as being so common in society. "Cultural acceptance of misogyny, often in the form of entertainment, lulls us into believing that harm motivated by a victim's sex or gender expression is normal and inevitable. Historical and contemporary versions of racism, homophobia, and patriarchy offer the behavior refuge, just as misogyny harbors racism and homophobia."[304]

Monica Hesse, a *Washington Post* reporter, wrote about the power of Hill's testimony to bring workplace harassment to the front page in her article, "Anita Hill's testimony compelled America to look closely at sexual harassment."[305] The hearings brought to light how abuse and harassment infect society—the pervasive impact of sexual harassment. Hesse continued with an observation: "The hearings expanded the common understanding of harassment. Harassment wasn't just a man physically forcing himself on a woman, as it had been in the early part of the 20th century. It wasn't just a man pinching a woman's behind or demanding sex in exchange for keeping employment . . . It was something that could happen casually. It was something women could be blamed for or shamed for—Can't she lighten up?—and it could happen entirely in secret."[306]

Sexual abuse does not exist in a vacuum; every element of society, including business, media, culture, and politics, plays a hand in reproducing the conditions of violence.

Professor Hill's media coverage relayed the dominant culture's values, expressed in male arrogance. Senator Joe Biden became the messenger of patronizing language expressed in veiled Senate politeness. Her testimony became the lightning bolt that electrified women worldwide. The backlash of Hill's treatment changed the battlefield, exposing a public display of men dismissing, objectifying, and insulting women.

History—Written by Whom? The Rise of Patriarchy

You have to know the past to understand the present.

—Carl Sagan

The history of rationales for violence persists to the present, obscuring the many cultural and social threads of sexual violence throughout history. Patriarchy established social relations, ideas, and practices that were, in turn, codified into law to impose women's oppression for much of history.

Anthropologists of early history describe many matriarchal societies where women had influential positions in society. Describing the transformation from matriarchal to patriarchal societies relies on who writes history. The first anthropologists were all men whose views and biases permeated their studies. As a result, these studies described the transition from a matriarchy to a patriarchy from a male perspective. Since the victors wrote history, a patriarchal version of history was accepted as true and accurate, justifying social relations of subjugation and exploitation of women in the modern world.

Just as it was *obvious* to medieval farmers to say that the earth was flat, it was just as *obvious* for cultural and religious leaders centuries ago to say that women must submit to men. Neither is true, but society accepted these beliefs and practices as truth, a truth that held sway for centuries—until it was challenged in the modern era.

At all costs, those men of privilege labor to preserve the power and privilege of previous eras. Historically, they used their social and economic power to codify unequal social relations into laws. They presented the existing conditions of misogyny and social division as natural and inevitable, the oppressor and the oppressed as a natural condition.[307] As a result, social relations reproduced the social structure, enforcing women's subjugation.

Social practices and institutions maintained the legacy of gender inequality through laws, such as inheritance laws, which allowed property to be passed only along male lines. Women were forced into home life and child-rearing, excluded from jobs, and prohibited from owning property. In the eighteenth century, English common law permitted a man to discipline his wife and children with a stick or whip no wider than his thumb. This "rule of thumb" prevailed in England and America until the late nineteenth century.

Historical Rationales

A common misperception is that male supremacy has always existed and is natural; this falsity continues to invade modern popular culture. One influential rationale that feeds the misconceptions suggests that men rule because they are stronger and more aggressive. Others argue that men produce more value through their labor—they are the breadwinners of the family! Therefore, it is natural that they are dominant. Ideological rationales developed to explain the male-dominated role, such as those following Judeo-Christian teachings, promote the idea that male supremacy is a divine right, a belief many followers hold today.

Charles Darwin placed gender roles as part of a deterministic biological evolution, describing the rationale for men dominating society as the "natural order."[308] Darwin's views reflected Victorian values on gender roles. While he wrote that both genders play a role, he also had his take: "The average of mental power in man must be above that of woman."[309] Darwin's rationale may be the most common and harmful as it falsely claims gender roles are genetic, pre-determined, static, and unwavering. It relies on determinism to justify genetic superiority; in other words, *men are born to rule*. As the preeminent authority of his time, Darwin's philosophy became an accepted *fact*. Recent anthropological studies refute his theories.[310]

Ancient History

Matriarchy thrived in North America as matriarchal Indian tribes greeted early European settlers. Matriarchal societies evoked the ire of anthropologist Lucien Carr in 1884, who studied the Iroquois. He was offended by their egalitarian society. Carr's critical review of the clan mothers' powers, rights, and duties nevertheless described a functioning matriarchy, declaring the system a "pure mockery of man's helplessness. From the cradle to the grave, there was never a time when the Iroquoian man was not subject to some woman."[311]

In her book *Women's Evolution*, Evelyn Reed points to several developments during the transition from matriarchal communal property to private property under patriarchy.[312] Previously, society was organized along a clan social organization, where the clans provided the social and economic foundation of matriarchal societies. Male status was determined by relationships with their sisters and mothers.[313]

Each gender had an essential role in maintaining the clan. Complementary roles in matriarchal societies implied a duality where each gender contributed differently but ultimately contributed equally to the clan's success. While genders were not always equal, they were not exploitative, as each gender had its place to ensure that the clan thrived.

The transition from subsistence living and communal ownership to private property shifted property relations between genders, enabling patriarchy to impose its will by dominating the economy. The move from communal subsistence living to private property compelled women to a secondary status, sometimes condemning them to property.[314] The transference of power changed the social relationship between men and women, creating a new society that used violent (rape, slavery, enforced subservience) and nonviolent (laws, codes, enforced social practices) means to ensure dominance. Male dominance enforced economic prohibitions against women owning property. The rape of a daughter was seen as a violation of the father's property rights, and violators paid a penalty to the father.[315]

Power and wealth flowed to the male line through other mechanisms, such as girls being sold through bride price and dowries. Property was passed down through male lines, cutting out clan or community ownership under the matriarchal regime. This process fortified gender stratification and the dominance of men.

World War II as a Turning Point

As much of the male population was drafted to fight World War II, women were put to work in the war industries, providing them with more independence and opportunities. After the war ended, those social and economic advantages continued. Empowered, they engaged in social activism, addressing equality and respect outside the home. Growing awareness accompanied independence, gave women power, and created a foundation that grew alongside the emerging Civil Rights Movement. The Child Abuse Prevention and the Women's Movements asserted their independence and liberty to challenge existing norms of abuse and exploitation. They became mentors of the new movement of survivors.

Child Abuse—A Tragic Legacy

All the mechanisms of subjugation and oppression of women are equally valid for the violence inflicted on children, as children have less power and less ability to defend themselves.[316] Children held little value or power. Children's secondary position in society made them very vulnerable and susceptible to abuse and exploitation.

The written history of abuse in the Americas began over 400 years ago when Christopher Columbus arrived and recorded the rapes of its indigenous residents by his crew. The Virginia Company, an entity formed at the service of England, petitioned the King requesting permission to import children from England to settle in America. They asked permission to do "whatever necessary to force the children into the ships." The Virginia Company was "desperate for child labor and went to great lengths to import unwilling youths [. . .] and were placed in the custody of the masters to whom they were apprenticed [. . .] [without] any concern for the best interests of these children."[317]

Similar demands forced impoverished families to send their children to work in factories. While reformers attempted to raise the age of child workers to fourteen in 1876, it was not until 1938 that children became protected by working conditions and a minimum age for labor.[318] Sadly, children's agricultural work has historically been exempt from labor law.

We are born into a system where social relations, structures, practices, and corrupted beliefs are defined and solidified in previous generations. We inherit the viewpoints, biases, and practices of the societies we are raised in; in all instances, the preexisting social and political power reproduces its dominant role in society and is solidified through legacy culture, including religion, schools, and media.

The Child Abuse Prevention Movement that arose a century ago has a long history of building awareness that began over a century ago. The first recorded initiative was the New York Society's formation of the Society for Prevention of Cruelty to Children in 1875.[319] Historian Steven Mintz gave startling evidence of child sex abuse in this era: "An 1894 textbook reported that the "rape" of children is the most frequent form of sexual abuse."[320] It must be noted that the creation of the Society for Prevention of Cruelty to Children was modeled after the Society for the Prevention of Cruelty to Animals, which was founded in 1866, nine years previously.[321]

The horrors of WWII heightened awareness of social ills and community responsibilities, which pushed individuals and institutions to examine the welfare of children. After the war, doctors, the American Medical Association (AMA), and social workers engaged in research and activism surrounding child abuse. Rising concern by academics, social reformers, and legislators fueled this growing movement.[322] There were few sustained actions of reform addressing the rights and safety of children until the 1930s.[323]

Sexual abuse of children was not medically or socially recognized until the 1960s.[324] The first record of child abuse was noted by the radiologist Caffery, who saw unusual bone fractures in children in the early 1960s.[325] The *Journal of the American Medical Association* published the 1962 article titled "The Battered Child-Syndrome" by pediatric psychiatrist C. Henry Kempe, which ignited widespread attention among medical professionals and the national media.[326] His article presented the moment when child maltreatment entered mainstream awareness. Before the article's publication, injuries to children—even repeated bone fractures—were not commonly recognized as the result of intentional trauma. Instead, physicians often looked for undiagnosed bone diseases or accepted parents' accounts of accidental mishaps such as falls or assaults by neighborhood bullies.

Kempe's "Battered Child" opened the floodgates to community outrage, scientific investigation, and legislative action. "By 1966, every state had passed legislation requiring better reporting and intervention in cases of child abuse."[327] Increasing community awareness followed by laws and regulations created a foundation for a safer community. New research on child abuse led to new areas of medical specialties, and significant articles appeared in academic journals. Social activists and state legislators responded with new laws protecting children and holding abusers accountable.[328]

In 1969, a study by Vincent DeFrancis, "Protecting the Child Victim of Sex Crimes Committed by Adults," revealed that abuse was underreported. He concluded, "Child victims of adult sex offenders are a community's least protected children. Frequent victims of parental neglect, they are, almost always, also neglected by the community, which has consistently failed to recognize the existence of this as a substantial problem."[329] In the article "A Short History of Child Protection in America," John Myer described how advocates pushing for reform achieved significant legislative changes and advances in academic research. The growing reform movement led to the protection of children becoming more normalized, socially and politically, and codified in laws protecting children.

The article continued with a section titled, "Child Abuse Becomes a National Issue," which describes how, before the mid-1960s, society did not recognize child abuse. "The 1960s witnessed an explosion of interest in child abuse, and physicians played a key role in this awakening. Before the 1960s, medical schools provided little or no training on child abuse, and medical texts were largely silent on the issue. Even pediatricians were widely uninformed."[330] The consolidation of child advocates, parent groups, schools, and government agencies led to the formation of dozens of child advocacy organizations, setting the stage for the emergence of the Child Abuse Prevention Movement.[331]

Child Village started in 1976, serving for over forty years with support for children.[332] Beginning as a campaign against child abuse, it grew into a residential treatment center. In 1983, their expanded nationwide advocacy prompted the name change to Childhelp. Two years later, they established a national hotline.[333] Their advocacy for preventing child abuse grew to a national presence, helping to raise awareness. As a result, Childhelp has been a leader in the national campaign pushing for reform legislation. As the most vulnerable, children are a bellwether of sexual abuse. They have no power, economic viability, or physical stature to resist. Childrens' very existence depends on others, not only for food and housing but also for love and attention.[334]

Child Abuse Exposed in 1979

Recognition of child abuse expanded to include attention to sexual violence against children. In 1979, David Finkelhor published *Sexually Victimized Children*, a major contribution to exposing child abuse: "Child protection workers from all over the country say they are inundated with cases of abuse."[335] Finkelhor's call to health workers about the scope of abuse became a clarion call to all. "Public outrage, which has for several years focused on stories of bruised and tortured children, is shifting to a concern with exploitation. Between 1977 and 1978, almost every national magazine had run a story highlighting the horrors of children's sexual abuse."[336]

Society could no longer "unsee" the harm suffered by children. The combination of medical science and social activism set the stage for significant legislation protecting children. Some legacy institutions continue a path of resistance to change by wrapping themselves in the backward views of parenthood, patriarchy, and religious beliefs.

The Child Abuse Prevention Movement continued to be a moral center for reform through advocacy to make communities safer. As partners and allies, the Child Abuse Movement joins the Women's Movement and other social justice movements. Together, they intersect and overlap many spheres of shared additional concern, such as domestic violence and incest. The Child Abuse Prevention Movement, the Women's Movement, and the Survivors Movement share mutual and complementary interests in each other's success. Each movement bolsters the work of the other; differences in focus and mission become opportunities for future collaboration.

Justice Denied

Early American laws provided little protection from rape and no protection for women of color. In 1855, the Supreme Court case, *State of Missouri v. Celia, a Slave*, addressed the issue of rape, race, women, and slavery when a woman was tried and executed for killing her enslaver after years of rape.[337] The decision established Black slave women to be the property of their owners with no right to defend themselves.[338]

Susan Brownmiller, in her book, *Against Our Will: Men, Women and Rape*, described the laws of the plantation, with "the slaveholding class that created the language and wrote the laws pertaining to slavery, it is not surprising that legally the concept of raping a slave simply did not exist. *One cannot rape one's own property.* The rape of one man's slave by another white man was considered a mere 'trespass' in the eyes of plantation law."[339]

Early US legal decisions ruled that women had to prove their "good character" to pursue charges against their assailant to the satisfaction of attorneys, prosecutors, and judges, all men. A New York judge issued a ruling in 1838 that served as legal guidance for many decades: "She must resist until exhausted or overpowered for a jury to find that it was against her will."[340] Only men could serve on juries in New York state until 1937, providing little hope of justice for women. Married women had no legal recourse if raped by their husbands; South Dakota was the first state to prohibit marital rape in 1975.

Prosecutors, juries, and judges weighed women's testimony against the standing of the alleged rapist, in effect diminishing her testimony. That meant a rapist was much less likely to be punished if he had higher social status than his victim—or if he was White and she was not. As late as 1975, California courts were "required" to give the following jury instruction in rape cases: "A charge such as that made against the defendant, in this case, is one which is easily made and, once made, difficult to defend against, even if the person accused is innocent. Therefore, the law requires that you examine the testimony of the female person named in the information with caution."[341] It wasn't until 1993 that marital rape was outlawed in all fifty states, though some religious commentary continued to support the right of spousal rape.[342] Some religious communities adhered to the scripture that says that women are "under the man."

Misogyny, Patriarchy, and Male Supremacy

Discussion is incomplete without outing the pernicious bigotry of misogyny, giving excuses and protection for predators and their crimes, which in turn shaped society, especially forcing women's subjugation into society.

Corporate office managers talking about the "girls" in the secretarial pool cruelly demeaned them socially. They reinforce women's diminished status in the workplace and reduce them economically as employees highlighting male supremacy and patriarchy all at once. Predators repeat and reproduce the dogma of the subordinate, the other, the person with less rights, and rob women of status, dignity, power, and wealth. Predators not only look for vulnerability but also reproduce the conditions that create it.

Maintaining supremacy by the powerful requires oppressing those perceived as beneath them to keep their social position. Women, people of color, immigrants, and children become fodder for predators to preserve their privileged status. Job discrimination, low wages, stymied promotions, education level, and limited options for advancement reinforce this process. The contention for power between perpetrator and victim emphasizes that the community's safety is not just a fight in the legal sphere. This struggle also points to the importance of winning ideological battles in culture, social relations, and day-to-day practice.

Women's Liberation

A wellspring of activism addressing violence came from women who participated in the Civil Rights Movement in the 1950s and early 1960s. Historian Danielle McGuire, in her brilliant book, *At the Dark End of the Street*, provided many examples of Black women engaged with anti-rape activism as part of the Civil Rights Movement.[343] Leaders in this movement fostered the fight against violence in all communities by developing the Women's Movement's "Second Wave," which continued the fight in the late 1960s.

Consciousness-raising groups emerged in the 1970s as an enduring contribution, becoming a powerful tool for demonstrating the harm women suffered and raising awareness to build a common bond. The peer consciousness-raising groups in the early 1970s exposed the harsh truth: abuse in society was ubiquitous in the home, workplace, schools, universities, and churches. The shared experience showed women that they were not alone. This fight was a social movement that began as an embryo and later exploded throughout society.[344]

Nationwide, consciousness-raising groups provided a feminist foundation for addressing rape. The organization New York Radical Feminists, founded by Shulamith Firestone and Anne Koedt in 1969, held a speak-out against rape in April 1971 in New York City, which led to a body of writing describing rape in all sectors of society.[345] A central theme was the oppression of patriarchy and how intimidation, threats, exploitation, and oppression silenced women.

The practices of peer consciousness-raising groups developed in-your-face street advocacy, with slogans such as "the personal is political" and "sisterhood is powerful," providing a fundamental cultural shift from previously accepted social norms. The *New York* Times quoted author Alix Kates Shulman, feminist and coeditor of the book, *Women's Liberation! Feminist Writings That Inspired a Revolution & Still Can*, describing the liberation of consciousness-raising groups: "What made the discussions so powerful was the sense we had that a great flood light had been turned onto the world, lighting up all our experience; it was as though all the murky and scary shadows we had been living with all our lives were suddenly wiped away."[346]

Peer consciousness-raising groups and women's empowerment initiatives of the "Second Wave" became influential contributions to awareness, the first step to engaging politically.

Most women in my circle of social and political activists (anti-war, anti-racist, social justice) in the late sixties moved from civil rights, social justice, and anti-war work to forming Women's Liberation activism and consciousness-raising in the early 1970s. The holdover of old chauvinistic politics of both the traditional left and *new* left offended the growing militancy of feminists and Women's Liberation activists. Women vigorously challenged men with their chauvinistic attitudes, sexist behaviors, and blindness to full equality in and out of the home. Society floated along for centuries on a sea of male supremacy and misogyny, unquestioned and unchallenged, until the Women's Movement stood up and fought back.

Organized—Rape Crisis Centers Form

The Washington Rape Crisis Center, founded in 1969, established the first of its kind, a center that was a direct result of the conscious raising groups. Within a year, other centers opened, including San Francisco, Seattle, Chicago, Boston, and Philadelphia.[347] Soon, there was a rapid explosion of emerging rape crisis centers across the country.

Take Back the Night (TBTN) marches also appeared in the 1970s.[348] The power and influence of the Women's Movement led to significant reforms such as the federal program Title IX. This 1972 law, which was added to the education code, prohibits discrimination based on sex in any school that receives federal funding.[349] By 1978, the grassroots organizing of rape crisis centers expanded nationally, creating the National Coalition Against Sexual Assault.

Persistence by these grassroots activists began to influence lawmakers as they fought to make a difference. The actions of the movement and their established successes led to other forms of activism, lobbying politicians, and effective interventions in electing women politicians, leading to successes. The Victims of Crime Act in 1984 and the Violence Against Women Act (VAWA) in 1994 were landmark legislation protecting women. VAWA set up the Rape Prevention and Education (RPE) Program that helped fund the rape crisis centers.

In 2024, there were over 1500 rape crisis centers throughout the USA, serving communities with sex education, prevention, support, and political advocacy.[350] As the centers grew in number, they provided a foundation for forming fifty-six statewide and regional "coalitions against sexual abuse," or CASAs.

Racism

Any discussion about modern American culture must embrace the conversation about how the social vulnerability of women intersects with racism.[351] The historic underreporting of rape in communities of color is partly the result of police and prosecutors dismissing valid accusations, leading to the alarming statistic provided by the American Psychological Association, "For every Black woman who reports rape, at least 15 Black women do not report."[352] The underreporting compounds the harm as racism and misogyny rob communities of justice. The preponderance of evidence demonstrates the broad scope of crimes and widespread ignorance of such violence.[353] The failure of America to address these crimes against Black women is a crime in itself.

The book *At the Dark End of the Street* by Danielle McGuire describes hundreds of horrifying instances of injustices that Black women suffered in the Civil Rights Movement era. During those fifty years following WWII, rape and lynching coexisted.[354] McGuire's observations apply to the enforcement of laws for both. She says that laws may have been on the books, but having laws is worthless without enforcing those laws.[355]

The cruel mix of inequality in social power and economic standing, combined with a long history of American racism, creates little freedom and even less justice. The history of rape without justice for Black women is not new.[356] Writer and self-described "organizer and geek" Samhita Mukhopadhyay observes in the book, *Yes Means Yes*, "Technically, it is illegal to rape a black woman since rape is officially illegal. However, the cultural legacy of previous laws has maintained a set of conditions, including dominant narratives, structural inequities, class inequities, and cultural practices, that make it difficult for black women to prove they have been raped."[357]

The National Sexual Violence Resource Center reveals disturbing statistics of abuse in minority communities:

> Research on the prevalence of sexual violence helps us to understand how individuals who are members of groups that have historically been devalued continue to face higher rates of sexual harassment, assault, and abuse.
>
> - People with intellectual disabilities are assaulted at a rate more than seven times higher than people with no disabilities.
> - 47%—Almost half of all transgender people have been sexually assaulted at some point in their lives, and these rates are even higher for trans people of color and those who have done sex, work, been homeless, or have (or had) a disability.

- Black non-Hispanic women (44%) and multiracial non-Hispanic women (54%) are significantly more likely to have experienced rape, physical violence, or stalking by an intimate in their lifetime, compared to White non-Hispanic women (35%).

- 1 of 3 Native American/Alaskan Indian (NA/AI) women will be raped or assaulted in her lifetime, making the average annual rate of rape; and assault among American Indians 3.5 times higher than for all other races.

These statistics serve as a reminder that violence is rooted in inequality and disparities of power."[358]

Racism and sexual violence in modern America weave several methods of maintaining power. If you subjugate the weakest sector of society, those within the sectors at the intersection of race, gender, and class, it obscures the privilege of the dominant society. Predators have a strong interest in fostering inequality and vulnerability in all facets of society, ideology, social relations, and laws.

In the *History of Sexual Violence in Higher Education*, the authors Jody Jessup-Anger, Elise Lopez, and Mary P. Ko highlighted the Combahee River Collective Statement, published in 1978. This group of Black feminists outlined the contributions of African American women to the feminist movement. The statement "illustrated the intersections of racial, sexual, heterosexual, and class oppression. It discussed the complexity of working in solidarity with Black men to address racism, while also struggling with the same men to address sexism." The authors proposed a collective, collaborative movement against all oppression and highlighted the reality that their intersecting oppressions necessitated that they work together to address sexism while also addressing racism in the women's movement."[359]

Vulnerability

Vulnerability is a critical element of sexual violence. Women's secondary position in society and children's absence of standing identify them as easy targets. The power differential ensnares men as well, leading to the abuse of the most vulnerable—young boys. The predator priest who raped me had previously abused boys and girls who were older; their fightback pushed him to look for younger children. The use of power and control to abuse the vulnerable appears in family relationships, workplaces, religious institutions, sports teams, and doctor-patient relationships.

The uneven distribution of wealth creates a condition where the powerful exploit the most vulnerable, including the poor and immigrants. This contradiction appears in a culture of boss and servant, where the label *immigrant* automatically diminishes and erases them as less than human. Viewing a farmworker or housecleaner as a servant makes it easier for predators to exploit and abuse them. If the predator reduces the victim to an object of no importance, it raises the predator's power and robs the victim of power.

The words we use to describe others carry social significance. The example of the immigrant farmworker applies equally to all people of color, women, American Indians, and people with disabilities. Words can intervene as a material and ideological force in reproducing relations of power.

Activism Challenges the Legacies

The Survivors Movement emerged from the mentors of the past with the rise of Women's Liberation and the second wave of the feminist movement, as those previous social movements exposed the plague of sexual violence to broad social consciousness. The work of Susan Brownmiller's influential book, *Against Our Will: Men, Women and Rape*, in 1975, ignited public consciousness by observing "Rape had been cloaked in stigma and silence for much of American history.[360] Before the women's movement of the 1970s, it was understood to be a rare occurrence, as few survivors came forward."[361]

The second wave created new organizations, forms of cultural intervention, and ways to look at the world; they challenged the hierarchical, male-centric leadership. As survivors shared stories of abuse, it became an enlightening moment of liberation. However, although laws were established against rape, we also know that having a law is no guarantee of justice.

In the anthology, *Women's Liberation*, the contributor Susan Griffin in her selection, "Rape: The All-American Crime," recounted court testimony from a victim in 1971. After enduring intense shaming by the rapist's attorney, the victim asked, "Am I on trial?"[362] A summation of her trial experience was expressed in a leaflet distributed afterward: ". . . rape was committed by four men in a private apartment in October; on Thursday, it was done by a judge and a lawyer in a public courtroom."[363]

This new social movement of survivors emerged as it addressed abuse and created a unique and focused mission that separated it from the parent movements. Over 240 survivor organizations were formed, primarily focused on their program missions and clientele.[364]

The growing movement of survivors and survivor organizations challenged the legacies of oppression, institutions of power, and ideologies of exploitation. The contending forces of ossified ideas of the past on one side and the forces of justice on the other continue to battle in every sector of society. Survivor advocates win many battles but have not won the war.

The Survivor's Movement did not begin with one historic moment. It emerged from and alongside other great social movements that guided activists in organizing survivor-led organizations and mobilizing advocates. The successes of previous social movements created the conditions for this new social movement to thrive and emerge as an independent and distinct social force. As a result, survivors created a unique and focused mission. It became evident that collaborating with other survivor organizations helped advance each organization's power and impact. As we see in the next chapter, activism led to engagement in civil society.

CHAPTER 8

PRIVILEGE OF POWER AND POWER OF COMPLICITY

The Vulnerable

Betty, a classmate of one of my younger brothers, called me after my story of clergy abuse appeared in the local newspaper in Sioux City, Iowa, interested in sharing her abuse by two nuns when she was a first-grade student at my elementary school, Blessed Sacrament. During class, a nun would take her to the attached cloakroom and molest her.[365] Sometimes, a second nun would use the cloakroom for a similar attack.

Predators search for the most vulnerable and then pounce. Many predators join organizations and institutions where they have access to potential victims, seeking positions that can establish access, authority, and power. Like predators in the wild, human predators seek vulnerability, targeting youth, the emotionally wounded, and those isolated and crippled by previous abuse. Tactics include trolling for dysfunctional families, broken marriages, and those suffering from economic distress. Predators then offer help with the actual intention to gain access and exploit.

Institutions are complicit as they provide the access, the authority, and the status to exploit. Professor Marci Hamilton, in her 2017 article "Listen Up: There Is a Solution to the Sex Abuse and Harassment Epidemic Unfolding Before Your Eyes," published in the law review journal *Verdict*, quotes a retired FBI expert, Ken Lanning. "The reason that these guys have succeeded at harming others is because they earn people's trust, either through accumulated power or through being the super nice guy. Their trustworthiness creates access. So the fact that you have known someone "forever" and never seen them do one bad thing is basically irrelevant when it comes to those who sexually abuse, assault, or harass."[366]

Schools provide predators with an endless and revolving pool of targets. Sue, an attendee at an annual SNAP Conference, shared her dream of being a musician at a Southern California Catholic high school. Taking private lessons with a notable teacher, she felt honored when the music teacher showered her with attention. Over time, the private lessons set the stage to allow the teacher to isolate her from the classroom. Grooming and attention led to abuse. Years later, Sue understood how she was identified as vulnerable, becoming prey to the predator.

In a conversation at a SNAP meeting in 2012, I spoke with Juliette, who, as a child of a dysfunctional home, found refuge volunteering at a church associated with her elementary school. Her experience was similar to that of SNAP founder Barbara Blaine, as described in chapter 2. Her volunteering to arrange flowers on the altar led to grooming and eventual molestation by a priest.

During my volunteer work with SNAP, I heard hundreds of stories of clergy taking advantage of vulnerable people, such as the young woman immobilized by traction in a hospital bed and assaulted by the hospital chaplain, a priest.[367] Then there was the case of two priests assaulting two developmentally disabled kitchen staff working in the rectory.[368]

Target

Survivors have expressed that predators seem to have a *sixth* sense of vulnerability due to previous abuse, which creates insecurity and weakened defenses. Victims become victims once again. There is a great article pointing to the revictimization of rape victims by Farahnaz Mohammed, "The Repetition Compulsion: Why Rape Victims Are More Likely To Be Assaulted Again." This online article, posted on the Girls' Globe website, points to the danger. "Being sexually assaulted greatly increased the risk of future assaults, with one study purporting that being sexually assaulted once meant a woman was 35 times more likely than others to be revictimized." [369]

Authority and Access

Marci Hamilton gets to the truth of predators and prey in her book *Justice Denied*.[370] As mentioned in the book's preface, "The truth is that pedophiles go where children are, and they seek jobs and hobbies to further their goals. So if you know where kids gather, you can assume that pedophiles are not too far away."[371]

The 2016 Pennsylvania Grand Jury's 2018 investigation into the Catholic Church uncovered a "ring of predatory priests" within the Diocese of Pittsburgh who "shared intelligence" regarding victims, exchanged the victims amongst themselves, and manufactured child pornography. The group included (priests) George Zirwas, Francis Pucci, Robert Wolk, and Richard Zula, who used whips, violence, and sadism on their victims. An article in the *York Daily Record* by Anthony J. Machcinski titled "Priests Used Gold Crosses to ID Kids as Abuse Targets and Other Horrors from Pa. Report" described the deviant practices.[372] "He (Zirwas) had told me they, the priests, would give their boys, their altar boys, or their favorite boys these crosses," George testified. "So he gave me a big gold cross to wear." The report stated that "the crosses were a signal to other predators that the children had been desensitized to abuse and were optimal targets for further victimization."[373]

Great Power Bestows Great Responsibility—Or Not

Coach Jerry Sandusky used his position as an assistant football coach at Pennsylvania State University (Penn State) to identify and groom his victims. He was caught raping a child in 2002 but was not investigated until 2008 and arrested in 2011. Nationally famous Penn State coach Joe Paterno and three university officials were notified but failed to act.[374]

As the trial proceeded and testimony became public, Penn State fired Paterno. University officials were also arrested due to their failure to act on an eyewitness report of Sandusky raping a ten-year-old boy. Penn State valued its reputation by hiding child sex abuse rather than protecting children. Newspaper columnist Maureen Dowd compared the coverup at Penn State to the Catholic Church. "Like the Roman Catholic Church, Penn State is an arrogant institution hiding behind its mystique."[375]

Sandusky took additional steps to widen his pool of prey when he created a nonprofit, The Second Mile, serving underprivileged youth to train even younger victims.[376]

Another example is Dr. Richard Strauss, who used his position as team physician of the wrestling team at Ohio State University to abuse 177 athletes, beginning in 1979 and abusing hundreds until his arrest in 2019.[377] Even though reports were made to Ohio State University officials, no action was taken.[378] As a university and sports physician, Strauss used his position to exploit those in his care. University authorities ignored the complaints for decades, leading to complicit silence. Ohio State eventually paid $40 million to over 150 victims.[379]

Penn State, Ohio State, and Michigan State universities are just a few examples of university officials hiding and covering for predators. Ignoring and covering up abuse was not unusual—Michigan State was exposed as an example when several university officials were complicit in ignoring and covering up abuse in gymnastic training, as we saw in chapter 3. The testimony of gymnasts Rachael Denhollander and Sarah Klein exposed the hubris, arrogance, and indifference of university officials when reports of abuse first surfaced. It was not the first or last institution to cover up administration failures to protect its students from predation.

An NBC report documented the many failures at MSU, reporting on the article from the *Journal of Child Sexual Abuse*. The review of

MSU and Dr. Larry Nassar, dated February 10, 2020, excoriated MSU. "The university's persistent failure to take swift and decisive action to detect and stop Nassar's two-decade-long predatory and abusive behavior indicates a lack of institutional control, especially in light of the credible information reported to institutional officials at several points over many years. This failure, alone, clearly demonstrates the institution's most serious administrative impairments."[380]

The journal article mentioned how MSU administrators minimized the harm inflicted on hundreds of gymnasts, many of whom were children. One, they were accused of complicity in covering up a crime, which is a crime, not just a failure to report. Michigan law requires mandatory reporting for child abuse, something MSU and the journal failed to declare. Two, the failure to stop rape and sexual abuse and covering up reports are not "administrative impairments"; they are a crime.[381]

We learned about many hundreds of abuse cases by Boy Scouts leaders. Long-term coverups by the organization continued to draw fire. Fighting over the original $1.9 billion settlement, resistance from insurance companies, and strategic differences between plaintiffs' attorneys led to a jumble of claims and counterclaims.[382] As abuse survivors fought for justice and compensation, the judgment of a $2.46 billion settlement was finally settled by the Supreme Court after decades of legal fighting through bankruptcy court.[383] The settlement granted awards to 82,000 victims.

Power, Authority, Status

Many predators have powerful friends who help facilitate abuse. Institutions tend to *circle the wagons* to protect one of their own, a theme consistent with all complicit institutions, whether corporate, academic, or religious.

This tragic added component played out in the case of Dr. Thomas Havel, a psychiatrist and former priest who practiced at El Camino Hospital since 1980 for over four decades. When the Archdiocese of

Los Angeles released its list of hundreds of clergy predators, the list included the name of the then-Catholic priest Father Havel, now Dr. Thomas Havel, who served as a psychiatrist in El Camino Hospital and was accused of molesting three young girls.[384] Melanie Sakoda, my SNAP coleader, and I called on the hospital's governing body in a letter to take action to prevent other children from being abused, but they ignored the accusations and effectively disregarded the request for the safety of patients, especially young patients.[385] The governing body of the hospital never responded. Sakoda and I issued a press release and held a press event with supporters in front of the hospital on December 5, 2014, calling for an investigation and Havel's removal.[386] While the press event evoked several local TV news stories and notices in local newspapers, the dominating power of the establishment evaded a public response.

The hospital board of directors chose to protect its reputation and the reputation of Dr. Havel instead of supporting the two young girls who had stepped forward. One girl had come to Dr. Havel seeking help with problems that arose from abuse when she was thirteen. Instead of helping her, Havel abused her until she was eighteen years old.

Priest-psychiatrist's offer to settle sex suit is rejected

By Jeff Gottlieb
Mercury News Staff Writer

The Catholic priest who heads the psychiatric unit at El Camino Hospital in Mountain View has offered $135,000 to a Pasadena woman to drop a lawsuit alleging he had sex with her when she was a teen-ager.

The woman, ▓▓▓▓▓▓▓▓, rejected the offer, according to a document written under penalty of perjury.

The document also offers ▓▓▓▓ version of how she got involved with Dr. Thomas Havel and provides more details of their alleged sexual relationship, including the places where they had sex and specific sexual acts. The details are contained in interrogatories, answers to questions Havel asked ▓▓▓▓▓▓▓.

▓▓▓▓▓▓ said the sex acts started in 1968 when she was 13 and lasted until she ended the relationship when she was 18 or 19 and a student at UCLA.

Havel declined comment. His attorney, Edward Hinshaw of San Jose, said ▓▓▓▓▓▓▓'s version of events contained numerous inaccuracies, but he declined to specify them.

▓▓▓▓▓▓ said she "was lonely and was confused by her feelings brought on by her awakening sexuality" when she went to Havel for counseling in the summer of 1968.

At first, according to the document, Havel counseled her. But soon, she said, the counseling sessions turned to sex.

Tragically, the *San Jose Mercury News* article refers to the abuse of a thirteen-year-old girl as a "relationship." This harmful description hides the true nature of the abuse; it was not a "relationship" between a doctor and a thirteen-year-old girl—it was *abuse*.[387]

There are public databases of Catholic, Baptist, Hollywood, Boy Scouts, and Mennonite accused predators. There are currently no databases for therapists, psychologists, and psychiatrists who have been accused, arrested, and jailed for abusing patients while under their professional care. The class structure of power lets those with power stand above accountability. They operate in a sea of immunity and privilege, threatening the community with exploitation and abuse. How do we keep these professions accountable? How do we keep hospitals and mental institutions accountable if they are ruled by "professional courtesy" and insular oversight?[388] Arrogance and class privilege in these professions smother accountability and justice. But hey, offending psychiatrists can just use electro-convulsive therapy (ECT) to erase memories for patients in their care, erasing previous abuse by the doctor.

Power and Authority

Carolyn was a victim of domestic abuse when she approached me in my role as a SNAP leader and described her efforts to get marriage counseling from a priest. The Catholic prohibition against divorce left her with no option but to remain in the abusive marriage. Carolyn felt trapped and alone, especially when the priest exploited her vulnerability and emotional distress by initiating a sexual relationship. The priest used the therapy sessions to take advantage of her vulnerability and use his spiritual authority and counselor role to abuse her.

Robert, a Catholic soldier who questioned his sexuality, sought counseling while serving in Korea. As a young soldier far from home, he felt alone and isolated and sought connection with a priest who served as chaplain to seek counsel. What was supposed to be a supportive and helpful process turned into an opportunity for the priest to groom and then sexually abuse the young soldier.[389] When researching the database at BishopAccountability, I found that this priest had been repeatedly transferred from parish to parish, indicating problems.[390] The transfer to the military indicated the bishop wanted to remove him from the diocese and transfer him away from suspicion.

The military chaplaincy was an easy fix for Catholic Bishops to dump an accused predator away from parishioners and media exposure. The bishop can assure the parishioners that he is addressing the problem, while in reality, he is merely *passing the trash*, a common practice.[391]

Clergy who were caught in parishes for abuse were frequently transferred by bishops to outlying parishes, Indian reservations, hospitals, and the military.

Workplace

Famous researcher Diana Russell noted in her book, *Sexual Exploitation: Rape, Child Sexual Abuse, and Workplace Harassment*, that the prevalence of abuse and harassment in the workplace was widespread for both men and women, quoting a survey of 23,000 office workers in state government.[392] The results were startling: "Forty-two percent of all female employees and fifteen percent of male employees reported being sexually harassed at work."[393]

If predators have power in an institution, they use this authority and privilege to exploit their behavior. Sometimes, as a measure of protection, predators take additional steps to groom and manipulate coworkers so that abuse is overlooked or rationalized as *consensual*.

Two decades after testifying against Supreme Court Justice Clarence Thomas, Professor Anita Hill—commenting in her book, *Believing*, about how Gen X could play a role in gender equality and preventing harassment—warned the audience "that individual oppressive behavior was only possible because institutions sanctioned it."[394]

Adama Iwu, a corporate lobbyist in Sacramento, says she considered the same risks after she was groped in front of several 2018 colleagues at an event. She was shocked when none of her male coworkers stepped in to stop the assault. The next week, she organized an open letter for 147 women to sign, exposing harassment in the California government. When she told people about the campaign, she said they were wary. "Are you sure you want to do this?" they warned her. "Remember Anita Hill."[395]

Hollywood

Hollywood producer Harvey Weinstein exemplifies the power of misogyny and male supremacy. Lauren O'Connor, one of his employees, nailed the situation in a letter to the management of the Weinstein Company: "I am a 28-year-old woman trying to make a living and a career. Harvey Weinstein is a 64-year-old, world-famous man, and this is his company. The balance of power is me: 0, Harvey Weinstein: 10."[396]

Another Hollywood director to be accused by multiple victims was film writer and director James Toback—accused in civil court by forty victims, just some of the over 400 victims who stepped forward to report him.[397] As a director of major Hollywood films, Toback used that power and influence to exploit. And a predator he was, as exemplified in the *Los Angeles Times* headline, "395: The Number of Women Who Have Contacted the *Times* With Allegations of Sexual Harassment Against James Toback," dated January 7, 2018.[398] It is important to note that Toback exploited and abused women for forty years, with over 400 victims. Please note that the 400 victims may be underrepresented as the count does not include more victims who did not come forward publicly. In 2025, forty women were awarded a symbolic victory in a New York civil case for $1.68 billion.[399]

Statute of limitations laws, which severely limit the reporting of crimes, prohibited the criminal prosecution of Toback due to time limitations.[400] However, in 2022, a New York bill called a "lookback window" was passed, giving a one-year opportunity and expanding the time to sue Toback.[401] The SOL was an opening to sue outside previously prescribed time limits.[402] That law gave victims an opportunity to file civil complaints seeking damages in civil court.

The public exposure and the New York civil lawsuit gave many victims an opening to share their experiences. "It was the one secret I never shared about myself with my husband or anyone else," said Sarah MacKay, who was an aspiring actress studying musical theater at the American Musical and Dramatic Academy in New York when she met

Toback in 2004, adding that, because she blamed herself, she felt too much anger and shame to talk about what happened to her. Hearing others, so changed that. "I started to feel an overwhelming sense of relief, validation, and encouragement in knowing I wasn't alone," MacKay said. "And, for the first time ever, feeling that it wasn't my fault that I'd been assaulted."[403]

Racism

Discrimination, immigration status, income, misogyny, and racism significantly impact the selection of potential victims.[404] For instance, Black and Hispanic children in foster care are particular targets.[405] The conditions of historical racism have reduced the social standing and power of people of color and marginal communities who collectively have fewer resources (social, political, and economic). The more subjugated, oppressed, and vulnerable the community, the more likely they are to be victims of abuse.[406]

Cultural Exploitation on Indian Reservations

At the age of five, Charbonneau-Dahlen, a member of the Turtle Mountain Band of Chippewa Indians of North Dakota, was sent to St. Paul's Indian Mission School, a boarding school on the Yankton Sioux Reservation in Marty, South Dakota, where she said she and her eight sisters suffered horrific abuse. Native News Online points to 1950 when Mary Lou, one of the nine sisters, was seven years old: "Father Francis took me to the church basement where they stored coffins when somebody died," she said. "He would lift me up and tell me that if I didn't do what he told me to, he would put me in a coffin." She said he forced her to perform oral sex on him and knows of other girls who became pregnant. "They aborted the babies right there at the school," she said, "and burned the fetuses in the incinerator. I worked in the incinerator room, and anything Sister brought down in that bucket, I just had to put it in the incinerator."[407]

In 2010, nine sisters came forward seeking justice in the civil court after they were abused at a residential school in South Dakota.[408] As they began that case, South Dakota legislators responded by amending the state SOL laws to limit the Catholic Church's accountability for decades of abuse in Indian residential schools. The nine sisters were blocked from taking civil action.[409]

When I was president of the board of directors of SNAP, I traveled to Sioux Falls, South Dakota, on May 24, 2019, to extend support for the nine women.[410] American history tells many stories of the rape of Native Americans, from Christopher Columbus to modern America to the Catholic and Mormon residential schools.[411]

Sexual violence against Native American Indians is not just a historical event. It requires an understanding of the past to address the current crimes. The author, Robin Whyatt, in her article "Violence Against Native Women Has Colonial Roots," addressed the problem by providing a subtitle of "Understanding Today's Violence Against Native American Women Requires Confronting Our Brutal Past."[412] Over two hundred years of occupation, systematic abuse, and economic exploitation leave a mark on present-day society. Whyatt continues, "More than half of Native American women experience violence at some point during their lifetimes, and one out of three are raped. On some reservations, people say they do not know a single woman who has not been raped, and they tell their daughters what to do when—not if—they are raped."[413]

Indian residential schools in the USA and Canada removed children from their homes and reservations to institutionalize Catholic facilities. The impoverished communities of Native Americans reduced their power to demand safety and justice. With limited local resources and isolation, victims have little ability to protest or report crimes. The Indian residential schools of the Catholic and Mormon churches highlight a form of cultural imperialism.

There is a long history of Native American children being removed from reservations and their homes to live in Catholic religious residential schools, where abuse was rampant. Native languages, clothing, and customs were forbidden; Western clothing and uniforms robbed Native culture of its expression. Up until the mid-1960s, religious residential schools forcibly removed children from their family homes and stripped them of their culture. Widespread abuse and violence in Catholic residential schools are compounded by the accompanying ills of racism, poverty, and social isolation. For a hundred years, the Catholic residential schools gave predators free rein.[414]

The schools were run chiefly by religious institutions, primarily Catholics and Mormons. However, other faith communities were also involved and made the children vulnerable by dehumanizing them to a foreign culture. The ripping away from their culture, language, and dress at an early age, combined with being transferred hundreds of miles from home, made these children especially vulnerable. The Carlisle Indian Industrial School opened in 1879 and operated for thirty years; its mission was to "Kill the Indian in him and save the man."[415] Similar sentiments were held by other Catholic "missionaries" who wanted to eradicate Indian culture; they had the racist sentiment of "rip the Indian out of the child."[416]

The isolated Indian communities were a convenient dumping ground for clergy caught in parishes nationwide, as tens of thousands of children were sent to these boarding schools. The children were isolated, abused, and beaten. Researchers documented over sixty-five articles on violence at Indian residential schools, which requires more investigations into this painful history.[417]

The overwhelming scope of abuse of Native American women indicates that racism, misogyny, and privilege combine to make them targets. "Non-Indigenous perpetrators commit an estimated 86–96 percent of the abuse of Native women and are rarely brought to justice. Sexual assault has been experienced by Native women for centuries. Used as a tool of war and colonization, rape was a way to conquer the people during attacks from the beginning of colonization."[418]

Rape has been used to destroy the will of subjugated populations. Used as a tool of oppression and exploitation, it is a crime against humanity.

Inaction Negates Justice

Weak laws, compromised legislators, compliant judges, and lazy prosecutors hamper the prosecution of criminal offenders as they operate within a system of power relations. They are the foundation of the meme *old boys' network*. Social position, cultural (White) background, and class solidarity are bonds of solidarity, connection, and identity working against accountability.

Sarah Ransome, one of Epstein's victims and the author of the book *Silenced No More*, shared in an article her observation of the levers of power, starting with a string of powerful men: "Powerful figures, Kenneth Starr and Alan Dershowitz made a secret deal with Miami's US attorney, Alexander Acosta, that protected Epstein from federal charges and allowed him to work at his office during the day throughout his 18-month sentence for state crimes. Acosta later became Donald Trump's labor secretary."[419]

How easily we have seen adjudicated predators escape with little consequence like Epstein, Donald Trump, and others.[420] Money, power, influence, and connections help the predators escape justice too many times, such as we saw in the Brock Turner case where the judge thought, and ruled, that a rapist, coming from a "good family," deserved leniency. This raises a few questions for prosecutors and judges: Can family and personal connections justify a lenient sentence? Would you throw your brother in jail? Would you prosecute your buddy from the Freemasons or the Shriners' lodge? Would you arrest your golf buddy with whom you share membership in the same country club?

Legislators rely on the political contributions of the fortunate; prosecutors rely on the largesse of the well-to-do public, which contributes to their public campaigns; and judges cater to the privileged few, who are friends and neighbors who swim in the same social circle.

The legal system reinforces prey and predators through inaction. If there is no justice when a predator comes before the court, it allows violence to continue. Even when judges allow a case to proceed, rapists commonly receive an inconsequential sentence, as seen when only less than 3 percent of sexual predators serve jail time.[421] If all the players in the justice system acted with the highest motives, then hundreds of victims could be saved. If there had been timely reporting of known abuse by an administrator acting ethically, such as in the case of Michigan State doctor Nassar, who abused over 200 women, it might have prevented the abuse of dozens if not hundreds of other victims going back decades.

Raids

In October 2018, police raided the offices of all six Catholic Diocese of Michigan as a result of a request from the Michigan AG.[422] The raids were investigating the dioceses' handling of clergy abuse of minors with a broad search that included diocesan offices, pastoral centers, and church archives. Several months later, in May 2019, the Dallas police raided the Catholic Diocese of Dallas, Texas, due to suspicions that officials were hiding information.[423] "According to police, church officials repeatedly stonewalled investigators' attempts to get information about allegations made against at least five priests."[424]

State and local agencies carried over legacy inaction and institutional resistance to aggressively enforcing the law. They were slow to reform. *The Boston Globe's Spotlight* investigation revealed several instances of lax enforcement by police and resistant prosecutors who had a responsibility to pursue consequences for the predator.[425] The institutional power and authority of the church in Boston smothered any serious challenge to its actions by civil authorities.

Predators diminish human life by wielding tools of privilege. How can a survivor of violence achieve justice in a system based on the inequality of predator and prey? The child rapist Jeffrey Epstein's ridiculous light sentence is another example of the powerful using their wealth to escape justice. The numerous accusations against him melted away with payoffs, public and private, allowing him to escape accountability. Again, the powerful escape accountability, such as in the case of England's Prince

Andrew, who famously engaged in these criminal acts and escaped one accusation by paying $16 million to a victim as part of a NDA.[426]

Justice awaits an answer; the fight against abuse is an ongoing site of contention between institutions that cover abuse and those fighting to protect the vulnerable, support the harmed, and prevent future abuse. The more we understand and address a victim's vulnerability, the more we can prevent abuse and achieve a just society. As we shall see in the next chapter, the rising social movement of survivors intervenes to raise public awareness through conventional media and social media, sounding the alarm.

CHAPTER 9

MEDIA SOUNDS THE ALARM

Media Pays Attention

Oprah Winfrey took the initiative to address sexual abuse of men and publicly introduced the scope of a previously unknown crime. She assembled two hundred male victims, filling the recording TV studio, for her syndicated *Oprah Winfrey Show* in 2010. Women make up the majority of abuse victims, maybe 90 percent of all cases of abuse, but less is known about the abuse of men. Winfrey introduced her audience of fifteen million viewers to the men who shared their stories, and the difficulty they had in telling them due to low self-esteem, self-silencing, and shame.

Oprah hosted a two-part episode titled "200 Men Step Forward to Speak About Childhood Sexual Abuse."[427] The audience visibly expressed compassion, some in tears, upon hearing the suffering of each survivor.[428] Winfrey had previously revealed that she was raped by a relative when she was nine years old.

Tyler Perry, the actor, director, and producer, suggested that Oprah have a show on male survivors, emphasizing the importance of sharing survivors' stories to extend support and solidarity. He explained on the show, "I'm hoping that in talking about it, that it's helping a lot of other men to be free because there are so many of us who don't say anything," Tyler says. "The pressure lifts every time you talk, every time you are able to help someone else."[429]

Oprah later reflected on the importance of the episodes: "In my 25 years of doing this, I'm more proud of these two shows than almost anything else I've done in my career. These are two of the most phenomenal shows I've ever done."[430] Oprah's popular TV program reached tens of millions of viewers in over 150 countries, raising awareness.

Mainstream Media Emerges From the Sidelines

Before the modern era of public disclosures, there was a long history of mainstream media ignoring the social plague of sexual violence. They carried forward all the ills of society by dismissing or ignoring violence as a social problem. For too long, the media saw abuse within the framework of sensational reporting to satisfy readership and viewership. Undue influence on the corporate bottom line prompted sensational, lurid, and inflammatory headlines, which sold newspapers. Racism and misogyny, the curses of social discourse, also infected media reporting of violence.

Despite the dangers of speaking out during the Jim Crow era, Recy Taylor, a 24-year-old Black mother and sharecropper, refused to stay silent after being kidnapped and gang-raped by six White men while walking home from church in Abbeville, Alabama, on Sept. 3, 1944. Although the men threatened to kill her if she told anyone, Taylor bravely testified against the men who attacked her. Yet two grand juries failed to indict the men. When Taylor reported the crime and went to the press, she received support from the NAACP and Rosa Parks.[431]

Her courage in reporting generated little mainstream media attention. The case received little media attention outside the African American press. The *Pittsburgh Courier*, an African American newspaper, ran this headline: "Alabama Whites Attack Woman; Not Punished."[432]

The Recy Taylor case points to the previous public indifference to rape and the inability to see rape as a crime against women of color.

Taylor did not receive justice, as Black women rarely received justice in Southern courts. As the Civil Rights and Women's Movements grew, they reflected the legacy of past heroes, like Taylor. Danielle McGuire wrote in her book, *At the Dark End of the Street*, "When radical feminists finally made rape and sexual assault political issues, they walked in the footsteps of generations of Black women."[433]

Recy Taylor and Rosa Parks formed an advocacy organization, The Committee for Equal Justice (also known as the Committee for Equal Justice for the Rights of Mrs. Recy Taylor), to raise awareness and promote justice for women of color. Eighteen chapters nationwide advocated for justice leading to organized advocacy against violence, interracial rape, and White attacks on Black women.

The Legacy of Silence

The bravery of Recy Taylor stepping forward marked a new era in public disclosure. The perversions of justice, racism, and misogyny held a long history of silencing women of color that carried over from the Civil War and slavery. "One cannot rape one's own property," Susan Brownmiller wrote, "[t]he rape of one man's slave by another white man was considered a mere "trespass" in the eyes of plantation law."[434]

The history of buried accusations highlighted Taylor's bravery in naming the accused. Writer Samhita Mukhopadhyay, a MediaJustice [formerly: Center for Media Justice] coordinator, pointed out in her 2019 essay, "Trial by Media," the lasting legacy of media silence "The rape of women of color rarely makes the front page of any national newspaper."[435] Explaining some background, she wrote: "The cultural legacy of previous laws [. . .] dominant narratives, structural inequities, class inequities, and cultural practices [. . .] make it difficult for Black women to prove they have been raped."[436]

McGuire agreed in *At the Dark End of the Street*, pointing out that women made "tremendous legal and political inroads, partly because of the legacy of the civil rights movement and the African-American activism on sexual violence."⁴³⁷ The media's historical blindness to sexual violence in general and dead silence on violence against women of color remains as baggage, obscuring the culture of abuse in modern society.

Oprah Winfrey referred to Recy Taylor when she received the Cecil B. DeMille Award acceptance speech at the Golden Globes, commenting on how social justice campaigns benefit from the help of the press. "They threatened to kill her if she ever told anyone, but her story was reported to the NAACP, where a young worker by the name of Rosa Parks became the lead investigator on her case, and together they sought justice. . . . She lived as we all have lived, too many years in a culture broken by brutally powerful men. For too long, women have not been heard or believed if they dared to speak their truth to the power of those men. But their time is up. Their time is up."⁴³⁸

The first victory for Black women who were victims of rape arrived in 1959 in Chattanooga, Florida, the first time that White men were charged with raping a Black woman in that state. Four White men were prosecuted and found guilty. McGuire observed the historical significance of this verdict on her website, DanielleMcGuire.com. "The Tallahassee verdict was a major break from the past. From slavery through the bulk of the 20th century, white men assaulted and raped Black women with impunity. The conviction and life sentences sent a powerful message. For the first time since Reconstruction, Black women could imagine state power being used to protect them and hold white men accountable for their actions."⁴³⁹

While the (White) mainstream press ignored the Tallahassee case as they did with Recy Taylor, the case received attention and coverage from the *New York Amsterdam News* and several African American newspapers, highlighting a historic verdict.⁴⁴⁰ The media refrained from lurid and sensationalist reporting, which was a step forward.

Opening the Doors to Public Discourse

The mid-1980s saw progress when several media outlets reported on the crimes of the Catholic Church. One brave reporter, Jason Berry, tackled the issue, spotlighting the 1985 case of a prolific child abuser, Catholic priest Fr. Gilbert Gauthe, in Abbeville, Louisiana. He became the first priest to face a criminal trial, which received national attention due to Berry's reporting. Gauthe pleaded guilty to abusing thirty-seven children and received a twenty-year sentence.[441] He served ten years and moved to Texas, where he abused a three-year-old child.

Berry revealed the dark secrets of the church, created a scandal, and electrified the local community. It was a scandal that could not be dismissed, reaching a national audience and prompting the Vatican Embassy in Washington to send three church-appointed *investigators* to learn more and mitigate the stain on the church's reputation. Berry's reporting prompted the exposure of other cases of clergy abuse across the country, and he followed up with a book, *Lead Us Not into Temptation*, in 1992, about this trial and the failure of the Catholic Church to protect children.[442]

The articles established a historic moment that led to decades of continued reporting of abuse in major institutions. Previously, all public mention of abuse was reported as individual depravity, not as social ills or through institutions of power. The Gauthe case was one of the first "outings" of an institution covering up violence as a corporate action.

In 1985, Barbara Blaine, the founder of SNAP, read Berry's report on violence in the Louisiana parish while working in Chicago. The national media's attention to the Gauthe case in 1985 sparked the formation of SNAP, pointing to the power of media to mobilize and activate survivor advocacy. We saw similar developments after the first media accounts of the abuse of the gymnasts and the formation of the Army of Survivors.[443]

Pioneers in Exposing Violence

Before the internet became an information source, around the year 2000, traditional media played a dominant role in community awareness, expanding opportunities for victims of abuse to learn of other victims and survivor organizations. Phil Donahue's TV talk show of the 1990s provided an opportunity when he interviewed Barbara Blaine of SNAP, Father Andrew Greeley, and reporter Jason Berry.[444]

David Clohessy, the executive director of SNAP for twenty-five years, commented on the significance of this 1993 interview on the Phil Donahue show in an article in the *National Catholic Reporter* on August 26, 2024. "Perhaps most important, talk shows like Donahue brought forth more victims than absolutely any other source. His producers put the SNAP phone number on the screen, and hundreds would call seeking support."[445] Donahue was so helpful that "we in SNAP resolved never to turn down the opportunity to appear on one, regardless of how tawdry or exploitative they might seem."[446]

Blaine praised Donahue, who "gave support to clergy sex abuse survivors like us" in the early days of the fight against abuse.[447] Decades later, Clohessy pointed to the significance of the media becoming an engine for reaching thousands of survivors nationwide, an event that was impossible for an organization without a budget. "Without talk shows—especially *Donahue* and later the *Oprah Show*—— we would have been able to reach and help far fewer survivors trapped in shame, silence, and self-blame."[448]

At the turn of the millennium, attention to sexual violence expanded dramatically, increasing social awareness. SNAP's network grew tenfold with the national attention of the *Boston Globe Spotlight* series, demonstrating the media's immense power to reach millions of victims. Media exposure and social awareness led to the emergence of advocacy and survivor organizations throughout the mid-1990s and early 2000s, which continued to grow and thrive, reaching all sectors of society.

Media as an Advocacy Tool

Most reporting of sexual violence before 2000 focused on individual cases without addressing the social context of widespread abuse. As addressed in previous chapters, predators and institutions go to great lengths to maintain public ignorance by compelling silence. Historically, when a predator was exposed, you might see a paragraph or two in the newspaper and a ten-second spot on local TV news. That legacy of overlooking abuse began to erode with the reporting of Jason Berry in the late 1980s and the testimony of Anita Hill in the mid-1990s.

SNAP, along with its local leaders in a hundred different locations, became a powerful resource for public advocacy by engaging with the media. SNAP held media training exercises at its annual winter leaders' meetings and annual national conferences. These exercises and instructions were a form of professional development for volunteers to develop the skills to hold press conferences and to prepare press releases. This training had several aspects, including how to craft a press announcement by outlining the basics of who, what, when, and where for any event—interviews required practicing beforehand. The practice also gave us experience in responding spontaneously. As preparation for any media interview, we also learned to focus on assembling three main points to avoid wandering and getting lost in a dozen topics. One exercise had a volunteer take center stage with a pretend microphone, giving a statement while being questioned by the trainer, David Clohessy, who posed as a reporter asking questions. The practice gave me and others the confidence to speak up without wilting, highlighting the importance of being prepared for press events and practicing, practicing, practicing. This exercise enabled leaders to respond to local issues independently of the national organization.

One participant, Bob, a local SNAP leader in Oregon, shared his media experience: "I was terrified. The first few times I spoke out to the media, I feared what the Cardinal would do to me. But after a while, I realized they were more afraid of what the media would do to them if they did anything to me. That was very liberating."⁴⁴⁹

Press events and protests by survivors accomplished four important mission goals: 1.) to point out an accused predator to protect the community from future abuse, 2.) provide evidence that violence existed in the church without accountability, 3.) to deliver the message to survivors of abuse that have never reported it that they are not alone, 4.) to raise awareness in the community about sexual violence.

The Myth and the Media—I Am the Only One

The research and advocacy organization CHILD USA cites a statistic mentioned earlier in the book that the average age of a victim of child sex abuse stepping forward publicly to disclose their abuse is when they are fifty-two years old.⁴⁵⁰ I buried my memories for fifty years, going public in 2016 about my abuse in Iowa that took place there in 1959. I initiated news interviews in my hometown of Sioux City, Iowa, and in cities nearby, such as Omaha, Nebraska, and Des Moines, Iowa. I received front-page news in the Sunday edition of the *Sioux City Journal*, several local TV interviews, and a public radio interview in Des Moines, Iowa.⁴⁵¹

As a result of my public disclosure, fifteen of my classmates came forward and shared that the same priest had abused them! Surprisingly, no one had previously reported Fr. Murphy until I went public fifty-five years later. I was the first to call out the child abuser. The "#MeToo" phenomenon of one victim stepping forward and dozens following demonstrates how the media brings previously silent victims forward.

We have also seen how media investigations, such as the *Boston Globe Spotlight* and investigations of Bill Cosby, Jeffrey Epstein, and Harvey Weinstein, brought hundreds of previously silent victims forward, saying, "Me too." One of the most dramatic demonstrations of the power of the media was when one gymnast stepped forward in response to an article about Olympic coach Larry Nassar in the Indianapolis daily newspaper, the *IndyStar*, and 200 victims followed.⁴⁵²

Catching the media's attention was an important element in reaching silent victims. Standing in front of a church, holding a sign, may reach a hundred or so parishioners and the few cars whizzing by. Getting a local newspaper or television station to cover our event could reach an audience of tens of thousands.

The importance of media attention was the focus of the National Sexual Violence Resource Center's report in March 2023, "What is the Connection between Media, Sexual Violence, and Systems of Oppression?" "Social media, television shows, movies, advertisements, celebrity events, and other large public viewership happenings are powerful tools in setting cultural trends, social norms, and lifestyle benchmarks. These norms include subtle (or not-so-subtle) cues about how certain people should look, act, what they should wear, and how they should live. This doesn't just create changes in material culture (styles, trends, and aesthetics) but creates internal changes within us, between us, and internally in our own community. It changes how we see ourselves, how we see others, and how others see us."[453]

Similarly, the *Boston Globe Spotlight* series exposed the breadth of violence in Catholic schools and churches in 2002.[454] More than a decade later, a CBS "60 Minutes" program broadcasted an episode titled "Before Spotlight" that pointed to the long-standing problem of clergy sexual abuse.[455]

Four months after the *Oprah Show*, in March 2011, national news covered the arrest of Pennsylvania State University assistant football coach Jerry Sandusky. Victims filed dozens of allegations against Sandusky, as well as university administrators, for failing to act when notified of the abuse. "The former president of Penn State University and two other former administrators were sentenced to jail terms Friday for failing to report a 2001 allegation that assistant football coach Jerry Sandusky was molesting young boys."[456]

Media Reveals Institutional Crimes and Cover-Ups

As the leader of a national contender for the best football team in college sports, Penn State's Head Coach Joe Paterno, along with other university administrators, dismissed and ignored the many allegations of Sandusky's abuse for a dozen years. His arrest and trial led to a sentence of thirty to sixty years in prison. The scandal of Sandusky and complicit university officials made national news in 2016.[457]

The conviction was the first major blow to collegiate sports. Soon, other college sports scandals surfaced, such as gymnasts at Michigan State, wrestlers at Ohio State, and athletes at the University of Michigan. Other scandals surfaced, such as the billion-dollar settlement of the University of Southern California over a university gynecologist and the silence of administrators who knew of the abuse for at least a decade and did nothing.[458] One of the attorneys for the victims, John C. Manly, who represented the third group of plaintiffs, said, "The reason U.S.C. paid this money was that there was culpability—they knew early on, in the early '90s and through his tenure that this was happening."[459]

Larry Nassar's downfall started in March 2016, when *IndyStar* published its "Out of Balance" series, investigating USA Gymnastics' broken policies for handling sexual abuse.[460] Gymnast Rachael Denhollander of Louisville, Kentucky, wrote to the *IndyStar* on August 4, 2016, disclosing her abuse by Nassar. *IndyStar* continued covering the case alongside other reporters from the USA Today Network, including the *Lansing State Journal* in Michigan, where the Nassar trial occurred. After the initial report, five more victims came forward, then, "More than 500 women were abused by Nassar, who spent 18 years as the team doctor of the U.S. women's national gymnastics team and also worked at Michigan State."[461]

An academic study by the Media School of Indiana University titled "Media Framing of Larry Nassar and the USA Gymnastics Child Sex Abuse Scandal" pointed to a limitation of media coverage; however, once star athletes became involved, the news media paid more attention.[462]

The personal attachment of public media to focus on one athlete ignores the systemic failures and the larger discussion about the societal impact of CSA in sports.

The same academic study showed the number of news articles concerning the abuse of gymnasts from the first report. Five hundred monthly media reports appeared in the first dozen years. Once the trial took shape, Olympic stars became engaged. "The number of articles, both on the local and national sides, remained relatively low until the more prominent names of the sport, Gabby Douglas, Aly Raisman, and McKayla Maroney, came forward. Once the story achieved more salience, the media coverage shifted its emphasis, where themes emerged. The media effects were dramatic, based on the higher notoriety of the Olympic stars, and the number of media stories shot up; it rose from 500 to 10,000 stories in a month."[463]

In contrast to the silence of the MSU hierarchy, the *IndyStar* newspaper exposed a widely known predator preying on Olympic-winning gymnasts. The important investigation and reporting of the *Indianapolis Star* follows the examples of the *Boston Globe's Spotlight* investigative series of 2002 and the exposure of 7,000 Boy Scouts in the "Perversion Files" in 2012 published by the *Los Angeles Times*.[464]

Media Exposes FBI Failures

Even with victims reporting, many governmental agencies failed to act. For instance, gymnast McKayla Maroney went to the FBI, which failed to respond for over a year. Even then, the FBI falsely manufactured Maroney's testimony. A *PBS NewsHour* story titled, "WATCH: McKayla Maroney Says FBI Made Up Statements She Never Said to Protect Larry Nassar," called attention to the subservience of government officials to prominent institutions and individuals, effectively silencing victims and protecting predators: "She said the FBI fabricated her story to protect a '"serial child abuser"' instead of her and other athletes. They had legal, legitimate evidence of child abuse and did nothing."[465]

The academic study by the Media School of Indiana University titled "Media Framing of Larry Nassar and the USA Gymnastics Child Sex Abuse Scandal" also looked at the stories the media did not report. It pointed to the media's interests as they did not always report beyond the lurid details of individual stories. After all, the lurid sells newspapers. The fallout from this attitude of reporting is that the focus on the individual victims and perpetrators fails to examine the social causes that provide this environment for abuse to happen. This style of reporting neither helps the victim nor makes the community safer. The study observes that "reporting on one incident of abuse ignores society's systematic failures to prosecute."[466]

Media Events Promote Public Awareness

The SNAP network of over 30k contacts worldwide and over a hundred local leaders in six countries advanced the model that publicity, press statements, and press conferences were the best way to reach those harmed by abuse. During my leadership role as president of the board of directors from 2018 to 2021, I made efforts to hold public events, issue press statements, and hold press conferences. Local, national, and international media interviewed me hundreds of times, including media from seventeen countries, and national media, including the *New York Times*, *TIME* magazine, *Fox Nightly News*, *CNN*, *USA Today*, *Al Jazeera America*, *National Catholic Reporter*, *The Guardian* (US), *NPR Morning Edition*, and the *National Enquirer*. International media interviewed me, including media from Ireland, Croatia, New Zealand, Australia, Austria, India, South Africa, the UK, Brazil, Netherlands, Qatar, Russia, Turkey, Israel, Canada, Saudi Arabia, the Philippines, and Egypt.

After two years of investigation and testimony, the Pennsylvania Grand Jury released its report in August 2018, pointing to over 300 accused clergy and over 1,000 victims.[467] The report had been expected; SNAP leadership was prepared. As executive director of SNAP at the time, I knew that the number of victims and predators would be large, as the church had a long history of cover-ups in other dioceses. The researchers of BishopAccountability.com have already documented hundreds of cases of cover-ups in Pennsylvania.[468]

SNAP leaders Becky Ianni, Judy Jones, and I visited two cities each, covering the six Catholic dioceses. We prepared weeks in advance for the release of the report and held press conferences in front of six dioceses in six different cities in Pennsylvania. We also prepared media statements for local and national media, which provided background on the scope of abuse. Both local and national media covered the stories. According to news monitoring services, SNAP media preparation and press conferences generated over two hundred media stories in the following days. That week, I wrote a press release calling for grand juries in every state, saying, "What Happened in Pennsylvania Happens in Every Parish in America."[469]

In 2019, the *Houston Chronicle* headline put another religious organization on the spot. "20 Years, 700 Victims, Southern Baptist Abuse Spreads, as Leaders Resist Reform."[470] This series of articles led to the comparison of abuse in the Catholic Church. Most Baptist parishioners found it difficult to believe, whereas some took action, and some 19 percent moved away from the dominant association of the Baptist Church, the SBC.[471]

Reporting—Get the Language Right

Columbia University's Dart Center for Journalism and Trauma Tip Sheet gives guidance on reporting violence: "Get the language right. Rape or assault is not 'sex.' A pattern of abuse is not an 'affair.' Rape or assault is in no way associated with normal sexual activity; trafficking in women is not to be confused with prostitution."[472]

It is essential to add a clarion call: abuse of a young teenager by a coach or teacher is not a *relationship*; it is child abuse. Get the language right.

Modern media faces increased competition from social media while simultaneously consolidating into fewer news organizations. Published stories belong to an ever-shrinking number of companies and explosive media centralization across all fields.[473] Some may describe modern American media as continually demonstrating their shared interest in maintaining and reproducing legacy systems, not fully divesting in old ideologies, i.e., patriarchy, elitism, and class bias.

As survivors, activists, and social justice organizations raise social consciousness, the monopolies of media power have responded to that pressure. Public intervention, survivor advocacy initiatives, and the mobilization of survivor movement activists become a social force to call out weaknesses. The bastions of power rarely make reforms from within—they make reforms when forced to do so.

Media reporting maintains tension between two contending forces: one, to inform the public, and two, to hold and increase market and profit share for its owners. Traditional media bears the legacy of ignoring abuse in marginalized communities, such as communities of color, the less abled, the homeless, and the mentally ill.[474] The media have failed to address the unique circumstances of LGBTQ communities and their spectacularly high rates of abuse.[475] The scandal of Catholic residential schools in the USA mirrors the hundreds of cases of abuse exposed in Canada. The history of abuse in residential schools is yet to be unearthed in the USA. These historic institutional assaults have been long-hidden for over a hundred years, yet they are rarely examined in the news.[476] All marginalized communities have become targets, yet have not been fully explored in the media.[477]

Media reporting carries the legacy of damaging descriptions of abuse. Describing sexual assault in lurid language was designed to grab headlines, sell papers, and engage TV viewers, a practice not limited to sensationalist journals like the *National Enquirer*. Other media problems persisted, such as blaming the victim, as we saw in chapter 5, "Why Survivors Don't Report." Another problem was the characterization of child abuse in the media; instead of describing abuse in the case of an older man and a young teen as abuse, the press often resorted to identifying it as a relationship. We see that even in current times.[478]

Reporting Patterns

In May 2011, a Berkeley Media Study examined hundreds of news stories about abuse. Here were their clear patterns of news coverage: First, child abuse remains largely out of view. Second, when child abuse is covered, it is usually because an incident of child abuse has achieved some milestone within the court system. Third, prevention remains virtually invisible. Fourth, the language that describes child abuse in news coverage is often vague.[479]

Guide for Journalists

The Minnesota Coalition Against Sexual Assault created an online guide for journalists, "Sexual Violence: A Guide for Journalists," which challenges reporters with imprecise language and descriptions that can misconstrue violence. Such malformations of the situation deflect from the predator and end up blaming the victim. The following misleading descriptions of victims can arise, diminishing the victim and leading to victim blaming.[480]

- Dressed provocatively and/or was attractive
- Did not report immediately to police—or never reported at all
- Did not report use of a weapon in the assault (more often, coercion and threats are used)
- First said "yes" and then said "no"
- Did not fight back or call for help (a common reaction to trauma is non-resistance or silence due to frozen fear or "tonic immobility")
- Had no physical injuries (the case in the majority of assaults)
- Was young

- Was being prostituted, drunk, using drugs, or willingly accompanied the offender
- Had a history of mental illness
- Had made a prior false report about assault
- Had consensual sex with the offender
- Met or talked with the offender after the assault, or did not leave after the incident

Sarah Welliver, a former journalist and now a public information officer for the Utah Department of Child & Family Services, pointed to the framing of news stories. When it comes to child abuse and neglect, Welliver worried that the conventional news frame discourages communities from taking steps to protect children: "Newsrooms need to have these deeper conversations of how they cover crime and what is really necessary."[481] Newsrooms might choose to forgo the one-off stories and instead compile a database to track common factors in abuse cases in an effort to uncover causes.

Subject Areas as yet Unexplored

The stories of institutional violence continued to tumble into the news, such as the Boy Scouts, Jehovah's Witnesses, public and private schools, Mormons, and the systematic abuse of Native American Indian children in residential schools. These scandals strike at the moral center of America and remain areas requiring continued examination and reporting.[482]

The media have a foothold in several sectors of society as a profit-driven business, an ideological bulwark for maintaining and reproducing the existing social system, a political force carrying tremendous power, and an intervening influence when contending social/political ideas battle for dominance and popular hegemony. Since 2000, mainstream media have fallen on hard times, with hundreds of newspapers failing or being eaten up by large chains. Local media is vanishing. Even TV news is falling in both numbers and influence. Modern media has become a jungle of voices and contending forces, broken from mainstream to other forms, such as streaming, social media, blogs, and podcasts.[483]

The media shapes the focus and attention of opinions, values, and social awareness. Facts and stories can provide background and evidence—they can tell and expose lies. The media have the potential to awaken society to the severity of violence. Society owes much to the courageous reporters who uncovered the powerful, the institutions, and the politicians, such as Nicole Weisensee Egan, Julie Brown, Marisa Kwiatkowski, Ronan Farrow, the *Boston Globe "Spotlight"* reporting team, the *IndyStar* reporting team, Kirby Sommers, Jodi Kantor, Megan Twohey, and Jason Berry.[484]

Advances in Reporting

In her book *Not That Bad: Dispatches from Rape Culture*, Gay pointed to the necessity of reporting. "Sexual assault is no longer an undercurrent in political life; it shouts at us from news headlines, colors the electoral debates, shapes rally slogans and protest chants."[485]

The cacophony of accusations against American presidents, senators, and governors joins other accused predators such as disgraced Hollywood producers, high-ranking clergy, and corporate bosses who use their power to abuse and exploit. Reporting violence has made incremental improvements over time. For media, selling newspapers, getting TV sponsors, and generating a profit remains a compelling mission. However, rising public awareness pushed management to report more stories responsibly. Society and the media continue to be marked by and challenged by the legacy stains of past ideology (i.e., racism and misogyny), stains not yet washed from modern culture.

The public rise in understanding of violence has shifted the conversation. Survivor voices demanding to be heard pushed the media to pay attention and accurately report the information. As awareness of the issue grew, so did the activism. The formation of hundreds of survivor organizations and thousands of social media platforms formed by organizations and individuals since 2000 raised awareness of systematic abuse through media actions, enabling media attention to build the movement, such as the nineteen million who tweeted, "#MeToo,' following the first tweet.

A positive effect is that survivors are less likely to be subjected to victim-blaming due to the growing awareness of media entities that have changed the language in news reporting. The advocacy of survivors and survivor organizations continues to challenge the language and old myths used in reporting. The battle against modern media is not over.

Survivors of violence stepped forward and publicly named crimes and criminals in new articles, on social media, and in public demonstrations. They compelled the media to accurately and correctly report the harm of violence. Emerging as a spontaneous movement nationwide, survivors stepped forward, establishing the foundation for future actions and organizations. Media stories raise community awareness and act as a clarion call to all who suffer in silence.

Social media brought this new movement of survivors to the public's attention and helped announce its existence. The next chapter explores social media's impact on supporting survivors, raising awareness, and propelling social change.

Two resources for media reporters

Two sources of guidance for media reporting on victims of sexual abuse.

- The Dart Center is a project of the Columbia University Graduate School of Journalism, "Reporting on Sexual Violence," tipsheet, July 15, 2011, a guide for reporters of sexual violence https://dartcenter.org/content/reporting-on-sexual-violence#.VA8sM_ldXHs

- Minnesota Coalition Against Sexual Assault, "Sexual Violence: A Guide for Journalists," online guide, http://www.mncasa.org/, updated 2017, a guide for reporters of sexual violence https://mncasa.org/wp-content/uploads/2022/06/Reporting-on-Sexual-Violence_A-guide-for-journalists.pdf

CHAPTER 10

SOCIAL MEDIA AND #METOO

On October 5, 2017, several Hollywood actresses, including Rose McGowan and Ashley Judd, named Hollywood producer Harvey Weinstein in a *New York Times* article by reporters Jodi Kantor and Meghan Twohey, titled "Harvey Weinstein Paid Off Sexual Harassment Accusers for Decades."[486] Reporter Ronan Farrow followed with a *New Yorker* article October 10, 2017, "From Aggressive Overtures to Sexual Assault: Harvey Weinstein's Accusers Tell Their Stories," in which dozens of women spoke of coercion, intimidation, and economic repercussions,[487] including actresses Rose McGowan and Rosanna Arquette, and model and Miss Italy contestant Ambra Battilana Guiterrez, showing a pattern of abuse, coercion, intimidation, and economic repercussions. The list expanded Weinstein's accusers to at least eighty victims.[488] On October 15th, actress Alyssa Milano took to social media and tweeted, "If you've been sexually harassed or assaulted, write 'me too' as a reply to this tweet."

The tweet caught fire, leading millions of others to express their solidarity and shared experiences of sexual harassment, abuse, and rape. The tweet liberated those previously silent to step forward and speak their truth.[489] The world changed at that moment. The impact continues to reverberate throughout society, shaking the foundations of the previous understanding of the scope of abuse. The explosion of solidarity exposed a continent of hidden and silent victims who stepped forward and said, "Me too!" The tweet brought abuse into the public square for examination, discussion, and reform.

A Single Spark Can Start a Prairie Fire

The #MeToo tweet created a variety of related hashtags, unleashing an explosive reaction with 609,000 posts and a worldwide response within days, leading to nineteen million tweets within a month, touching every sector of society.[490] The aphorism, "A single spark can start a prairie fire," aptly describes the conflagration that followed the first tweet. The hashtag became a battle cry for millions.

Eventually, hundreds of women came forward with accounts of harassment or abuse by Weinstein.[491] In November 2017, *Vox Media* published a list of 262 accused Hollywood celebrities, primarily men, along with allegations of harassment and abuse[492] by many women who were included in *The New York Times* and *The New Yorker's* coverage, including Rose McGowan, Mira Sorvino, Laura O'Connor, Zelda Perkins, and Lucia Evans, as well as others who came forward following the release of the initial reports: Angelina Jolie, Cara Delevingne, Kate Beckinsale, Annabella Sciorra, Juliana de Paula, Trish Goff, Lupita Nyong'o, Lauren Sivan, Minka Kelly, Angie Everhart and Daryl Hannah.

Famous Hollywood actresses used their star power to become the vanguard in exposing the scope of abuse. Their stories highlighted how privileged and powerful Hollywood players like Weinstein used their power to exploit and abuse. The Hollywood vanguard created the fireworks that ignited all sectors of society. The fire continues to burn.

Over the next several months, media outlets followed up with reporting on Weinstein and other Hollywood predators, with accusations of hundreds of victims of assault and harassment.[493] These articles opened the door by describing the courage of survivors stepping forward and the elaborate tactics taken to silence and intimidate these victims.

Actress Rosanna Arquette shared her account in a 2018 *NPR* interview about a visit to Hollywood producer Harvey Weinstein's hotel room in the early 1990s.[494] She had an appointment to pick up a script and discuss a possible acting role. Instead of meeting in the lobby, she was directed to his hotel room, where she was met by Weinstein, wearing nothing but a bathrobe, and asking her to give him a massage before grabbing her hand and pulling it toward his penis.[495] Arquette "stayed rooted in the doorway of Weinstein's room" and resisted the assault.[496] Weinstein responded with intimidation, saying, "Rosanna, you're making a very big mistake."[497] He mentioned other actresses who he claimed submitted to his sexual overtures "whose careers he said he had advanced as a result. Arquette responded, 'I'll never be that girl,' and left." [498]

Arquette described how he continued to use his power to intimidate and silence her. "He made things very difficult for me for years." She warned that Weinstein would use similar tactics on other actresses coming forward. "He's going to be working very hard to track people down and silence people," she explained. "To hurt people. That's what he does."[499]

Arquette believes her career suffered; she lost at least one role because of it and, as a result, stayed silent for many years.

Weinstein, as a famous, rich, and influential Hollywood producer, used his power and prestige to exploit hopeful actresses and staff employees. "They range in age from early 20s to late 40s and live in different cities. Some said they did not report the behavior because there were no witnesses, and they feared retaliation by Mr. Weinstein. Others said they felt embarrassed."[500]

Many of the victims cited in *The New Yorker* magazine article confirmed that Miramax and Weinstein movie studios knew of the abuse but did nothing to stop it.[501] Women who stood up to his actions had few choices, such as signing an NDA with some compensation or facing sanctions and penalties in the industry.[502] They accused Weinstein of using his power, lawyers, and public relations staff to dissuade victims from reporting.

The public outing of additional Hollywood predators continued on the publishing platform *Medium*, with one story titled, "Weinstein Isn't the Only One: Screen Celebs Who Abuse Women or Children."[503]

Tarana Burke

Movement leader Tarana Burke coined "me too" in 2006 during her advocacy work with Just Be, a youth social center that empowers girls in Atlanta. She was a grassroots activist for over a decade before the hashtag #MeToo went viral. Burke became a visible and powerful advocate for survivors by forming the #MeToo Movement organization in 2017 to engage in support, advocacy, and political activism on a local and national level.[504] With millions of tweets and rising awareness, the #MeToo Movement fostered the rise of new leaders and organizations, opening the door for other victims worldwide to publicly acknowledge #MeToo!

Her work inspired millions of previously silent victims. Survivors across the globe mobilized with a single statement of solidarity, exposing the true extent of sexual violence in society and declaring connection and identification. The #MeToo hashtag and the "me too. Organization" that formed as a result, exposed the extent of violence and the overwhelming silence of the previous era. *No longer can society look away*. Victims understood—I am not alone.

The tidal wave of activism and the social power of #MeToo translated into political power in the following years.

Silence Breakers

The women who spoke out about Hollywood predators organized and became known as the Silence Breakers. In 2017, they received *TIME* magazine's prestigious front page cover as "Person of the Year." Social media embraced the hashtag #SilenceBreakers, which reflected the emerging voices expressing solidarity with courageous survivors who were breaking the silence.

In addition to his reports in *The New Yorker*, Farrow released a podcast and book titled *Catch & Kill*. The title refers to Weinstein's pattern of "catching and killing" accusations in the media before they reached the public.[505] Catching refers to getting the accuser before they go public and killing the story with intimidation or payoffs. According to an ABC timeline about Donald Trump's similar tactics: "Trump meets with David Pecker, the then-chairman and CEO of American Media Inc.—which owns the *National Enquirer*—at Trump Tower in New York. Pecker agrees to help with Trump's campaign by looking out for negative stories about him to "catch and kill," according to prosecutors' statement of facts."[506]

The most famous case of "catch and kill" arose from Trump's affairs with Stormy Daniels, an adult film actress, and Karen McDougal, an actress and former *Playboy* model. In July 2016, "The National Enquirer secures the rights to McDougal's account for $150,000 but never publishes her story, a tactic known as 'catch and kill.'"[507] Federal prosecutors later said the agreement was meant "to suppress [her] story so as to prevent it from influencing the election." Through his attorney, Michael Cohen, Trump also purchased the life story of Stormy Daniels for $130,000, another case of "catch and kill."

Farrow's reports also illustrated how New York District Attorney Cyrus Vance, Jr. helped protect Weinstein from facing criminal charges.

Survivors began communicating and networking, joining forces with the hundreds of survivors coming forward against other industry predators, like James Toback, Les Moonves, and Bill Cosby. They lobbied state representatives to change the SOL in New York and California, which are critical states for the entertainment industry. This led to important reform laws to hold predators accountable and opened the door for survivors seeking justice. Hollywood victims' immense influence and prestige translated into a new environment of laws and raised awareness. In February 2020, Weinstein was found guilty of rape and sentenced to twenty-three years in prison in New York, a sentence that in 2024 is under appeal with an upcoming retrial.[508] He remains in custody due to his California conviction, where he was sentenced to sixteen years in prison.[509]

#MeToo Hits the Powerful

The #MeToo Movement reached every sector of society. It shattered the dam of denial, resistance, and stonewalling as predators in Hollywood, universities, sports organizations, government, and businesses were outed in mainstream and social media.[510] The title of an article on the publishing platform *Medium* demonstrated an effect of #MeToo: "Weinstein Isn't the Only One: Screen Celebs Who Abuse Women or Children."[511]

In 2017, reporter and legal analyst Lis Wiehl received a $32 million settlement from *Fox News* after she alleged abuse by the popular *Fox News* host, Bill O'Reilly. What made this unique from other MeToo moments was the culture of *Fox* News, which criticized survivors as part of the backlash against the movement. By the end of that year, five more women had registered complaints against O'Reilly, alleging abuse and harassment.[512]

Fox News demanded that the victims sign an NDA in exchange for payments, some of which reached millions of dollars. Only when the web of deception was unraveled by reporters Emily Steel and Michael Schmidt of the *New York Times* did the public come to understand his crimes.[513] *The Times* reported payoffs to five women: *Fox News* producers Rachel Witlieb Bernstein and Andrea Mackris, host Rebecca Gomez Diamond, news anchor Laurie Dhue, and anchor and host Juliet Huddy. The exposure of the NDAs led to O'Reilly's dismissal; advertisers fled, and more victims stepped forward. According to Jodi Kantor and Meg Twohey's book, *She Said,* "On April 19, not even three weeks after the publication of the *Times* story, he was fired. Both he and Rodger Ailes, the Republican power broker and architect of the network, had lost their jobs, not due to claims of mistreating women—*Fox* had known about many of those—but rather because of public exposure of those claims." [514]

Fox News paid O'Reilly $25 million on his departure [my emphasis]. This payment emphasizes that rewarding an accused predator on the way out is the privilege of the powerful.

The Wildfire Spreads

The wildfire spread to all sectors of society, business, universities, sports, etc., exposing predators. The field of battle generated hashtags specific to each sector: #CSA (child sex abuse), #Believewomen, #Believesurvivors, #ChurchToo, #WhyIdidntreport, #SilenceBreakers, #MenToo, #Timesup, and #Survivor, among many others.

The #MeToo meme reached every sector of society. It shattered the dam of denial, resistance, and stonewalling as predators in Hollywood, universities, sports organizations, government, and businesses were outed in mainstream and social media.[515] Social recognition of the scope of abuse raised awareness to all sectors of society.[516]

Fallout

About a year after the #MeToo tweet, the *New York Times* ran a story with the headline, "#MeToo Brought Down 201 Powerful Men. Nearly Half of Their Replacements Are Women."[517] The article identified the 201 accused predators, and those who replaced them. "They had often gotten away with it for years, and for those they harassed, it seemed as if the perpetrators would never pay any consequences. Then came the report that detailed Weinstein's assaults and harassment and his fall from Hollywood's heights."[518]

The backlash reached all sectors of society, where the famous were outed. It wasn't just the vulgar Hollywood producers who abused, but also company bosses, senior attorneys at law firms, famous musicians, honored athletes in sports, politicians, and journalists. The *New York Times* article discussed some limitations after the initial #MeToo revelations:

> A year later, even as the #MeToo movement meets a crackling backlash, it's possible to take stock of how the Weinstein case has changed the corridors of power. Sexual harassment has hardly been erased in the workplace. Federal law still does not fully protect huge groups of women, including those who work freelance or at companies with fewer than fifteen employees. New workplace policies have little effect without deeper cultural change. And as the Supreme Court confirmation battle over Brett Kavanaugh showed, Americans disagree on how people accused of misconduct should be held accountable and what the standard of evidence should be.[519]

No Longer Hidden—Social Media Becomes an Expression of Solidarity

Many victims felt that they were the only ones or burdened with guilt and shame, as shown by the statistics of the National Research Council: "The research council, noting that some 80 percent of sexual assaults go unreported to law enforcement."[520] The #MeToo, then Twitter, meme upended the previous silence, as more victims stepped forward. Ending the silence ended the stigma carried by victims of sexual violence.[521] Social media took center stage in popular culture, arriving in 2000 and jumping to tens of millions of users within a few years. The founding dates of Facebook, Instagram, and X (Twitter) were between 2004 and 2010. In 2024, around 72.5 percent of Americans used social media sites, including Facebook, Instagram, TikTok, X, and Pinterest.[522]

Connection and Identification

Social media created a new power center that complemented mainstream media and the dominant social structure by becoming another social force for forming public opinion. Everyone can jump in with a post, opinion, and picture—you don't need a million-dollar printing press or a ten-thousand-watt TV station to intervene in society. Social media provides powerful tools to challenge political, social, and cultural dominance based on power and wealth.

The social media explosion opened opportunities for survivors to create online social media identities, allowing them to post personal stories, commentary, and interventions. Each Facebook post, X comment, and Instagram graphic starts as an individual contribution; as it gains ground in popular discourse, it becomes an intervention into the social and political conversation.

Social media initiatives also promote action and organizing. Many organizations referenced in this book use social media to promote their missions and agendas to effectively reach thousands of people. Each action provides support, cultivating links to other organizations with initiatives that help survivors. These efforts, in turn, can recruit hundreds more followers to take action. Social media is a powerful recruiting and organizing tool.

The tidal wave created by #MeToo created solidarity among the tens of millions of previously silent victims of abuse. This phenomenon has restructured social discourse and political organizing and fostered the creation of survivor organizations that stepped forward to create a new social movement.

Impact of Politics, Laws, and Social Practice

The combination of millions of victims saying #MeToo and the creation of tens of thousands of survivor social media entities compels changes within the institutions of power: Congress, state legislatures, newspapers, workplaces, Hollywood, religious institutions, and social structures. Social media's footprint makes its mark on all sectors of society. Before the influence of social media, many institutions responded to sexual violence as merely individual instances of depravity, not as a social problem. Social media exerted itself as another source of advocacy. Social media shifts the conversation from an individual tragedy to a social problem, where it becomes part of the social conversation, no longer hidden, creating improvements in social life, culture, and politics.

Slow Burn

The tsunami of #MeToo tweets created a tidal wave of popular cultural intervention. As social media thrives on a diversity of platforms, it slowly continues to gather members, influence, and power.[523] Survivors' social media provides a path to building connections. Organizing through social media provides a mechanism for solidarity. A single survivor organizer with limited time and resources can use social media to reach thousands.

Twenty million people tweeting #MeToo established a fertile ground for ongoing advocacy and action. However, creating formal organizations presents challenges due to limited resources and time commitments.

Thought and work are needed to discover funding sources, assemble resource material, create a nonprofit, find staff, and develop a compelling mission. Many survivor leaders started by creating entities that thrived on social media, independent of any formal organizational form.[524]

Social Media Mobilizes

Before #MeToo, many victims understood their abuse as an individual, as the knowledge of other victims was hidden. After the #MeToo awakening, solidarity emerged, as seen in the historic social response to #MeToo.

Social media has sparked tens of thousands of personal stories, expressions of mutual support, and hundreds of political actions. It enriches society's social life and raises awareness, leading to a healthy field of thousands of entities, hundreds of survivor-led organizations, statewide and regional initiatives, and national coalitions and associations, empowering those without power to challenge the reigning institutions.

The #MeToo hashtag became an easy and memorable meme for victims and survivors to express solidarity. At the same time, it became a site of contention between rising awareness and the old practices of misogyny and male supremacy. These contending political forces are between those defending the legacies of patriarchy and those creating a new social movement. Popular social media interventions supported the creation of new organizations, strengthened existing organizations, and emerged as political power.

CHAPTER 11

POWER OF CIVIL SOCIETY: NGOS AND COMMUNITIES ENGAGE

Civil Action: A Path to Accountability

Attorneys became a powerful force as they represented the interests of victims when challenging huge institutions and the rich and powerful. They compelled accountability from individuals and institutions through civil actions. They exposed those who hid behind wealth, power, and authority. Before the movement demanded change, justice was hobbled by weak laws, such as SOL laws that reduce the window to report crimes.

Previously, victims had few options for justice, as they faced powerful predators and worldwide organizations. The rising voice of survivors, media attention, and government intervention created a counterforce to the previous power structures. An individual has little power when they confront a powerful abuser or a huge organization; now, they confront crimes as part of a movement. As of 2024, there were challenges in most states to reform or eliminate laws on receiving damages and efforts to strengthen the prosecution of criminals.

Advocates were able to sue for damages, adding an effective means to achieve justice. Some of the awards to victims reached tens of millions of dollars, with several reaching a hundred million dollars awards—for instance, a $500 million payment to 327 victims of Michigan abuser Larry Nassar and the $800 million award to 710 victims of Dr. Tyndall of the University of Southern California.[525]

Since 2000, hundreds of attorneys have taken on the Catholic Church, including three notable attorneys representing survivors: Jeff Anderson, Mitch Garabedian, and John Manly. Anderson was one of the first attorneys to take on violence in institutional settings, representing a Minnesota victim in 1983 in the first legal challenge to the Catholic Church for abuse. Anderson stepped forward as a resolute and ardent advocate.[526] His early practice of civil rights and poverty law demonstrated his commitment to social justice, which gained the trust of survivors and led to his representation of tens of thousands of victims.

Anderson shared his story of drawing up those first court survivor complaints and then serving the papers; it was the first case of its kind. "While denying any knowledge of the priest's history of sexual abuse, the Catholic Church offered a $1 million settlement, provided the Riedle family would sign a confidentiality agreement."[527] The church representative told Anderson, "This is what we do." Anderson was stunned, as it indicated there was a "clear signal that the bishops had concealed child sexual abuse before."[528] That first case of a clergy abuse victim transformed him into a passionate advocate for a lifelong endeavor. *CNN* highlighted Anderson as the first attorney to take on the church for sexual abuse, as he was the first to file a lawsuit in 1983 and the first lawyer in the country to take on such cases. He says the abuse suit he took on, which targeted the Archdiocese of Saint Paul and Minneapolis and the Diocese of Winona, Minnesota, was the first against an American Catholic diocese.[529]

Anderson continued his tenacious fight against the church while understanding the necessity of reaching out to victims who remain silent. "Delivering the message is the key," said Anderson. "As a trial lawyer, I can take the case, but it takes months or years to get to the courtroom.

In the past, lawyers waited for the courtroom to reveal the truth. But when it comes to child protection, it can't wait. We have to remove priests immediately and report to the police immediately. I can't let them hurt another kid while I'm on watch. The media becomes the messenger and means of exposing peril."[530]

Anderson's law firm has sued the Vatican on five occasions without success due to several limiting factors. Anderson's practice now welcomes victims in many fields outside of clergy abuse, including schools, universities, sports teams, Boy Scouts, and the music industry.

Boston attorney Mitch Garabedian's work gained fame when the *Boston Globe* investigative team published the *Spotlight* series of investigative reports on the sexual abuse of children by clergy in the Archdiocese of Boston.[531] Garabedian had warned the Boston community of the church's practice of covering up abuse of children in 1994, years before *Spotlight*.[532] He represented a single mother and three young boys whom Father Geoghan molested, along with hundreds of other children in the Boston area. Geoghan had previously admitted to abusing young boys three decades before he was removed as a priest and imprisoned. Each bishop assigned him to parishes, covered it up, and moved him to another parish.

Garabedian contacted the church. "I figured they'd want to know about this, and the way they acted was really strange. They acted like, 'Oh, okay, we'll take care of that.' Like it was no big deal, I thought it was very, very strange."[533] As he pursued cases in court against the Catholic clergy, he received publicity that informed the community, leading to more victims and their families stepping forward. Fr. Geoghan harmed dozens, if not hundreds, of children. These initial efforts led to more cases, not just the Geoghan cases. As Garabedian began representing more families, his interactions with the church grew difficult; he concluded that "the Catholic Church really didn't care." Garabedian remembers the first time he filed a civil complaint in 1997, and he gave the complaint to the clerk. The clerk looked at me and said, "It's about time somebody did something about this."[534]

Cardinal Bernard Francis Law made extensive efforts to hide and protect Geoghan when accusations of his cruelty arose. During many meetings over the years, Garabedian confronted Cardinal Law and other diocesan staff, attempting to seek justice for victims; however, church officials were dismissive. The *Boston Globe Spotlight* series brought hundreds of new accusations that the church could no longer hide.

Eventually, justice won out. Garabedian held the Archdiocese of Boston accountable through a civil action case, representing eighty-six victims of Father Geoghan. He also represented 120 victims of clergy sexual abuse by forty priests in another Boston case. Cardinal Law was exposed for his crimes, coverups, payoffs for silence, and efforts to move predators out of town to avoid accountability.

The church attempted to keep a lid on the exposure of widespread clergy sex abuse, using its stature as a religious institution in a very Catholic community. Even so, pressure mounted from parishioners, the media, and civil society. Four days before Cardinal Law was to testify before a grand jury, he fled Boston to the Vatican to avoid testifying. The Vatican rewarded Law for fleeing by securing a cushy job in Rome, giving him a princely church and a kingly allowance. Law was given legal protection because of the Vatican's nation-state status, allowing Law to avoid accountability for his complicity in crimes and coverups.

As a local SNAP leader in San Francisco, I traveled to Stockton, California, to support a survivor who was part of a civil trial suit against Father Michael Kelly and the Diocese of Stockton. Over twenty days, I observed attorney John Manly and his partner Vince Finaldi vigorously represent the victim of child rape. Both Bishop Stephen Blaire and the Vicar General took the stand, replying with numerous variations of "I can't recall."[535]

The church provided a bogus *expert* on recovered memories in an attempt to discredit the victim, which failed to persuade anyone outside church functionaries. Manly produced substantial evidence supporting the victim's claim with testimony from family and church members. Documentation was provided about Fr. Kelly's absences, which he said were visits to family in Ireland. Instead, these absences were, in fact, his institutional therapy outside of the diocese because of previous accusations of child sex abuse. The mounting evidence foretold the verdict by the jury. Before they could assess damages, the accused predator, Father Kelly, fled to Ireland to escape accountability.[536] In response, the diocese settled and awarded the victim $3.75 million.[537]

In California, attorney John Manly represented thousands of victims. Manly's practice began in 1997 in a case where the jury awarded the victim over $5 million. Manly won additional settlements from important institutions in America and has challenged the USA Olympic Committee for failing to protect women athletes and gymnasts. For the Olympic gymnasts, the court awarded $380 million to hundreds of victims; 150 victims testified at trial.[538] He represented thousands of victims of abuse within several sectors of society, including representing 710 victims of USC gynecologist George Tyndall, and received a billion-dollar award from the University of Southern California, one of the largest settlements in history.[539]

Another huge settlement imposed on the Catholic Church occurred in Los Angeles when Manly, working with other attorneys, won a $660 million settlement from the Archdiocese of Los Angeles due to their decades-long practice of failing to report clergy abuse to the police.

The only avenue for any form of justice was through civil lawsuits. Judges and juries provided the forum for that justice. The hundred-million-dollar settlements reflected the severity of coverups by major institutions. A case in point, in May 2022, the *Los Angeles Times* published the headline: "UC Pays Record $700 Million to Women Who Accused UCLA Gynecologist of Sexual Abuse."[540] The following year, the University of Southern California paid $1.1 billion in settlements for victims of Gynecologist George Tyndall as a result of administrators "mishandling" complaints by victims.[541]

By their very nature, laws can hold many twisting paths to justice. International laws add another degree of complexity and challenge. However, in the case of the Vatican, the church claimed they were an independent nation and couldn't be sued. For instance, we saw that play out in the UN Committee on the Rights of the Child and the UN Committee on Torture. The Catholic Church participated as a nation in the inquiries, deflecting accountability demanded by UN committees as the church wrapped itself in religious rationales, citing its sovereignty over its faith and beliefs, and refused to cooperate with civil court case investigations. Many have challenged the Vatican hierarchy and the Pope to hold them accountable. However, as the oldest institution in the world, it continues to ignore or deny any outside challenge.[542]

We come into the world as individuals facing existing institutions, dominating ideologies, and encompassing economic systems. Yet our free will and social connections enable us to engage politically and culturally with the world as citizens within larger communities, not just as isolated individuals. We connect and engage our community through active involvement in society, not limited by what existed previously, but by what we want to see for our present and future. We have the opportunity to create the world we want to live in as we engage in civil society as active agents, not just passive recipients.

Non-Governmental Organizations Engage

Civil society knits us together through the community of non-governmental organizations (NGOs), social and fraternal associations, charities, religious groups, nonprofit organizations, and cultural initiatives.

The establishment of rape crisis centers in the early 1970s was a turning point in combating sexual violence.[543] They were not the result of government initiatives, nonprofits, and NGOs; they were *organic* social movements that began with women who stepped forward to do the work and serve a population with few resources. The Women's Liberation Movement created the first rape crisis centers and soon expanded to over

1,500 centers and fifty-six state coalitions nationally.[544] As these centers gained social acceptance, they became a resource and received funding from state and federal programs.

The National Institute of Health and other federal agencies provide a broad range of subsidies to advocacy organizations. Government and universities, public and private foundations, along with a multitude of organizations, initiatives, and programs, support and sponsor research and education to address sexual violence. All are active in responding to the rising evidence of widespread abuse. Altogether, survivor advocacy, charitable organizations, government programs, and local activism combined to form NGOs.

The 240 survivor-led organizations engage with and influence the entire panoply of NGOs through its coalition building, legislative advocacy, media outreach, and mutual support.[545] These interactions vary according to interest and mission, where some NGOs pursue a singular mission objective. As the collection of NGOs within the network of survivor organizations collaborate with common goals, it simultaneously knits a more cohesive social movement.

Heightened Awareness and Successful Organizing

This social movement sprang from activists, creating dozens of statewide and regional initiatives and forming organizations to reform laws, prevent abuse, and support survivors. At the same time, social media sparked tens of thousands of personal stories and political expressions of solidarity. These grassroots initiatives exploded in size and vigor after the #MeToo tweet in 2017, which activated tens of millions.

A parallel development to individual actions and initiatives was the development of survivor-led organizations beginning in the late 1980s, leading to hundreds of organizations formed since 2000. For instance, SNAP began as a collection of support groups in 1988, and RAINN began providing support in 1995.[546]

Most organizations are formed organically and created by survivor activists stepping forward. Some began as social media posts that touched a unique audience, such as Incest AWARE and Promoting Awareness—Victim Empowerment (PAVE), which began as Facebook pages.[547] The steady growth of initiatives started around the year 2000, driven by rising social awareness and social justice organizing, which led to the creation of hundreds of national support and advocacy organizations in 2025.[548] The surge of organizations in diverse sectors, each advancing unique missions, enriched this new social movement as they developed links through solidarity and cooperation.[549] A full review of the many survivor organizations follows later in the book.

Survivors and organizations arose through engagement with civil society, combining to create a formidable foundation for a new social movement. The force started with advocate leaders who created organizations and initiatives that will be introduced in future chapters. A second force is that they were empowered by attorneys who vigorously sought justice. A third force is the allies that support survivors and provide resources. The fourth force is civil society, the media, which has risen from its past lethargy to expose widespread violence, thereby raising awareness.[550]

No longer could the public, government agencies, and civil society deny the ubiquity of violence where one out of four women and one out of six men have been sexually abused; few knew that about 70 percent of victims never come forward.[551] The cruelty of child sex abuse causes such harm that it takes decades for a victim to come forward. The creation of organizations, initiatives, and coalitions served as the movement's foundation, starting at the most basic level: one action, one event, one survivor at a time.

Insiders and Whistleblowers Step Forward

Three faithful Catholics responded to the budding exposure of Catholic clergy abusing children in 1985. The three advocates, a priest, Fr. Thomas Doyle, an attorney, Ray Mouton, and a priest-therapist, Rev. Michael R.

Peterson, alarmed at the revelations in the Father Gilbert Gauthe abuse case in Louisiana, felt the issue of clergy abuse demanded attention from the church. Father Thomas Doyle, a canon lawyer and a member of the Vatican Consulate, was sent to New Orleans to investigate.

The three advocates wrote an eighty-five-page paper, "The Problem of Sexual Molestation by Roman Catholic Clergy: Meeting the Problem in a Comprehensive and Responsible Manner," pointing to the corruption and coverup within the church hierarchy.[552] The report was written for the United States Conference of Catholic Bishops in 1985, but tragically, not one of the bishops responded to their request to have the study distributed at the Bishop's Conference. Undeterred, Fr. Thomas Doyle, a Vatican scholar, sent the report to every bishop. Again, no response.[553]

The Vatican removed Father Thomas Doyle from his position with the Vatican Embassy in Washington, DC, as a repercussion for his public disclosure of abuse in the church. After a 20-year career in the military, Doyle became the canon law expert in legal cases, testifying on behalf of victims.[554] He aggressively challenged the church potentates through articles and research papers and testified as an expert witness in civil trials in hundreds of cases for victims.[555] Doyle expressed support for survivors of clergy abuse through his public advocacy for over two decades. He is a perennial speaker at SNAP's annual conferences, inspiring attendees by acknowledging previous successes and promising future ones.

When the *Boston Globe Spotlight* series exposed the true scope of abuse in the Catholic Church, Boston was aflame with righteous anger, and groups were formed to respond. One group, composed of faithful Catholics, formed Voice of the Faithful in 2002.[556] They mobilized parishioners to hold the church accountable for their complicity through educational meetings and establishing local chapters to widen their advocacy.

BishopAccountability

BishopAccountability (BA) is a research group that documents abuse within the Catholic Church, acting as researchers, archivists, and historians of the clergy abuse crisis in America. BishopAccountability has two essential demands of the church: that there must be a full accounting of abuse and that the bishops must be held accountable.

The two founders, Anne Barrett Doyle and Terry McKiernan, practicing Catholics from Boston, were morally outraged by the *Spotlight* series revelations. In response, they created BishopAccountability to support victims of clergy sex abuse and hold the church hierarchy responsible. As a national organization, they documented grand jury investigations in thirteen states, assembled data using newspaper articles, gathered court records in criminal and civil cases, and sought grand jury testimony. The combination of sources of information and documentation led to the database of over seven thousand accused clergy predators.[557]

The BA database provides government agencies, NGOs, attorneys, and investigators with backgrounds, photos, court testimony, timelines, and other forms of evidence of abuse by clergy. BishopAccountability established itself as a historian and archivist of abuse in the Catholic Church and became a model for other archives developed by similar NGOs, and examples include Baptists, Mennonites, and Boy Scouts.[558]

BishopAccountability assembled millions of documents over twenty years using survivor accounts, published documents, court records, grand jury evidence, and state investigations. Their documentation of over 7,300 accused Catholic predators has been crucial for communities.[559] Their website makes available more than "63,630 pages of church files, over 121,000 news articles, a collection of investigative and other reports and studies totaling more than 100,000 pages, and over 1,880 archived copies of lists of accused created by more than 150 dioceses and more than 25 religious institutes and provinces." Their office in Boston has a physical archive of "243,770 pages of publicly released church files; over a million pages of other church files; and the Demarest Archive of accused persons totaling more than 25,880 sources."[560]

BA's database has been used by police and state governments, as they highlighted in an email to supporters. "The Michigan Attorney General's recent report on the Lansing diocese cites BishopAccountability more than 50 times. Prosecutors tell us that our documents, data, and expert analysis are essential."561

Survivors, attorneys representing victims, and news reporters rely on BA for documented and researched information. Their documentation shows that about 10 percent of clergy are abusers, a secret tightly guarded by the church.562 BishopAccountability documents a timeline of the crimes that started in the 1940s and continues to reveal the church's secret documents, providing thousands of references in "A Documentary History of the Crisis, Timeline of Events, Documents, Reporting, and Commentary" from the 1940s to 2007.563

BishopAccountability provides a starting point for identifying and finding clergy predators. When my memories first surfaced in 1995, I checked to see if Father Murphy was on the BishopAccountability list of accused predators. He was not. After I went public in 2016 with my story, others came forward as victims of Fr. Murphy forty or fifty years previously. BishopAccountability now lists Father Murphy as an accused sexual predator.564

BishopAccountability increased its mission to include databases from other countries, such as Ireland, Chile, and Argentina. It hosts the daily news thread called Abuse Tracker, described as a "digest of links to media coverage of clergy abuse."565 They are the scribes and historians of survivors of violence in the Catholic Church.

The Next Step

The creation of many organizations, initiatives, and coalitions served as the movement's foundation, starting at the most basic level: one action, one event, one survivor at a time. The surge of multiple organizations in diverse sectors, each advancing unique missions, enriched this new social movement. As they developed links through solidarity and cooperation, their power expanded to intervene politically. The steady growth of initiatives beginning in 2000 led to the creation of hundreds of national support and advocacy organizations in 2025.[566]

The following chapter on survivors engaging in politics describes the vanguard and leading organizations that are at the core of this new social movement. Their combined advocacy creates a new social force that intervenes in politics, culture, and daily life to change the world.

CHAPTER 12

MANY WAVES, ONE OCEAN

We are the ones we have been waiting for[567]

—June Jordan

The spontaneous outpouring of activism spread nationwide following the first "Take Back The Night" marches in the early 1970s.[568] Local rape crisis centers expanded beyond major cities, including Philadelphia, San Francisco, Washington, DC, and Seattle. These actions started as a reclamation of women's independence to walk down the street without harassment.

These events became a clarion call for national organizing, signaling women's outrage that continues today and advancing the idea that sexual violence will no longer be tolerated. They served as the vanguard for future actions. The Survivors Movement gained momentum in 2000, as hundreds of leaders stepped forward to organize activist and advocacy organizations to raise awareness, prevent abuse, and change the laws. Their successful efforts set the stage for a new social movement. As victims moved from victim to survivor to organizer, they created organizations in all sectors of society and became the foundation of the new social movement.[569] This chapter describes several vanguard organizations, a couple dozen groups representing the diversity of hundreds of survivor organizations within the movement.

Can You Count the Waves in the Ocean?

The tremendous growth of survivor organizations reflects how these organizations and coalitions meet the needs of survivors through advocacy and support. This new, vibrant social movement has not finished growing and expanding. Just as we cannot count the number of waves in the ocean, neither can we count the number of groups and organizations working to change the world. Below is an examination of about fifty organizations that represent our new social movement.

Five Missions and Twelve Sectors

The defining directive of any organization is its mission: who it is, what it wants to accomplish, who it serves, and by what means it advances its work. The diversity of organizations in this new social movement embraces multiple objectives, audiences, and services. It is not a homogeneous assembly of similar look-alike organizations but rather a loose movement of organizations that weave a fabric that connects in a diverse tapestry with unique missions and audiences.

Just as weavings have a variety of colors, weaves, yarns, and patterns that create a tapestry, every organization combines its unique characteristics. Throughout this book, I refer to the 240 national survivor organizations, each unique. Below, I identify five unique foundational missions and a dozen sectors to highlight each contribution to the collective formation of a social movement.

The formation of organizations brings together activists around a common mission, such as mobilizing, advocating, and educating. Some organizations embrace numerous missions and overlap with the work of other organizations. When examining our grand social movement as a whole, we must recognize the contributions of each group, initiative, and coalition.

Five Organizations Take the Lead

Five organizations are notable due to their influence, history, and impact. They are the largest and most influential. We begin with RAINN, the "me too. Movement Organization," Darkness to Light (D2L), CHILD USA, and SNAP. RAINN and the "me too. Organization" are the largest and most influential, as they have more than ten times the social media presence of any other survivor organization.

Rape Abuse Incest National Network—RAINN

RAINN, founded in 1994, is the largest anti-sexual violence survivor organization in the world. It sponsors the anonymous National Sexual Assault Hotline at 800.656.HOPE [800-656-4673], and support in English and Spanish are available online.[570] RAINN was founded by Scott Berkowitz in 1994 and became the largest and most influential anti-sexual violence organization, providing support, information, and resources to millions of survivors. This vanguard institution also created a national hotline for victims, which has helped hundreds of thousands of callers each year. In 2019, RAINN had a staff of several hundred and over 4,000 volunteers.[571] It has a national presence in the news and advises the media.

RAINN works in partnership with thousands of local rape crisis centers and sexual assault service providers across the country and operates the DoD Safe Helpline for the Department of Defense. Their mission is to "prevent sexual violence, help survivors, and ensure that perpetrators are brought to justice."[572] RAINN identifies four major initiatives as part of its mission: victim services, public education, public policy, and consulting and training. It also sponsors a speaker's bureau and supports educational programs. Within each category, RAINN has links, analyses, guidance, resources, surveys, and help that reach over 300,000 annually. RAINN has engaged in political organizing and lobbying national politicians on prevention issues.[573]

me too. Movement Organization

After the "MeToo" hashtag went viral in 2017, Tarana Burke used the resulting movement to form the "me too. Organization," which grew rapidly and expanded internationally.[574] "The mission of the #MeToo Movement organization is to support survivors of sexual violence, connect survivors with resources, advocate for change, gain survivor justice, and raise community awareness."[575] They present themselves as a global, survivor-led movement against sexual violence dedicated to creating pathways for healing, justice, action, and leadership. A major initiative of the "me too. Organization" is the formation of a coalition of advocacy organizations called Survivors Agenda, which includes about fifty organizations aligned as allies.[576] The constellation of organizations within the Survivors' Agenda aims to foster healing, change conversations, support movement building, intervene in changing policy, and shift the narrative around sexual violence.

Darkness to Light—D2L

The year 2000 introduced the beginning of a new advocacy organization, Darkness to Light (D2L).[577] Their mission is to empower "adults to prevent, recognize, and react responsibly to child sexual abuse through awareness, education, and stigma reduction." Twelve community leaders formed D2L in response to a question: "What can we do to prevent abuse and keep children safe?" They mobilized community members to create an initiative around educating adults to protect children. Holding yearly conferences called "From Darkness to Light," they began to elevate the voices and stories of adult survivors of child abuse.[578]

This initial community advocacy laid the foundation for a new organization and established worldwide programs that promote prevention, called Stewards of Children—training to reach parents, teachers, and community leaders. Their prevention advocacy serves communities, schools, faith centers, youth, and parents around the world.[579] With the worldwide partnership, D2L has trained over two million people in 115 countries through its prevention programs.[580]

D2L identifies the four communities of its mission: adults in the family, the community, youth organizations, and the political sphere.[581] Their mission highlights their service to survivors and the community as a whole."[582]

D2L established programs in seventy-six nations, reaching over two million adults. It has also developed other programs, such as Prevent 360°, a program for prevention, and designed for "[t]he strategy of providing both children and adults prevention education to prevent, recognize and respond appropriately to abuse launches today. Combined, the programs include complementary language and strategies, so adults and children have a common language to talk about sexual abuse and other types of victimization."[583] Another initiative is the Honest Conversations webinar and streaming services that address many issues within diverse communities, including LGBTQ, communities of color, formerly incarcerated, immigrants, and other marginalized communities.[584]

D2L developed Prevent Now!, a workshop to help build a community-based and prevention-based "collection of best practices that create and sustain grassroots efforts aimed at cultural change" through training, tools, and resources.[585]

CHILD USA

CHILD USA describes itself as a "nonprofit think tank for children devoted to ending child abuse and neglect."[586] Led by law Professor Marci Hamilton, it has been the vanguard in reforming and eliminating SOL laws in over thirty states. Statute of limitation laws limit or remove the rights of victims of abuse to achieve justice. At the same time, these laws protect offending individuals, institutions, and companies from accountability. Professor Hamilton wrote a book in 2008, *Justice Denied: What America Must Do to Protect Its Children*, where she advocates for the repeal of SOL laws.[587]

Professor Hamilton created CHILD USA, providing resources for reform.[588] It is also known as the leading nonprofit think tank for children, "dedicated to protecting kids, preventing abuse, and working for the civil rights of children, conducts research, compiles evidence, promotes ideas, and proposes the most effective policies to prevent childhood abuse and neglect."[589]

The success of CHILD USA and other NGOs in raising community awareness compelled increased action by various state agencies. CHILD USA shines through its commitment to justice and accountability in all fifty states. It continues to make significant contributions to research, policies, and laws. It provides local, state, and national advocacy organizations with the fundamental information necessary to engage with policymakers, organizations, media, and society.

Survivors Network of those Abused by Priests—SNAP

SNAP arose in response to widespread sexual abuse within the Catholic Church in 1988.[590] Over time, SNAP broadened its mission beyond the focus of the Catholic Church and embraced all faith communities within its network, including Baptist, Mennonite, Lutheran, Jehovah's Witness, Mormon, Jewish, and others. It sponsors support groups in these faith communities as well as support groups centered around other modalities of abuse, including abuse as an adult, LGBTQ, ritual abuse, and Boy Scouts.

The SNAP network reaches worldwide with contacts in over sixty nations and SNAP leaders in nine countries: Austria, Germany, Serbia/Bosnia, Australia, New Zealand, Peru, Uganda, and Japan. It has made a complaint against the Catholic Church in the International Criminal Court, alleging crimes against humanity.[591] SNAP later provided testimony in hearings of the United Nations Committee on the Rights of the Child and the United Nations Committee on Torture.[592] It has a network of over 130 local SNAP leaders throughout the USA and several other countries. These local leaders provide support and advocacy for victims and host forty support groups each month.[593]

Fifty Organizations Doing the Work

Fifty organizations give a sampling of the 240 survivor organizations in this new social movement. They demonstrate the breadth of the movement with wide-ranging sectors of missions and communities.

Women and girls suffer the greatest harm as the victims of sexual abuse; according to RAINN, women suffer 90 percent of all sexual assaults.[594] They cite the statistic that "1 out of every 6 American women has been the victim of an attempted or completed rape in her lifetime" and about "3% of American men—or 1 in 33—have experienced an attempted or completed rape in their lifetime."[595]

Women have been the victims and grandest advocates of these hundreds of organizations, as demonstrated by extraordinary leaders who created powerful and influential survivor organizations that changed the world.

Children Advocacy

Childhelp

Childhelp has a long history of working for the safety and well-being of children, beginning in 1959 with the establishment of orphanages in many countries. They established and maintain a national hotline for those seeking support.[596] They also developed a program designed for Pre-K to twelfth-grade students called Childhelp Speak Up Be Safe for prevention education.[597]

Together for Girls

Together for Girls "is a global partnership working to end violence against children and adolescents, with special attention to sexual violence." Through data and advocacy, our global partnership drives action to break cycles of violence and ensure prevention, healing, and justice." [598] They seek, develop, and share evidence to illustrate the pervasiveness of sexual violence and inform effective solutions. They campaign for all children to live in safety. Together for Girls is an active organizer of the international Brave Movement, which will be described in the following chapter.

Speak Out to Stop Child Sex Abuse (SOSCSA) and Survivor Scouting

Speak Out to Stop Child Sex Abuse—SOSCSA and Survivor Scouting provide news, information, resources, and links for victims of sexual abuse in the scouting program.[599]

Thorn

Thorn builds technology to defend children from sexual abuse. "We join forces with the sharpest minds from tech, non-profit, government, and law enforcement to stop the spread of child sexual abuse material and eliminate the online exploitation of children."[600]

Empower Survivors

Empower Survivors is a survivor-led organization based on the peer support model.[601] It uses a mentorship program, peer support groups, and classes. Empower Survivors works to reduce the silence and stigma of childhood sexual abuse. Their peer support groups are individual and group-based. Elizabeth Sullivan, the founder of Empower Survivors, has shared her conversations with survivors on YouTube.[602]

Rights4Girls

Rights4Girls is "dedicated to ending gender-based violence in the US. We advocate for the dignity and rights of young women and girls so that every girl can be safe and live a life free of violence and exploitation."[603] They are active in training judges, lawyers, and politicians on the impact of gender violence. They work to raise public awareness of marginalized victims and advocate for laws where all girls can be safe.

National Center for Missing & Exploited Children—NCMEC

The National Center for Missing & Exploited Children—"NCMEC is the nation's largest and most influential child protection organization." They are the leader in finding missing children through their hotline, CyberTipline, receiving tens of millions of calls annually. "We are available 24 hours a day, 7 days a week: (800) 843-5678."[604]

Community Organizations

Promoting Awareness Victim Empowerment—PAVE

Promoting Awareness Victim Empowerment was founded in 2001 by Angela Rose with a mission to end sexual abuse and build communities to support survivors: "We support and empower victim-survivors and strive to prevent sexual violence through education, advocacy, and community action." They have a broad platform of services and support for survivors, including a hotline, information, and resources. They sponsor several campaigns for survivors: Shattering the Red Zone, Art for Awareness, Teen Dating Violence Campaign, and others.[605]

PAVE provides additional support for survivors at Survivors.org, which connects survivors with resources, links, and information. Survivors.org is a "tool that makes it easier for survivors to take control of their healing and find the resources they need to thrive."[606]

Sexual Assault Advocacy Network (SAAN)

SAAN provides support, empowers survivors, and advocates for justice. SAAN gives guidance and builds the community necessary to heal. They work to stop violence, foster awareness, promote prevention, and drive change. "We provide a supportive environment where survivors can find solidarity, resources, and hope as they navigate their journey toward healing and justice."[607]

Zero Abuse Project

Zero Abuse Project provides help and services for education, training, and advocacy, and they are "committed to transforming institutions in order to effectively prevent, recognize, and respond to child sexual abuse." They also work for "systemic legal change, guidance for survivor support, and leadership on emerging technologies."[608]

Zero Abuse Project has also supported the Jacob Wetterling Resource Center, an initiative that supports advocacy and training to end child sex abuse and address missing children.[609]

Echo Training

Echo Training educates "families, communities, and professionals about trauma and resilience to promote survivor empowerment, resolve individual and community-level trauma, and create safe, stable, nurturing relationships that break the cycle of generational trauma."[610] They support survivor empowerment through in-person and online trauma training courses for parents and teachers and also provide Spanish language training courses.

Religious and Faith-Based Communities

Ending Clergy Abuse—ECA

Ending Clergy Abuse is a worldwide organization of human rights activists and survivors who work to compel the church to end clerical abuse, especially child sexual abuse. They seek justice for victims harmed by clergy abuse in the Catholic community. The fundamental projects of ECA are the demands for global zero tolerance, stopping clergy sexual abuse, protecting children, seeking justice for victims, and ending the cover-ups by church authorities.[611]

Godly Response to Abuse in Christian Environment—GRACE

Godly Response to Abuse in Christian Environment has a simple, direct, and powerful mission: "Empowering Christian communities to recognize, prevent, and respond to abuse." With that mission, they have "accumulated and organized a wealth of resources from mental health experts, former prosecutors, and theologians to give you and your organization a well-rounded, robust, and deep understanding of abuse and how to prevent it."[612] GRACE developed prevention strategies and customizable training using videos and articles. They have created a program for independent investigations when troubles arise in faith communities.

Awake

Awake has a mission to "awaken our community to the full reality of sexual abuse in the Catholic Church, work for transformation, and foster healing for all who have been wounded."[613] They have three focuses: raising awareness of abuse, preventing, recognizing, and responding to sexual abuse, and fostering healing for all those wounded.

Mennonite Abuse Prevention—MAP

MAP "publishes credible allegations of sexual abuse and other abuses of power in Anabaptist-affiliated institutions" to ensure "safety and healing for all."[614] Since 2016, they've maintained a database of accused predators within the Mennonite community; they brought public knowledge of abuse in their community.

Silent Lambs

Silent Lambs provide victims in the Jehovah's Witness community with "a voice and a place to unite with others and find healing."[615] They sponsor education, support, and resources.

Hollywood, Entertainment, Music, and Broadcasting

Female Composers Safety League—FCSL

Female Composers Safety League "envisions a composing industry free from sexual abuse, harassment, prejudice, and marginalization."[616] FCSL provides safety, inclusion, restoration, and support groups for members. Founder Nomi Abadi established the mission in response to the "clear and urgent need to center the experiences of survivors of sexual assault in the music industry, who have lost their careers because they were abused and silenced."[617]

Hire Survivors Hollywood

Hire Survivors Hollywood supports survivors of sexual abuse within the entertainment industry by encouraging the hiring of survivors.[618] It also promotes opportunities, auditions, and interviews for survivors. Founder Sarah Ann Masse, "hopes that her initiative will create a safe, equitable work environment, increase representation in the industry, and encourage individuals who have faced sexual violence to come forward without fear of their careers being damaged."[619]

Maestra

Maestra envisions "an industry that is more diverse, equitable, inclusive, and accessible, across all intersections of race, sexual orientation, physical and intellectual ability, age, nationality, appearance, and gender identity and expression."[620] Their membership includes composers, music directors, orchestrators, arrangers, copyists, rehearsal pianists, and other musicians. They sponsor and support seminars, mentorship programs, technical skills workshops, networking events, and online resources. They promote equality to address historical disadvantages and practices that have limited women and nonbinary musicians and composers.

Schools and Universities

End Rape on Campus (EROC) "works to end campus sexual violence through direct support for survivors and their communities."[621] They provide resources and referrals to those harmed by abuse. They also advance "policy reform at the campus, local, state, and federal levels." EROC established a Campus Accountability Map & Tool that documents sexual assaults on 1700 campuses to foster transparency and accountability nationwide.

Stop Educator Sexual Abuse
Misconduct and Exploitation—SESAME

Sesame provides "support, resource materials, and research" for students, survivors, their families, teachers, professionals, and the media.[622] SESAME provides guidance for reporting abuse, training for teachers and staff, and information on reporting abuse to authorities.

Trafficking
Protect All Children from Trafficking—PACT

PACT protects every child's right to grow up free from sexual exploitation and trafficking through education, advocacy, and legislative action. "Together, we can protect all children from trafficking and create a world where every child is safe, supported, and empowered."[623] This advocacy and legislative reform advance justice, prevention, and healing. PACT sponsors educational, training, and legislative advocacy.

Polaris

Polaris connects "victims and survivors to support and services, and helps communities hold traffickers accountable."[624] For two decades, Polaris has been a leader in holding traffickers accountable, supporting survivors, and fighting the exploitation of those trafficked. Polaris provides statistics, analysis, and resources to inform the public. They also engage in advocacy for public policy. They sponsor the National Human Trafficking Hotline: "The Trafficking Hotline's mission is to connect human trafficking victims and survivors to critical support and services to get help and stay safe. The Trafficking Hotline offers round-the-clock access to a safe space to report tips, seek services, and ask for help."[625]

For Communities of Color
Sisters of Color Ending Sexual Assault—SCESA

SCESA "is an advocacy organization of Women of Color dedicated to working with our communities to create a just society in which all Women of Color can live healthy lives free of violence." They define their core work as "supporting and advocating for Women of Color and Organizations." They support the leadership of women of color through training, support, and policy advocacy. They aspire to end the silence and stigma they believe is "essential to building a world where every woman feels safe and valued." [626]

Alianza Nacional de Campesinas

Alianza Nacional de Campesinas is a national women's farmworkers' organization created by current and former women farmworkers to organize for worker health and safety, immigrant and migrant justice, and ending gender-based violence. "We work at the intersection of gender, migrant, labor, and climate justice." Alianza engages with national organizations to "advocate for changes that ensure their human rights."[627]

Ujima—The National Center on Violence
Against Women in the Black Community

Ujima "addresses the pervasive issues of sexual assault and domestic and community violence within the Black Community."[628] Ujima works to end violence by promoting social change and systematic reforms. They provide training, outreach, research, webinars, and forums.

National Organization of Asians and Pacific Islanders
Ending Sexual Violence—NAPIESV

National Organization of Asians and Pacific Islanders Ending Sexual Violence advocates for victims from the Asian and Pacific Islander (API) communities so that they can live in "safety, dignity, and equality." They work to dismantle the systemic barriers and advocate for a society where "all individuals can thrive, free from the impacts of sexual violence."[629] They authored the 2023 Safe Spaces Report for Survivors of Sexual Violence in Asian & Pacific Islander (API) Communities.[630]

Native American
Missing and Murdered Indigenous Women USA

Missing and Murdered Indigenous Women USA addresses a large number of missing Indigenous women, who disappear at an alarming rate within American Indian communities.[631] Their advocacy and support work provides information, statistics, and resources to raise awareness.

Minnesota Indian Women's Sexual Assault Coalition—MIWSAC

MIWSAC works to end "dating violence, sexual assault, stalking, and sex trafficking." They created a training and sustainability Toolkit to respond to Missing or Murdered Indigenous People (MMIP) cases.[632]

SouthWest Indigenous Women's Coalition—SWIWC

SWIWC is a statewide organization serving the Tribes in Arizona that addresses and responds to "violence through education, training, technical assistance, policy advocacy, and culturally sensitive supportive services."[633] It focuses on training, technical assistance, policy advocacy, education, and outreach.

Strong Hearts Native Helpline

Strong Hearts Native Helpline provides support and advocacy. They address crisis intervention, education and information, service provider referrals, and health options. It also sponsors a hotline and a 40-hour sexual assault advocacy training.[634]

Men

Male Survivor

Male Survivor was founded in 1995 and is "committed to preventing, healing, and eliminating all forms of sexual victimization of boys and men through support, treatment, research, education, advocacy, and activism."[635] Providing a 24-hour chat support team as well as scheduled support groups, they have support for survivors, their families, and partners. Their resources reach over 200 countries around the world.

1 in 6

1 in 6 addresses the negative impact of sexual abuse of boys and men, a crime that happens to one out of six men. They provide resources, a 24-hour helpline, and an online chat. They have also recorded video chats, giving guidance and information designed for trauma recovery. In addition, they have dozens of survivor stories recorded in videos.

In late 2024, 1in 6 partnered with the Zero Abuse Project.[636]

Military

Protect Our Defenders—POD

Protect Our Defenders is dedicated to ending sexual violence, victim retaliation, misogyny, prejudice, and racism in the military. They also work to change the cultural environment of the military to free it from misogyny and racism. POD works to provide policy reform, legal support, research, education, and advocacy to expose sexual abuse and create respect and dignity for service members.[637]

Service Women Action Network—SWAN

SWAN works to "support victims of military sexual assault, to hold perpetrators accountable in the military justice system." Part of their advocacy is having sexual assault recognized as one of the sources of PTSD. SWAN offers support and resources for mental health, sexual assault, and VA claims. They also sponsor a 24-hour hotline for one-on-one support. SWAN advocates for supportive policies with Congress, the Department of Defense, and the Veterans Administration.[638]

Glass Soldier

Glass Soldier supports and promotes "education and prevention initiatives that empower individuals and drive cultural change within the military" to reduce sexual abuse.[639] It provides support, education, and prevention initiatives to drive cultural change within the military.

Incest

Incest AWARE

Incest AWARE offers "services and solutions to end sexual abuse in families through prevention, intervention, recovery, and justice." The mission is to "keep children safe from incest in the first place, secure safe methods of intervention, support survivors in recovery, and end recidivism by transforming people who harm." They provide many support services, referrals, training, a speaker's bureau, workshops, and self-study courses.[640]

Survivors of Incest Anonymous for Adult Survivors of Childhood Sexual Abuse—SIA

SIA "is a 12-step, self-help recovery program modeled after AA. Our mission is to empower survivors of childhood sexual abuse and to help them thrive." SIA started in 1985 and is one of the longest-serving organizations addressing sexual abuse in America. Their principal work is the sponsorship of their network of support groups.[641]

Mothers* Of Adult Survivors of Incest and Sexual Abuse—M*OASIS

M*OASIS provides resources and support, through empathy and compassion, for those closest to us to understand what they may be struggling with.[642] It provides guidance on how to lend support and essays on the many challenges facing those harmed by incest, an excellent source of helpful resources for those supporting an incest victim.

Worldwide Awareness Voice, Education, and Support—5Waves

5Waves views sibling sexual abuse as a silent epidemic that must be challenged. Five Waves provides resources to support victims/survivors to "bring sibling sexual trauma out of the shadows so people around the world can talk about it, heal from it, and prevent it." Their website provides many helpful resources for parents, advocates, academics, teachers, medical staff, researchers, youth, and families.[643]

Foundations Supporting Survivors

Joyful Heart Foundation

Joyful Heart Foundation works to end sexual abuse, domestic abuse, and child abuse through education and advocacy. Its mission is to raise awareness, advocate for reform policies, and work for legislation that brings justice to survivors. They initiated The Heal the Healers (HTH) micro-grant fund that was created to provide financial support for professionals working directly with survivors. They sponsor the End the Backlog initiative to "improve the criminal justice response to sexual violence" by reducing the processing time of rape kits. They also support retreats for victims to promote healing in mind, body, and spirit.[644]

Leila Grace Foundation

The Leila Grace Foundation "provides sexual assault awareness for college students across the country" to provide education that can reduce the risk of assaults on college campuses.[645]

Moore Center for the Prevention of Child Sexual Abuse

The Moore Center for the Prevention of Child Sexual Abuse advances the goal of helping "stop the cycle of abuse and prevent the lifelong pain and injury caused by child sexual abuse."[646] They embrace many steps to prevent child sex abuse, including investing in protecting, engaging with allies, developing policies, educating, and advocating on a worldwide scale.

Sanar Institute

The Sanar Institute supports healing from the "impact of trauma caused by interpersonal violence" by providing services, education, and support to victims and communities.[647] They provide support for victims of human trafficking, sex trafficking, labor trafficking, sexual violence, and domestic and family violence. Sanar supports various healing modalities, including EMDR and individual and group therapies.

Oak Foundation

The Oak Foundation aims to "make the world a safer, fairer, and more sustainable place to live."[648] The foundation has programs in forty countries worldwide. The Oak Foundation has been working with CHILD USA to reform "the statute of limitations for child sexual abuse cases . . . which will help shift the cost of the abuse from the victims to the ones who caused it."[649]

A Breeze of Hope Foundation

A Breeze of Hope Foundation focuses on preventing childhood sexual violence and promoting safe and healthy communities for children. They advocate internationally, engage in legal and policy reform, and advance public information campaigns, utilizing various media outlets including radio, television, printed press, and social media.[650]

Elizabeth Smart Foundation

The Elizabeth Smart Foundation promotes "social change in the fight against sexual violence" by adopting "a thoughtful, trauma-informed approach and includes the perspectives of survivors and victims." It envisions "a compassionate society where survivors are heard, individuals are empowered, and sexual violence is eliminated." Their slogan expresses their mission: "Bringing hope, empowerment, and change in the fight against sexual violence."[651]

Many Waves, One Ocean

Organizations are often formed organically by visionary leaders, with some starting modestly through social media posts that resonate with a unique audience. Some grew into national organizations. Whatever the source of organizing, the surge of multiple organizations arose in diverse sectors, each advancing unique missions, enriching this new social movement as they developed links through solidarity and cooperation. Mission focus varied considerably, but solidarity and mutual support set the stage for the coalescing of social movement over time.

These initiatives appropriated many of the lessons of the great social movements of the past, such as the Women's and Civil Rights Movements. The 1970s slogan of the Women's Movement, *Many Waves, One Ocean*, applies to the rapid development of survivor organizations in the diversity of missions and sectors combined to define a movement.

My website, StandUpSpeakUp.org, has a database of over 240 survivor organizations.[652] The National Sexual Violence Resource Center also compiled a searchable database of over 500 local and national survivor organizations.[653] Together, these databases give an introduction to the breadth of survivor organizations. These lists continue to grow, indicating support and advocacy organizations that help survivors and make the community safer.

Suzanne Isaza, an advocate for incest awareness and a leader in the fight to end the exploitation and injustice of sexual violence, created the organization Incest AWARE.[654] She also founded the survivor nonprofit, SAAN, whose mission is to "champion the rights and well-being of sexual assault survivors."[655] She provides an observation of the current organizing efforts: "When I think of a survivor's movement, I think of people emerging and forming a wave, like building waves in the ocean, and as it gets bigger and bigger and bigger, it draws more power."[656]

As Wide As the Ocean and As Deep As the Sea

Previous chapters demonstrated that violence affects every community. This chapter explains how organizations sprang up to respond to the diversity of abuse that touches every corner of society and the organized response in each sector. Altogether, survivor organizations weave together a social movement and become the foundation of a safer community.

As wide as the ocean and as deep as the sea, survivors forming hundreds of organizations have met with success in all sectors. Over time, these previously *siloed* organizations coalesced to form associations and coalitions, establishing a unique mission to address sexual violence as a social force, a movement.[657]

CHAPTER 13

COALITIONS, ASSOCIATIONS, AND ALLIANCES LINK UP

A single voice in politics is a single voice in the wilderness. . . .

A hundred voices in a chorus sharing one message speak louder than hundreds announcing their pleas individually. As each group links up and aligns with coalitions and associations, its power increases, and all members benefit. When each organization succeeds, so does the movement. When the movement succeeds, so does each organization. Organizations coalesce around shared mission objectives and harmonize advocacy to build a social movement chorus.

Organizations enrich our movement with their diversity of missions, strategies, and audiences, establishing the foundation for associations and coalitions that bring those organizations together. The organization centers and conglomerates around several defining categories of audience and mission.

Coalitions form to achieve a common goal with members sharing a mission, collective work, and agreed-upon objectives.[658] There are six categories of coalitions: children's, trafficking, Native American, Asian and Pacific Islanders, broad, multi-mission, and global initiatives. The following seventeen coalitions and alliances comprise a diversity of platforms, audiences, and agendas.

Children's Coalitions

National Coalition for Child + Family Well-Being

The National Coalition for Child + Family Well-Being (formerly the National Child Abuse Coalition) is one of the oldest survivor coalitions, formed in 1981. This group includes a powerful membership in civil society of over thirty leading organizations, including the American Academy of Pediatrics, American Bar Association, American Psychological Association, Childhelp, National Children's Alliance, Prevent Child Abuse America, and two dozen other organizations. They promote education, policy development, and advocacy. The Coalition also works to strengthen families and communities to prevent abuse and neglect.[659]

National Coalition to Prevent Child Sexual Abuse and Exploitation

National Coalition to Prevent Child Sexual Abuse and Exploitation, formed in 2005, embraces "multiple strategies and policies" to prevent abuse. It has created a "framework for effective, comprehensive, and holistic prevention interventions" called the "National Plan to Prevent Child Sexual Abuse and Exploitation." The coalition includes Prevent Child Abuse America, the National Center for Missing and Exploited Children, the National Sexual Violence Resource Center, the National Children's Advocacy Center, MassKids, StopItNow, the Committee for Children, and others.[660]

Online Sexual Exploitation and Abuse of Children—OSEAC

The Online Sexual Exploitation and Abuse of Children assembled a coalition of survivor organizations to fight sexual, exploitative, and abusive material directed at children that have, at some stage, a connection to the online environment and "child sexual abuse materials, grooming, sextortion, and live-streaming of abusive acts." This coalition includes coalition members Brave Movement, Darkness to Light, Enough is Enough,

Keep Kids Safe, RAINN, Rights for Girls, Thorn, and other members. OSEAC works to "support and contribute to developing legislation and government programs that respond to identified gaps and weaknesses within the U.S.'s current legal framework and government-led initiatives related to preventing and responding to OSEAC."[661]

Trafficking Coalitions

Alliance to End Slavery and Trafficking—ATEST

The Alliance to End Slavery and Trafficking "advocates for solutions to prevent and end all forms of human trafficking and modern slavery around the world." Over a dozen advocacy organizations allied for "solutions to prevent and end all forms of forced labor, human trafficking and modern slavery around the world." This alliance works to inform and create public policy to combat human trafficking.[662]

Coalition to Abolish Slavery and Trafficking, Los Angeles—CASTLA

Coalition to Abolish Slavery and Trafficking is "working to put an end to modern slavery and human trafficking through comprehensive, life-transforming services to survivors and a platform to advocate for groundbreaking policies and legislation." CAST provides counseling, legal resources, housing, education, leadership training, and mentorship for those ensnared in slavery and debt bondage. CAST advocates for policy reforms and public awareness.[663]

Coalition Against Trafficking in Women—CATW

The Coalition Against Trafficking in Women is "working to end the trafficking and sexual exploitation of women and girls by advocating for strong laws and policies, raising public awareness and supporting survivor leadership globally." They support and work with survivors to "develop life-changing prevention and protection policies," and mobilize the public to reform laws and policies to achieve justice. They have developed resources and connected with allies to support those harmed by trafficking.[664]

Native American

Coalition to Stop Violence Against Native Women—CSVANW

Coalition to Stop Violence Against Native Women has a mission to "stop violence against Native women and children by advocating for social change in our communities." Their advocacy addresses domestic violence, sexual assault, dating violence, stalking, and sex trafficking in New Mexico's tribal communities. They use their collective strengths, power, and unity toward the creation of violence-free communities to eradicate violence against Native women and children. They champion social change through support, education, and advocacy.[665]

Alliance of Tribal Coalitions to End Violence—ATCEV

The Alliance of Tribal Coalitions to End Violence works to end violence and "provide safety of American Indian and Alaska Native women" by addressing domestic violence, dating violence, sexual assault, and stalking. They provide training and technical assistance to dozens of Native organizations in thirty-nine states. They are also active in advocating for policy changes to end abuse in American Indian communities.[666]

National Native American Boarding School Healing Coalition—NABS

The National Native American Boarding School Healing Coalition was created to increase "public awareness and cultivate healing for the profound trauma experienced by individuals, families, communities, American Indian and Alaska Native Nations resulting from the U.S. adoptions and implementation of the Boarding School Policy of 1869." This policy ripped children from their homes and sent them to residential schools, the majority run by Catholic institutions, where many were severely abused.[667]

Asians and Pacific Islanders

National Organization of Asians and Pacific Islanders Ending Sexual Violence (NAPIESV)

The National Organization of Asians and Pacific Islanders Ending Sexual Violence was "created by a group of API anti-sexual assault advocates to center the experiences of survivors of sexual violence. It is a program under Monsoon Asians & Pacific Islanders in Solidarity that focuses on enhancing services to survivors in the Asian and Pacific Islander communities with practices and programs specific to their culture." They envision "a world where every individual within API communities lives in safety, dignity, and equality" and "strive to build a society that embraces diversity, uplifts survivors, and eradicates all forms of sexual violence."[668]

Coalitions With Wide Missions, Broad Agendas, and Diverse Audiences

All Survivors Day

All Survivors Day celebrated the advances made by survivors in building a movement of support and advocacy, prompting the organizing of a global celebration of survivors on November 3, 2018. The year after the social media explosion #MeToo in 2017, survivor organizations mobilized the first call to action, bringing together an international coalition of survivors and organizations to host international rallies, speakers, and marches in fifteen cities in fourteen countries worldwide to raise awareness of sexual violence.[669]

Developed through the collaboration of Marci Hamilton of CHILD USA and me as president of SNAP, it brought together sixteen national survivor organizations as the sponsoring coalition.[670] My call for the All Survivors Day event was a call to action to all citizens to come together and help change the culture that surrounds sexual abuse and assault. Hamilton called for action, "This is a day to stand with victims of sexual abuse and assault. They have been silenced and ignored for too long."[671]

All Survivors Day was organized to honor the survivors of sexual abuse, foster solidarity among survivors, raise awareness of the widespread nature of the issue, and change the culture that allows abuse to happen.[672] The event followed the headline trials of Bill Cosby and Larry Nassar, the Pennsylvania Grand Jury report, the U.S. Department of Justice investigations, four state investigations, and a social media flood of #MeToo disclosures that highlighted the ubiquitous abuse in society.

All Survivor Day blazed across the world with broad support to raise awareness and support survivors as the first international coalition addressing sexual violence. However, the reality of meager resources, diverse missions, the absence of an organizing center, and other factors undercut the political will to establish All Survivors Day as an annual event. It went silent. Members of the coalition of allies stepped out of one coalition and into another alliance a couple of years later to form Keep Kids Safe.

Keep Kids Safe (KKS)

Keep Kids Safe was formed in June 2020 to advocate for the safety of children by promoting policies and programs that address "prevention, healing, and justice" as a political intervention. In November 2021, KKS published a "National Blueprint to End Sexual Violence Against Children and Adolescents." This document became the instrument for unifying the groups and advancing their agenda in influencing federal policy.[673]

The KKS Movement "is focused on inclusive, comprehensive, bold, and transformative action from leaders, including prevention to protect this and every generation to come, healing for victims, survivors, and their families, and justice for victims and survivors, and accountability for perpetrators and institutions who covered up the abuse."[674] It assembled major survivor organizations, including RAINN, SNAP, TAOS, Together for Girls, D2L, CHILD USA, National Children's Alliance, Prevent Child Abuse, and the Monique Burr Foundation for Children.[675]

This coalition presented the National Blueprint as its uniting principle. The UN General Assembly adopted and passed a resolution based on the National Blueprint affirming their desire to "eliminate and prevent all forms of child sexual exploitation, abuse, and violence and to promote dignity and rights."[676] They proclaimed November 18th of each year as the World Day for the Prevention of and Healing from Child Sexual Exploitation, Abuse, and Violence. The World Day announcement acknowledges the success of the organizing effort of the survivors' movement to bring sexual abuse to the international stage.

The KKS coalition organized a visit to the U.S. Capitol in April 2023 to lobby for the "National Blueprint" and met with Senator Durbin of Illinois and representatives of the Bipartisan Task Force to End Sexual Violence. Two dozen coalition members also visited the Senate and congressional representatives to lobby for KKS principles addressing access to prevention, healing, and justice. KKS and the Brave Movement engaged with the White House Gender Policy Council to introduce the National Blueprint and rallied in front of the White House to raise awareness.[677]

While the KKS coalition dissolved shortly after those lobbying efforts, it established a template for future partners to join for mutual benefit. Parallel to the organizing and development of KKS was the emergence of another coalition of groups.

Survivors' Agenda

Survivors' Agenda is a "me too. International, Inc." project formed in 2020 following the initial founding of the "me too. Movement" organization in 2018. Its original mission aimed to build power and change the conversation about sexual abuse. It described itself as survivor-centered and led a "collective of organizations and survivors who believe that survivors should be the ones shaping the national conversation on sexual violence." Survivors' Agenda established a steering committee of twenty-one organizations. Over sixty community partners committed to "laying the foundation for future movement building, policy changes, narrative shifts, and accountability efforts." As an introduction, Survivors' Agenda hosted a national call on June 25, 2020, "with over 700 participants focused on the mobilization of survivors and the necessity of confronting systemic sexual violence."[678]

They also sponsored the online Survivors' Agenda Virtual Town Hall from September 24th to 26th, 2020, centering survivors in the conversation about sexual violence. Survivors' Agenda began as a program of the "me too. Movement organization" and several dozen allies and sister organizations. They assembled a diverse coalition of organizations, including "me too. International, Inc.," the National Association of Asian and Pacific Islanders Ending Sexual Violence, the National Survivor Network, Ujima, Safe Before Anyone Else, SAFEBAE, the National Organization of Sisters of Color Ending Sexual Assault, and several additional organizations. As of 2025, the Survivors Agenda's work had been subsumed into the work of "me too. International, Inc." a project explored in the next chapter.[679]

National Alliance to End Sexual Violence—NAESV

National Alliance to End Sexual Violence is "the voice in Washington for the 56 state and territorial coalitions and 1300 rape crisis centers working to end sexual violence and support survivors."[680] Statewide organizations joined with local rape crisis centers to create NAESV to advocate in Washington for state coalitions and local programs. Their range of services includes policy recommendations on upcoming legislation, advocating for appropriations to help end sexual violence by providing analysis, media interviews, and advice for members of Congress and the executive branch.

National Center on Sexual Exploitation—NCOSE

The National Center on Sexual Exploitation wants to "build a world where people can live and love without sexual abuse and exploitation" by mobilizing legal, corporate, and legislative action.[681] They implement their work through research, litigation, advocacy, policy, and training. They have been active in making social media safer through their support of de-platforming Pornhub, combating trafficking, removing child sexual abuse material, and eliminating AI image-based abuse. A Catholic advocacy organization, Morality in Media, founded in 1962, changed its name to the National Center on Sexual Exploitation (NCOSE) in 2015, focusing on sexual violence, child abuse, prostitution, and sex trafficking.[682]

Every Voice Coalition

Every Voice Coalition shouts in its headline: "Believe Survivors, Support Survivors, Empower Survivors."[683] It is active in fifteen states to combat sexual violence in schools and university campuses. Their coalition includes End Rape on Campus, National Alliance to End Sexual Violence, National Women's Law Collective, National Organization of Victim Advocacy, No More Foundation, It's On Us, and others. Every Voice Coalition is "a student and young alum-led non-profit bringing together students, community organizations and universities to combat campus sexual violence by empowering survivors and students to write, file, and fight for their own protections and support into law."[684]

The movement of allies and sister organizations, coalitions, and associations signal the diversity and strength of this movement.[685]

Survivors Go Global

"me too. International"

"me too. International," was formed in 2018 by Tarana Burke following the explosion of the #MeToo tweets of the previous year. Burke has been a leader and vanguard in raising awareness, organizing, and mobilizing survivors worldwide. "me too. International" focuses on helping survivors access resources and building communities of advocates to create solutions. Their work shifts the narrative around sexual violence, centers on survivors and their healing, and provides ways for supporters to take action in their communities. They promote a commitment to cultivate a multi-sectoral, multi-racial, and multi-gender movement to end sexual violence.[686]

"me too. International" described efforts to work with other organizations in their "Measuring the Economic Impact Of Covid-19 On Survivors of Color," report to develop and advance "a global survivor-led movement to end sexual violence." They announced conversations with activists and movements to build an infrastructure that addresses "the prevalence of sexual violence and the immediate needs of survivors in those countries." Their 2020 Impact Report announced the beginning stages of organizing a global network with "me too. International, Inc." serving as "convener, thought leader, and organizer."[687]

That objective established the formation of the Global Network of "me too. International" and announced it on December 3, 2024. This initiative recognized "the urgent need for a worldwide response to the phenomenon of sexual violence." The Global Network assists survivor-led movements in building power for resistance and healing to transform culture, society, and relationships that perpetuate SGBV (sexual and gender-based violence).[688] They also joined forces with the Global Fund for Women to address violence around the world. The Global Network focuses on building power for resistance and healing in communities in Latin America, the Caribbean, and Africa. It will work to transform culture, society, and relationships that perpetuate SGBV. The network currently has 134 organizations across thirty-three countries.[689]

This initiative recognized "the urgent need for a worldwide response to the phenomenon of sexual violence. The Global Network assists survivor-led movements in building power for resistance and healing to transform culture, society, and relationships that perpetuate SGBV (sexual and gender-based violence)."[690]

Brave Movement

The Brave Movement is a survivor-led global advocacy movement that aims to create a world where all children are safe and protected. "We must be brave so that children can be safe," describes the initiative to mobilize the power of survivors to build political power and take action. The Brave Movement works to mobilize the collective power of survivors to demand action from leaders and decision-makers.

The Brave Movement is hosted by Together for Girls, a survivor-led global movement campaigning to end childhood sexual violence "led by fourteen survivors and allied partners" and "focused on prevention, healing, and justice worldwide."[691] They aim to "abolish statutes of limitation in every nation and create a safer internet for children."[692] The creation of the Global Statute of Limitations Reform Task Force brings together two powerful forces—the Brave Movement and CHILD GLOBAL—to eliminate SOL for child sex abuse worldwide and open the door to victims' access to justice.[693]

The Brave Movement was active in the first Global Ministerial Conference on Ending Violence Against Children, which was held in Bogotá, Colombia, in November 2024.[694] This global conference was the first time that all governments of the world convened to commit to preventing violence against children. They created and coordinated the Global Survivor Council (GSC), placing "survivor voices at the heart of the discussion, ensuring their voices are heard."[695]

"Their lived experiences shape policies that guarantee children are safe," said Dr. Daniela Ligiero, CEO of Together for Girls and Founder of the Brave Movement.[696]

The Conference collected and represented survivor-led organizations to engage with world leaders to speak about all forms of violence against children. "The Global Ministerial, hosted by the Governments of Colombia and Sweden in collaboration with the World Health Organization (WHO), UNICEF, and the United Nations Special Representative to the Secretary-General on Violence Against Children (SRSG VAC), will provide an unprecedented opportunity to secure robust commitments to ending violence against children."[697]

To Zero

The organization To Zero supports and organizes the global community of individuals and organizations working to end child sexual violence (CSV). It works to address the lack of resources and root causes to combat cultural taboos that keep abuse in the shadows. Another objective is to "create a safe and healthy world for children, adolescents and youth" by removing "the threat of sexual violence throughout the life course, starting in childhood." To Zero works to prevent CSV, support healing, and develop a "stronger culture of justice and accountability that prioritizes the rights, needs, and safety of survivors."[698]

An Orchestra

Eighty musicians circled in a music hall and playing their favorite songs is not an orchestra; however, a central music score and unifying theme, a set tempo, and a marriage of musical rhythms, with musicians acting together, do perform as an orchestra. Similarly, two hundred unique survivor organizations advancing their missions, objectives, and practices do not make a movement. Organizations working together, engaging with a common and coordinated mission, become a movement; their combined power exemplifies solidarity. We witness organizations move from unique, separate organizations to coalesce into collective formations, coalitions, and associations—the Survivors Movement.

Over a period of twenty-five years, there was a dramatic progression toward unity of action and solidarity of associations. The coalitions described above are concrete manifestations of the emerging movement. Collectively, this movement is taking steps to form a powerful social and political force by redefining social relations, creating support for victims, preventing abuse, eliminating restrictions on reporting abuse, and holding predators accountable. The influence of this new social movement uses its social and political successes to influence national legislation and statewide investigations and hold predators accountable.

The success of these coalitions and the rise of survivor organizations demonstrate the emerging political power of this new social movement.

CHAPTER 14

MOVEMENT ENGAGES IN POLITICS

When I first stepped forward and joined other survivor advocates in 1995 to take action as part of the SNAP network, we faced restrictive laws, the immense power of the institutional Catholic Church, an unaware community of parishioners, mainstream media emerging from sensationalism to factual reporting, and a compromised legislative system failing to protect the vulnerable.

Just as one pebble can trigger an avalanche, the Survivors Movement aggregated the activists who stood up, spoke up, took action, organized, and engaged to change society. Hundreds of separated individual actions propelled forward a mighty avalanche of social change. Like the Civil Rights or Women's Movement, the Survivors Movement emerged from the initiatives and organizations in dozens of sectors scattered across a couple of decades.

> *Our challenge is to organize the power*
> *we already have in our midst.*
>
> —Martin Luther King

Since about 2000, the creation of over two hundred survivor organizations propelled the movement forward, establishing major reforms, instigating state investigations, compelling new laws, and raising social consciousness. Survivor organizations and coalitions stepped up to *organize the power* and use that power in four political interventions.

Our movement is defined by its interconnection, communication, and shared interests. By any definition, we are a movement busting out of silos of individual actions to collective action; the movement is not the sole agent of this reform, yet it is a powerful engine of change that continues to expand its influence. The Survivors Movement blossomed from the explosion of the hundreds of organizations and coalitions seeking paths to health, justice, accountability, and prevention. This chapter explores four paths to seeking justice.

Four Successes—Political Interventions

Four interventions illustrate manifestations of survivor political power: legislative reform, initiation of investigations, creation of state and national legislation, and engagement in international advocacy.

I. Statute of Limitation Reform

Survivors demonstrated a strong interest in reforming or eliminating the SOL laws because they restrict the time limit when predators can be held accountable for a crime. The SOL laws impose time limitations for reporting and a deadline for pressing criminal charges and filing civil lawsuits for sex abuse. Murder, however, can be prosecuted anytime. Before the year 2000, most laws limited reporting of abuse due to SOL laws after the age of eighteen years.[699]

Previous to the present reform movement, SOL laws prohibited the prosecution of a child abuser if the victim reported three years after they reached eighteen, among similar limitations.[700] However, in the earlier chapter on why survivors don't report, we pointed to the statistic that the average age of a victim reporting child sex abuse is over fifty years old.[701] In practice, the delay in self-discovery of abuse and restrictions of SOL laws prohibited accountability.

Earlier, I described how some buried memories did not surface until I was forty-eight, and the most horrific memories were buried until I was sixty-three! When I attempted to file a police report in 1995 to hold the predator and the church accountable, the opportunity to press criminal charges or seek civil damages in Iowa, where the abuse happened, was prohibited. My attempt to make a police report failed as it was long past the Iowa SOL reporting period. The Iowa SOL laws restricted civil lawsuits for child abuse to victims coming forward four years after reaching eighteen. I had no path to justice.[702]

When I submitted testimony to the North Dakota Legislature on January 30, 2021, I described the harm of SOL laws in removing justice and accountability. The opposition to reforming and eliminating the SOL was not limited to the Catholic Church; it included other vested interests, including insurance companies, public and private schools, and others.[703] Many children suffered due to restrictive SOL laws that failed to provide justice and hold predators accountable.

For decades, tens of thousands of victims met with the same roadblock until the rise of the Survivors Movement, which forced a dramatic shift in eliminating and reforming SOL laws. Many predators abuse for decades, using their position to present the facade of amiability, power, and authority, as we have seen with clergy, coaches, teachers, and doctors. Institutions want to protect their reputations and pocketbooks. Politicians want and need the support of powerful institutions to get elected. As a result, they all have a vested interest in keeping SOL laws in place.

Challenge Statute of Limitation Laws

The patchwork of SOL laws addressing abuse in the United States embodies a variety of time and age limitations and effective enforcement dates. Prompted by advocates, but written by legislators and attorneys, these laws became fodder for legal battles, as we saw in the results of the Maryland case after an eight-year struggle, "Maryland's Highest Court Upholds Ending Statute of Limitations on Child Sex Abuse Lawsuits."[704]

Each state has its unique take on reporting crimes and holding predators accountable.[705]

As of 2025, cumulative advances have been made in reforming and eliminating criminal SOL laws in forty-four states. Nineteen states had eliminated age limitations for civil claims. SOL is an issue stirring reforms and opposition, with challenges remaining. The forces working for accountability and reform battled with the church, Boy Scouts, schools, and other large institutions that fought to keep SOL restrictions.

In a news story on *CNN* in August, 2018, a Pennsylvania father emphasized the tragic consequences of justice denied by SOL laws. Arthur Baselice said his son was abused by two clergymen who were not charged because the SOL had expired. His son died at twenty-eight from a drug overdose. "If I had an opportunity to meet with the Pope, I would want to hear his confession. I would tell the Pope, make Jesus proud of you. Come to Pennsylvania and demand that the (statute of limitations) be removed . . . and stop protecting the enablers and abusers. Those actions of prayer, penance, and fasting, he does have that to ease his conscience, but that does nothing for the victims."[706]

As of 2025, reforming SOL laws remained a challenge, with Maine, Massachusetts, Pennsylvania, and Rhode Island refusing to enact reform.[707]

II. Grand Juries, State and Federal Investigations

Terry McKiernan, the codirector of BishopAccountability, an organization that documents sexual abuse within the Catholic community, said it could take "decades before a victim comes forward after being abused as a child. By then, the statute of limitations, which might allow prosecution—has often run out. In lieu of prosecution, you at least have the thorough criminal investigation that's done by an AG's team, expressed in a report, even if the person who did the crime can't be prosecuted."[708] My history, as described in the first chapter, explained how memories of my abuse were buried for decades.

"[State investigations] do not have the standing in law of an indictment, a prosecution, and a conviction. But because the investigations are done by professionals and are done carefully, the reports have a kind of authority that is important to survivors and also important to the community as a whole."[709]

Professor Hamilton called out legislators to legislate: "For all the years that victims have been prevented from seeking justice and that pedophiles have benefited from the law and the disregard of those in power, the states need to enact legislation that will reverse these injustices."[710]

Pennsylvania Grand Jury

The public release of the Pennsylvania "40th Statewide Investigating Grand Jury Report," published in August 2018, showed the impact of state investigations.[711] The report found that more than 300 Catholic clergy had abused some 1,000 children over the previous six decades.[712] "The clergy sexual abuse hotline in the attorney general's office has been ringing day and night for six weeks, tallying 1,181 new calls as of Thursday," according to Pennsylvania AG's Josh Shapiro.[713]

"As a result of the heroism of the survivors (who testified before the grand jury), more and more survivors are finding voices," Shapiro said.[714] Calls flooded the Pennsylvania District Attorney's office, relaying the message: me too.[715] At the same time, local SNAP leaders in Pennsylvania and the SNAP hotline received hundreds of calls and email inquiries seeking help and information in the two weeks following the report's release. According to the media monitoring organization Meltwater, the Grand Jury Report generated over 2,000 articles establishing nationwide interest.[716]

When the Pennsylvania Grand Jury report came out in August 2018, I called for a series of actions to broadcast the scope of widespread abuse in the church.[717] SNAP leaders and I mobilized press conferences in six cities and towns in Pennsylvania in the two days following the report.[718] These press conferences prompted hundreds of local and national articles. The wildfire of interest nationwide confirmed a theme that we advanced—what happened in Pennsylvania happens in every parish and community in America.[719]

I urged SNAP local leaders and the network of survivors to call for a grand jury in every state.[720] The public outrage and mobilizing efforts pushed other states to investigate. Between 2002 and 2025, there have been twenty-six state investigations of the Catholic Church as documented in the nonprofit BishopAccountability list of state investigations.[721]

Rising Social Awareness Pushes Nationwide State Investigations

The State of Illinois AG Lisa Madigan succinctly described the failures of the Catholic Church to investigate and report clergy abuse. The Illinois investigation, published on December 19, 2018, stated: "By choosing not to thoroughly investigate allegations, the Catholic Church has failed in its moral obligation to provide survivors, parishioners, and the public a complete and accurate accounting of all sexually inappropriate behavior involving priests in Illinois." Madigan commented, "The failure to investigate also means that the Catholic Church has never made an effort to determine whether the conduct of the accused priests was ignored or covered up by superiors."[722]

The *New York Times* reported on the follow-up to the 2018 investigation, highlighting that the AG of Illinois, Kwame Raoul, "found more than 450 credibly accused child sex abusers in the Catholic Church in Illinois since 1950. Almost 2,000 children under 18 were victims."[723] The investigation uncovered a massive history of abuse and coverup by the Catholic Church, "detailing decades of child sexual abuse by Catholic clergy in the state."[724] This disclosure of 451 accused predators exposed the coverup of Catholic bishops who posted notice of only 103 accused predators.[725]

Due to the Pennsylvania Grand Jury investigation, the State of Michigan raided the offices of the six dioceses in Michigan.[726] In 2020, a report revealed 454 accused priests and 811 victims. The AGs of Maryland released a report on their investigation in September 2023, identifying 156 accused clergy abusers.[727] SNAP activists on September 4, 2024, urged the AGs "to complete the investigations into the Archdiocese of Washington and the Diocese of Wilmington, Delaware."[728] The Dallas police also raided the diocesan storage facility, searching for documents of abuse and attempting to investigate cover-ups, stating that the diocese was blocking their investigation. Again, the headline tells the story: "Missing and Incomplete Sex-Abuse Files Spark Dallas Police Raid Of Catholic Diocese Storage Facility."[729]

Other states, like the AG of Missouri, declined to investigate, merely compiling the data provided by each church diocese. SNAP called out the Missouri AG's for its "sweetheart" deal with the Archdiocese of St. Louis, allowing it to self-report. SNAP argued that instead of relying on church officials, each diocese should be under investigation by a grand jury, like the Pennsylvania Grand Jury, that "has the power to subpoena documents and to compel current and former church officials and staff to answer tough questions under oath."[730]

The AG of Massachusetts, the home of the 2002 *Boston Globe Spotlight* investigations, began their investigation in 2020 and continued to delay the release of their results into 2025. The same delay happened in California.[731]

The variations in scope and schedule of individual state AG investigations led to a patchwork of investigations across dozens of states.[732] However, the overall momentum looked promising for investigations in every state. The *New York Times* of June 2, 2023, reported twenty recent state investigations looking at Catholic Churches.[733]

Rising Influence of Survivors Movement Compels Federal Investigations

The Pennsylvania Grand Jury report prompted a joint letter from the Center for Constitutional Rights and me, as president of SNAP, to the

Department of Justice calling for a federal investigation.[734] The letter, dated August 15, 2018, called for the initiation of a "full-scale, nationwide investigation into the systemic rape and sexual violence, and cover-ups in the Catholic Church, and, where appropriate, bring criminal and/or civil proceedings against the hierarchy that enabled the violations."[735] The letter referred to an earlier request by Peter Isley of SNAP calling for a DOJ, federal investigation of the church in 2003, written on "behalf of the children, men and women who have been and will be victimized by Catholic clergy in the United States"[736] to then AG John Ashcroft. The Center for Constitutional Rights and SNAP brought "complaints and reports to international bodies including the International Criminal Court and the United Nations since 2011."[737]

SNAP issued a press statement on August 15, 2018, supporting an investigation, pointing out that "SNAP asked for such action in 2003, and again in 2014. We will never know how many children would have been spared harm if decisive action had been taken in 2003 or even in 2014. Today, we are again demanding that the federal government take action. Please do not waste any more time waiting for the Catholic Church to reform itself."[738]

Advocates welcomed the FBI's initiative to investigate. Reporters Candy Woodall and Brandie Kessler wrote an article: "Feds Put Catholic Church Across the Nation on Notice: Don't Destroy Any Evidence of Abuse."[739] The article in the *York Daily Record*, dated October 26, 2018, showed the federal government's growing interest.

> ### FBI Investigation
>
> **The FBI is actively interested in hearing from survivors of sexual abuse. There are certain criteria that have to be met:**
>
> - *Were under 18 at the time of the abuse,*
> - *Were abused after November 29, 1985,*
> - *Were born after 1978,*
> - *The abuse involved interstate or international travel, the production of pornography, or payments,*
> - *The perpetrator is still alive.*
>
> **If you or someone you know matches these criteria, Please contact the FBI at (215) 521-3647.**

Southern Baptist Church and Department of Justice

Survivors within the Baptist community called on federal authorities to take action by investigating Baptist churches, which, like the Catholic Churches, were unwilling to investigate and impose reforms.

An article by Sarah Stankorb in *Vice News* described Christa Brown's advocacy, pushing for Southern Baptist Church (SBC) transparency. "The Southern Baptist Church Ignored Its Abuse Crisis. She Exposed It," dated January 4, 2023, detailed Brown's mission to bring to light the scope of abuse within the Baptist community. Brown "renewed a call for a Truth and Justice Commission modeled on the U.S. Justice Department's probe of Pennsylvania Catholic dioceses. She called upon state attorneys general to launch thorough investigations into sexual abuse, institutional enablement, and maltreatment of survivors by SBC. She'd been lobbying for a federal investigation since at least 2018."[740]

"SBC's executive committee announced that the U.S. Department of Justice had initiated an investigation of multiple SBC entities. With such an investigation comes subpoena power and the collection of evidence that can be used by state and local law enforcement. SBC wouldn't be controlling the process."[741] Brown responded, "May justice flow down like waters."[742]

The FBI had a mixed history of investigation and prosecution of sexual predators. We explored in an earlier chapter the FBI's botched investigation of abuse suffered by gymnasts and athletes at the hands of Dr. Larry Nassar at Michigan State University. An *Associated Press* article reported on a dramatic example. "In one case, a victim was abused for 15 months after the FBI first received a tip about a registered sex offender, the report said."[743]

An attorney and advocate for victims of abuse, John Manly, of California, commented on the results: "This report makes clear that the FBI is simply not doing its job when it comes to protecting our children from the monsters among us who stalk them. Despite years of promises and numerous congressional hearings, it's now clear that the Larry Nassar scandal could happen again today."[744]

A DOJ report, titled "Audit of the Federal Bureau of Investigation's Handling of Tips of Hands-on Sex Offenses Against Children," dated August 2024, followed another 2021 audit on the failures of the FBI to address Nassar's hundreds of victims.[745] It disclosed that the FBI failed "to report to local law enforcement in about 50 percent of the cases."[746] The audit made a dozen recommendations to address loopholes, provide resources, and take corrective action to ensure that proper abuse investigations are supported.

After criticisms of the FBI in the Epstein and Nassar investigations, survivors expected that the FBI and other federal agencies would address child abuse and sexual violence with dedication. A vigorous and active

Survivors Movement can play an important role in forcing investigations and prosecutions of predators.

III. Federal Legislative Acts

Clery Act

The Clery Act requires greater transparency and timely warnings from colleges and universities about crimes committed on campus, including crimes of sexual violence. It also imposes civil penalties of up to $25,000 per violation. In 1985, the Federal Victims of Crimes Act gave victims resources and support to address sexual violence.[747] Several years later, in 1990, the Clery Act required colleges to report to civil authorities.[748] A number of schools have violated the Clery Act: "The Department of Education has found that about 340 colleges have violated the federal Campus Security Act since the law was enacted in 1991, according to the national watchdog organization Security on Campus."[749]

Michigan State University likely set a record in 2019 it wants no part of—the most rapes ever reported by a university on its annual Clery Act report.[750] In the *Detroit Free Press*, reporter David Jesse documented the extent of rapes and abuse of Larry Nassar at MSU.[751] The enforcement of the Clery Act forced a full disclosure of the extent of abuse at MSU. "It's all because of Larry Nassar. There were 933 reports of rape and 137 reports of fondling attributed to Nassar in 2018."[752]

SNAP Calls for Racketeer Influenced and Corrupt Organizations Investigation

For almost two decades, SNAP has been calling for reform of laws, especially SOL laws in dozens of states. Previous to the call for reform, in 2003, SNAP and the CCR took another avenue, requesting a federal Racketeer Influenced and Corrupt Organizations (RICO) investigation. They filed a request to the DOJ to initiate a RICO investigation of the widespread abuse in the Catholic Church.[753]

SNAP and CCR sent a renewed request to the DOJ for a national investigation in 2018, as the DOJ did not respond to the 2003 request. The new request letter was titled Demand for Investigation and Prosecution of High-Level Officials in the Catholic Church for Widespread and Systemic Rape and Other Forms of Sexual Violence, dated August 15, 2018, signed by two CCR senior staff attorneys, Katherine Gallagher and Pamela C. Spees, and me. The letter laid out the complaint:

> Yesterday, the Pennsylvania Supreme Court released a grand jury report which sets out in clear, unmistakable terms and in horrifying detail widespread sexual violence by priests involving more than 1,000 victims and a coherent, cohesive, pattern and practice of coverup by high-level officials in the Catholic Church in Pennsylvania and the Vatican.[754] The Pennsylvania report is comprehensive and the latest in a tragically long line of such reports from around the country and, indeed, the world.
>
> It is long past time for the U.S. Department of Justice to initiate a full-scale, nationwide investigation into the systemic rape and sexual violence, and cover-ups in the Catholic Church and, where appropriate, bring criminal and/or civil proceedings against the hierarchy that enabled the violations.[755]

Trafficking Legislation Advances

Advances have been made since 2020; Congress passed two laws, reflecting the public's rejection of SOL laws. The passage of Senate Bill "SB 3103—Eliminating Limits to Justice for Child Sex Abuse Victims Act of 2022" eliminates SOL laws for minor victims of trafficking. Equally important is the passage of "SB 4524—The Speak Out Act," which prevents the enforcement of NDA in instances of sexual assault and harassment. Both are major victories in limiting the time to report crimes.[756]

Violence Against Women Act

The Violence Against Women Act protects women from domestic violence, sexual assault, dating violence, stalking, economic abuse, and emotional abuse. Title IV of the Violent Crime Control and Law Enforcement Act became law in 1994.[757] Political successes followed with funding of $1.6 billion to investigate and prosecute violent crimes against women and offered services for women in housing, legal assistance, and prevention.

The VAWA endeavors to protect victims, provide resources and support services, eliminate gender-based violence, and provide justice for victims. This act was reauthorized in 2000, 2005, and 2022. Each reauthorization added new provisions to improve the existing law and expand its scope. For instance, the majority of grants addressed the victims' and justice system's needs in response to violence that already occurred rather than prevention of VAWA-related offenses, leading to guidance "toward programs aligned with the goals of violence prevention and changing attitudes about gendered violence."[758]

Some key provisions of VAWA include

- The creation of the National Domestic Violence Hotline, which provides 24/7 support and resources for victims of domestic violence.
- The establishment of the Office on Violence Against Women within the DOJ to oversee and coordinate federal efforts to combat violence against women.
- Protections for immigrant victims include access to immigration relief and protection from deportation.
- Programs and services for underserved populations, including Native American tribes and individuals with disabilities.
- Mandatory arrest policies for domestic violence incidents in some jurisdictions.

- Training for law enforcement officers, prosecutors, and judges on how to respond effectively to cases of domestic violence, dating violence, sexual assault, and stalking.[759]

Respect for Child Survivors Act

The Respect for Child Survivors Act, passed on January 5, 2023, "requires the Federal Bureau of Investigation (FBI) to use a multidisciplinary team with investigations of child abuse and related crimes. The act also reauthorizes grants for children's advocacy centers (CACs). CACs use a multidisciplinary response to coordinate the investigation, treatment, and prosecution of child abuse cases." This act provides guidance when investigating "child sexual exploitation or abuse, the production of child sexual abuse material, or child trafficking." The act requires the FBI to use a "trained child adolescent forensic interviewer in these investigations" and "use and coordinate with multidisciplinary teams based at CACs."[760] This team approach "ensure[s] federal cases of child sexual abuse, exploitation, and trafficking receive an effective multidisciplinary team response."[761]

Civil Action, Chapter 11, and Bankruptcy Law

When a Catholic diocese, the Boy Scouts, and other large institutions get hit with thousands of accusations, they protect themselves and their treasure by declaring bankruptcy. Not only does bankruptcy protect the institution from millions of dollars in damages, but it also has an equally nefarious role in hiding evidence. Bankruptcy allows offending institutions to stop the discovery of facts, which, in turn, silences survivors. Any complaint can be tied up in bankruptcy court for years and remain sealed forever. Of course, institutions love bankruptcy.

Such was the case of the Catholic Archdiocese of New Orleans.[762] According to an article in *The Guardian*, "The archdiocese filed for bankruptcy after paying $11.7 million in out-of-court, abuse-related settlements during a 10-year period beginning in 2020. The proceeding cost the archdiocese nearly $34 million in legal and other professional fees; remains unresolved as of 2025; and therefore has not yet resulted in any compensation for those with pending abuse claims."[763] The Archbishop would rather pay his attorneys three times as much as the victims to hide child abuse.

Congresswoman Deborah Ross (NC), a reform bankruptcy bill sponsor, commented in April 2024 about the drawn-out process of bankruptcy complaints. "Dozens of Catholic dioceses and other organizations, including the Boy Scouts of America, sought bankruptcy protection in recent years after being hit with thousands of sex abuse claims. Most of those Chapter 11 cases have been mired in litigation for years."[764] The Boy Scouts' bankruptcy was tied up in court for over three years, ending in April 2023 with an award of $2.5 billion to be shared with 80,000 claimants.[765]

Ross introduced legislation to support survivors of child sex abuse through bankruptcy reform called the Closing Bankruptcy Loopholes for Child Predators Act on April 18, 2024. This bipartisan bill addresses the misuse of declaring bankruptcy by institutions, such as the Boy Scouts and the Catholic Church, when faced with lawsuits for child sex abuse. The act addresses "how youth groups, sports' governing bodies, and religious entities, among other organizations," have used bankruptcy courts to "evade accountability" for hundreds of child sex abuse lawsuits. "By obstructing discovery and silencing victims, these entities prolong court proceedings and deprive victims of the justice they rightfully deserve," coauthor Claudia Tenney said in a press release.[766]

Bankruptcy law remains a smelly, rotten egg for victims and a golden Easter egg for abusers and complicit organizations in 2024.

Potpourri of Legislation

RAINN provides an introduction to legislation and its impact on supporting survivors, promoting accountability, and protecting the vulnerable.[767]

- "The Debbie Smith Act, reauthorized in 2024, intends to eliminate the backlog of untested and unanalyzed DNA evidence by providing the resources to process evidence and add these samples to the national DNA database. The grant program helps state and local governments improve the collection and analysis of DNA evidence, including evidence in sexual assault kits. Since its initial passage in 2004, funding from the Debbie Smith Act has resulted in more than 300,000 hits on CODIS [Combined DNA Index System], the national DNA database system."[768]

- The Campus SaVE amended the Clery Act in 2013 to increase transparency requirements for colleges, guarantee rights for survivors, establish disciplinary proceedings, and require education programs. This act has four elements:

    1. Every college must be transparent about crimes of sexual violence on campus and is required to provide an annual report documenting the crimes committed on and near campus over the past three years.

    2. A college must make accommodations for survivors, whether or not they decide to report to law enforcement. These accommodations can relate to a survivor's academic, living, transportation, or working situations. Institutions must provide victims with contact information about existing services on and off campus, including counseling, health care, mental health, victim advocacy, and legal assistance.

    3. Institutions must provide education and awareness programs, including sexual violence prevention education. Also, it provides information on awareness programs, bystander intervention, prevention, consent, and risk reduction.

4. Colleges must set standards for disciplinary proceedings, including a description of sanctions that might be levied against an accused student through impartial disciplinary proceedings in a timely manner.

- The SAFER Act—Sexual Assault Forensic Evidence Reporting—supports efforts to audit, test, and reduce the backlog of DNA evidence in assault cases and bring perpetrators to justice. This act is part of VAWA 2013.

IV. International Engagement—The International Criminal Court

Previous chapters demonstrated the scope of sexual violence and the rising movement fighting back within American society. There is also a corollary development of international fightback due to abuse worldwide. SNAP and the CCR made a complaint to the International Criminal Court (ICC) in The Hague in 2011 asking for the investigation and prosecution of Catholic Pope Benedict XVI and three Vatican officials.[769] The complaint detailed its accusations of crimes against humanity for abetting and covering up the sexual assault of children by priests.

This charge "marks the most substantive effort yet to hold the pope and the Vatican accountable in an international court for sexual abuse by priests."[770] CCR Senior Staff Attorney Pam Spees said in a statement announcing the filing, "Crimes against tens of thousands of victims, most of them children, are being covered up by officials at the highest level of the Vatican. In this case, all roads really do lead to Rome."[771] SNAP and CCR provided prosecutors with over 20,000 pages of supplemental materials, including reports, policy papers, and government and judicial inquiries.[772]

The ICC in The Hague decided not to investigate or prosecute the former Pope and other leaders of the Roman Catholic Church, stating that "the decision not to proceed may be reconsidered in the light of new facts or information" and suggesting that the cases can be brought to "appropriate national or international authorities."⁷⁷³

While the ICC never took action, they never dismissed the complaint.⁷⁷⁴

UN Committee on the Rights of the Child

In 2013, SNAP and CCR presented testimony to the UN Committee on the Rights of the Child concerning widespread abuse by Catholic clergy. On behalf of SNAP and the victims, the CCR presented dozens of pages of documentation and arguments for holding the Vatican responsible. These remedies and recommendations were suggested by CCR:

- Affirm the best interests of the child and ensure protection;
- Adopt disciplinary measures for higher-ranking officials, including bishops and cardinals, who engage in a coverup of sexual abuse cases and fail to report instances to secular authorities;
- Require mandatory reporting to secular authorities;
- Educate children about their rights under the Convention;
- Require background checks and psychological assessments by independent specialists;
- Open the ecclesiastical proceedings to the public.⁷⁷⁵

The Vatican testified before the committee and submitted its response to critics on which CCR, SNAP, and others commented. The UN Committee responded, calling for action. The headline captured the reaction of the UN Committee on the Rights of the Child: The CCR statement quoted the UN report: "The Holy See has consistently placed the preservation of the reputation of the Church and the protection of the perpetrators above children's best interests." The UN Committee demanded that the Vatican "must undertake a series of reforms to meet its obligations under the Convention on the Rights of the Child and disclose records on all cases of child sexual abuse committed by Catholic clergy around the world."[776] This testimony helped create an adverse finding against the church, which claimed immunity as a nation-state, avoiding sanctions.

UN Committee on Torture

The CCR and SNAP submitted a report to the UN Committee Against Torture (CAT) in April 2014 documenting the harm survivors suffered by Catholic clergy. They called on the UN to examine the Vatican's human rights record on "addressing the ongoing worldwide crisis of sexual violence and cover-ups."[777]

CCR Senior Staff Attorney Pam Spees called out the Vatican for ignoring abuse: "Months ago, Vatican officials submitted a report to the Committee Against Torture that makes no mention whatsoever of the rape, sexual violence, and cover-ups within the church, which carry severe and long-lasting harm. But the Committee Against Torture and international human rights law recognize rape and other forms of sexual violence as torture and cruel, inhuman, and degrading treatment, and the Vatican has fallen woefully short of its obligation to prevent and protect against these crimes."[778]

The CCR report described the long-term harms "suffered by survivors of clergy sexual violence, including increased risks of suicide and attempted suicide; mental illness, including depression, anxiety, post-traumatic stress, and addictive disorders."[779]

> The United Nations Committee Against Torture finds that the widespread sexual violence within the Catholic church amounts to torture and cruel, inhuman, and degrading treatment prohibited by the Convention Against Torture. [. . .] The committee expresses serious concerns about the Vatican's failure to prevent and punish rape and other sexual violence and about the Vatican's failures to meet its obligations under

the UN Convention to provide redress, including financial compensation, rehabilitative support, and a guarantee that the crimes will not be repeated. [. . .]

The committee expressed deep concerns regarding church policies and practices such as moving priests rather than reporting them to civil authorities for investigation and prosecution, failing to properly monitor known perpetrators, refusing to cooperate with national authorities, and lack of accountability for bishops and cardinals who have participated in cover-ups and enabled the crimes. The committee further finds that the Vatican's obligations reach beyond the Vatican City State to all those acting under the Church's effective authority and control.[780]

These are the recommendations of the "UN Committee on Torture Addressing Failures of the Vatican":

- Ensure monitoring of all individuals under their control and immediately suspend individuals suspected of abuse and prevent their transfer;
- Report allegations of abuse to civil authorities and cooperate with their investigation and prosecution;
- Apply meaningful sanctions to those who fail to exercise due diligence and react to allegations;
- Establish an independent complaints mechanism for victims; and
- Ensure that victims of sexual abuse receive redress, including fair, adequate, and enforceable rights to compensation and as full rehabilitation as possible.[781]

Barbara Blaine, founder and president of SNAP, pointed out in 2014 that on the "church's continuing abuse crisis, many Catholic officials talk compassionately in public but act recklessly and callously in private," endangering children and vulnerable adults.[782]

'Out of the Shadows' Steps Onto the World Stage

Out of the Shadows is a global research organization that addresses child sexual exploitation and abuse (CSEA) at the national level.[783] It works to prevent and respond to CSEA in sixty countries, covering about 85 percent of the global child population. It developed an index that tracks the implementation of programs to "build the framework for a holistic, government-led and civil society and private sector-supported approach to ending child sexual abuse around the world."[784] This Index is "organized around two governance dimensions: prevention and response. The prevention dimension comprises protective legislation, policy, and programs. The response dimension comprises support services and recovery, and justice process."[785]

Out of the Shadows commented that the USA "does not have a holistic, child-centered system in place to prevent and respond to CSEA. [. . .] The U.S. Pilot OOSI builds on the Global Out of the Shadows Index and helps uncover how 12 states are tackling CSEA both in person and online. Using 182 individual metrics aggregated into 22 indicators and four pillars." The index assessed each state's

~ legal frameworks
~ policies and programs to protect and educate children and key stakeholders
~ provision of support services for victims and offenders
~ and the justice process for victims[786]

Out of the Shadows examined the degree to which governments across sixty countries have enacted legislation to regulate how the private sector engages with children. This assessment included issues related to data protection, child labor, and the role of internet service providers in preventing the spread of child sexual abuse material online.

The Arc of History

> *The arc of the moral universe is long, and it bends toward justice. We've all heard this quote. But somebody has to bend it. The possibility we create in this movement and others is the weight leaning that arc in the right direction. Movements create possibility, and they are built on vision.*[787]
>
> —Tarana Burke,
> quoting Dr. Martin Luther King, Jr.

Individuals stepped forward and organized. Many are organized online through other social media, using their story as a seed to connect with others harmed in similar circumstances. The gymnasts coalesced from a newspaper series that brought survivors forward, leading to a court case. Others connected through civil actions like the Boy Scouts and their historic settlement. My involvement started by connecting with SNAP organizers demonstrating in front of a church. All these efforts grew and matured, fostering connections leading to organizations' coalitions and creating a movement.

As survivors' organizations and coalitions organized, their intervention in politics strengthened their ability to prevent future abuse, hold predators and their institutions accountable, and ensure a safer society. The activists of this movement, with a long history of peer support and personal healing, stepped up to engage in political actions to solidify gains and to compel actions to solidify those gains.

We have become more powerful by assembling individuals, organizations, and coalitions for a common purpose. The movement thrives in these thousands of points of light, exercising power by making a call to action, as seen in the next chapter.

CHAPTER 15

REMEDIES & CALLS TO ACTION

We Have the Power

My first public event protesting clergy took place in 1995. I stood in front of a church in Santa Rosa, California, where I joined a handful of other SNAP survivors and supporters, facing disbelieving parishioners and a challenge from the parish priest. Over time, I participated in other actions in the San Francisco Bay Area as a result of more disclosures of abuse in other parishes. I persisted. Others persisted. As my involvement in activism grew, I gained awareness of the scope of abuse locally and then nationally. The flood of revelations of clergy abuse within the Catholic Church connected with other sectors of society, equally burdened by abuse. Hundreds of organizations were formed. The #MeToo Movement brought millions of survivors forward and more organizations. Coalitions and associations assembled around shared missions and objectives. In 2025, over thirty years later, the Survivors Movement, a new social movement, has become a powerful social and political force.

Leaders stepped out of the wreckage of lifelong suffering, just as a phoenix emerges from the flames, to help themselves and others. Their courageous acts became the seed of social change; a social movement was born.

Activists took action with courage and commitment. Organizations and coalitions mobilized. Working together, survivors gained greater power to enact legislative reforms, eliminate or reform existing laws, and compel state investigations, thereby challenging society's legacy and institutional power. Survivors began to dominate the conversation.

What Is to Be Done?

This book shows how survivors have taken action, organized, overcome challenges, and accomplished successes. We still need to move mountains to achieve justice. Work is ahead as we face obstacles from the dominant social and political structures. Our movement must continue to work to achieve victories despite myriad challenges.

Obstacles remain in all spheres of society. Male supremacy and chauvinism continue to infect society and social actions. Legacy institutions and offending institutions present a façade of progress, but underneath, they undermine justice as they actively work to stifle legislation that would hold predators and institutions accountable. The mainstream media have reported on thousands of stories but continue to face headwinds in presenting fundamental issues of misogyny, child abuse, racism, homophobia, and other ills.

Lastly, there remains a massive deficit of knowledge of widespread abuse in several sectors: the scale of assault on the LGBTQ communities, the deficit of reporting in communities of color and its impact, the failure of the military to protect its soldiers, and the tragic underreporting of the horrific crimes inflicted on Indian communities. Yes, we have made progress, but we continue facing long-term challenges.

The Call for a National Convention

Like a weaving that incorporates many threads of varying size, color, texture, and material, our movement encompasses many diverse organizations whose missions form a patchwork of attributes and audiences. Calling for a national convention of survivors would assemble these organizations to develop solidarity and a common purpose. The announcement of such an event becomes a rallying point that can act as a magnet to bring more individuals and organizations to shared action. A convention would be a material expression of the movement.

> *When I think of a Survivor's Movement,*
> *I think of people emerging and forming a wave,*
> *like building waves in the ocean,*
> *and as it gets bigger and bigger and bigger,*
> *it draws more power.*
>
> —Suzanne Isaza,
> founder of Incest AWARE[788]

Now is the time to proclaim our power with a national "conference of equals" of survivor organizations, similar to the gathering of women's organizations at Seneca Falls, New York, in July 1848, which called for women's suffrage, equality with men, equal education, and jobs. The Seneca Falls meeting marked a time and place for the birth of the Women's Movement and became a sentinel moment in a two-hundred-year history of advocacy for women's rights. It sets the example for a survivors' conference of equals that would build cohesion and collective social influence.[789]

Such a meeting will help to cement the bonds of collaboration and solidarity with all organizations, associations, coalitions, and initiatives meeting as equals to address the needs of survivors. Let survivors have their historic moment, like the meeting at Seneca Falls, to build political power by establishing our Survivors Movement. Demonstrating solidarity and unity of action increases the movement's social and political power. When hundreds of survivor-led organizations and initiatives announce the Survivors' Movement, it becomes a magnet that attracts additional allies, bringing new organizations and individuals into the fold.

Like a community of nations that meet in the UN to develop a better world, we need a similar analogy for planning a survivors' "conference of equals," creating a platform for participation of the broad diversity of organizations, coalitions, missions, communities, and objectives in our movement.

Despite the disparity of mission and audience, all sectors share common themes of justice, support, prevention, and corrective action. Movement supporters, such as social workers, attorneys, therapists, doctors, feminist scholars, politicians, and law enforcement, can enrich the meeting with the combined force of all activists working to support the movement.

A "conference of equals" would announce and recognize the Survivors Movement's full power as a national political and social movement. It could gather hundreds of activists in a shared space to decide the future. The announcement would be a powerful intervention in popular culture, politics, media, and awareness.

Campaigns for Justice and Accountability

The activists of the Survivors Movement have compelling reasons to challenge the status quo in politics and legislation. Below are some campaigns addressing many of the outstanding challenges facing those harmed by sexual violence. All would benefit from active support in collaboration with other movement organizations.

Statute of Limitations Reform

The research and legal nonprofit CHILD USA provides a comprehensive program supporting the enactment of SOL laws in the fifty states. Advocacy groups have pushed dozens of states to reform and eliminate laws to make our communities safer and have been successful in over thirty states.[790] The challenge going forward is that each state has unique laws sprinkled across the nation to make further advances. Further reform needs to be made on the age of the victim and time limitations for reporting after abuse. Each state has differences in SOL criminal reporting and time limitations for seeking civil damages. While there has been great success in the reform of SOL laws, more needs to be done to bring justice for victims and accountability for predators and institutions that protect them.

Child Marriage

According to advocacy nonprofit Unchained at Last, "Nearly 300,000 minors, under age 18, were legally married in the U.S. between 2000 and 2018. A few were as young as 10, though nearly all were aged 16 or 17. Most were girls wed to adult men, an average of four years older."[791] While progress has been made, in 2025, child marriage, described as one or both parties entering a union while under age 18, "remained legal in 37 states."[792]

There are several other tasks to address in states that fail to protect children by allowing child marriage. CHILD USA considers "child marriage" to be a form of "forced marriage."[793] Their 2021 report points to the scope of child marriage in the United States, citing "data from all fifty states found that approximately 86 percent of these underage marriages involved girls and 14 percent involved boys. While the general public often assumes that child marriage is an issue limited to third-world countries, the practice is widespread across the United States today."[794] While the number of cases of child marriages has been reduced, there remains important work to be done to end child marriage.

Legislative Reform

Legacy legislation is marked by weak penalties for abuse. There are several tasks ahead for state and national legislators. For instance, major reforms must be made to end exemptions that hide abuse, such as religious exemptions and parental permission. Eliminate terminology and language to root out and eradicate those instances in law and legislation that excuse or tolerate old ideas—for instance, ending the misogynistic and patriarchal ideologies of believability, "he said, she said," and what she wore, or how late it was. These memes have been coded into law and legal practice, diminishing the status of the victim.

Work needs to be done to compel institutions to hold abusers accountable. So, legislators must enact strong laws that penalize crimes with jail terms and end sentencing where only 1 or 2 percent of convicted predators ever end up in jail.[795] As we saw in previous chapters, most victims don't report to the police! Legislators are responsible for supporting survivors as a form of restitution and restorative justice. For example, laws that compel individuals and institutions to pay for the restoration and restitution of their many victims must be enacted.

Investigations by State and Civil Society

There have been successful investigations of abuse in the Catholic Church in twenty states as of 2025.[796] The results of previous investigations suggest that investigations of other faith communities are necessary, as we have seen in the Southern Baptist churches covering up for abusers.[797]

There have been dozens of investigations by news organizations.[798] Further investigations must be made in communities of color and for LGBTQ survivors. There needs to be equal attention to corporations and social organizations, where power, authority, and money overwhelm justice and reporting. Attention must be given to doctors, physicians, and therapists who wield great power over their patients and have failed to protect those in their care. It is a common view that the American Medical Association, the American Psychological Association, and similar professional organizations have failed to protect patients and have provided cover for abusers. Civil society must step in to expose predators, no matter their professional status. Continued investigations are required to ensure a safe community.

AI-Generated Abuse

AI abuse happens in plain sight, although in disguise—a violation of human rights and a crime. AI is used by predators to demean, exploit, and degrade women and children while hiding behind a computer screen and computer-generated images. Law enforcement must have the tools to identify predators and victims behind the screen.

Advocates have called for an end to AI-generated child sexual abuse material (CSAM). RAINN defines CSAM as "any image, video, or content that depicts the sexual exploitation of minors. CSAM encompasses both real imagery and AI-generated or manipulated imagery."[799] RAINN has rallied for the prosecution of AI CSAM: "Deepfakes. Revenge porn. Sextortion. No matter what you call it, tech-enabled sexual abuse is harmful and unethical—and it should be a crime in every state."[800] CSAM demands widespread action by activists and advocates at every level of society; Congress and the government must take forceful action to end this exploitation.

Congressional Hearings and Legislative Action

Congressional hearings concerning SOL, child marriage, AI, and other issues can bring attention to the scope of abuse and propose legislative solutions. Hearings would also provide the platform to formulate new laws that protect the vulnerable, hold predators accountable, and give survivors hope for a safer world.

One constructive step would be to create and codify a Title Statute modeled after Title IX that gives global guidance on ensuring a safe and healthy society free of sexual violence. By codifying respect and dignity, it ensures the right to live free of violence and fosters safety in all vulnerable communities. Special attention must be paid to the health and safety of marginalized communities, such as nonbinary, gender-fluid, and transgender people.

Another legislative action would be to impose punitive sanctions on offending and/or complicit institutions and companies that hide sexual violence. Such sanctions would remove their business license and corporate protections, especially removing protection for executives. We have examined many examples of corporations that use their wealth to deny accountability. Hold powerful institutions responsible for their actions in perpetuating abuse through cover-ups and NDA payoffs. For example, we must also remove nonprofit status from complicit organizations, as we have seen with the Catholic, Baptist, and LDS churches, as well as civil organizations like the Boy Scouts, universities, sports teams, and the like. Further, remove corporation status from those companies and organizations that foster and cover up abuse.

Restitution and Restorative Justice

Those persons and entities responsible must be compelled to help mitigate the harm suffered by victims through compensation. I, like the vast majority of survivors, suffer lifelong consequences that compel the call for material support for various therapies (support groups, therapists, psychologists, and psychiatrists) and healing modalities (yoga, meditation, etc.). The trauma of sexual violence can cause emotional and psychological breakdowns, inability to hold a job, broken relationships and marriages, and general poor health. Healing is a lifelong journey that can be expensive. While compensation from the predator or institution can mitigate some effects, it can be an element of restitution. It is reasonable for survivors to demand some form of restorative justice as compensation for healing support.

International

UN Convention on the Rights of the Child

This book's primary focus is on abuse within the United States. However, abuse is not limited to the United States, either for the victim or the perpetrator. Solutions must be worldwide in scope, demanding worldwide investigation, action, and reform.

The United States has failed to ratify the UN Convention on the Rights of the Child, which was ratified by 193 other nations. Somalia was the only other country that failed to ratify the convention. Refusing to ratify avoids being held accountable to the international community for violations. Related, there is no law banning child marriage on the federal level.[801] Advocates and activists must organize to ensure the ratification of this convention and then its enforcement at the local, state, and national levels. We must weigh the rights of parental authority versus the safety and well-being of the child. Approval of this convention must be implemented in the United States, as no institution is allowed to violate children's basic tenets of respect and dignity.

Popular Action

Social and political change arises from popular power. Violence against women and children will not disappear without the demand for popular action. The history of the Women's Movement and the Civil Rights Movement shows that popular action compels politicians to act. We need similar action to compel the reforms outlined in this chapter.

Call for Ongoing Public Demonstrations

Previous monumental social justice movements, such as the Civil Rights Movement, changed the world through large events (March on Washington, 1963) and smaller events (Rosa Parks and the bus boycott, 1955). Similarly, we saw the Women's Movement, with large events (Women's March in 2017) and more minor (local demonstrations supporting reproductive rights), which led to great social and political power.

Popular actions like All Survivors Day in September 2018 provide a venue for exhibiting solidarity, bringing together survivors from many sectors. Public demonstrations also provide an opportunity to call out predators and institutions, draw media attention, and provide a venue for reaching a wider audience. Raising awareness offers comfort to those suffering, reminding them they are not alone.

Popular demonstrations complement high-level meetings of organizations and national campaigns, expanding political and social clout, creating a political power foundation, expressing the movement's depth and breadth, and increasing its political clout. Building the movement's base through mass actions expresses political power.

Going public can be a means to celebrate victories and demonstrate the movement's power in making social and political change. Honoring the heroes and celebrating the victories creates an atmosphere of confidence, so no victim will have to remain silent.

Activism—Large and Small

Every reader has an opportunity to engage. Connect with your local rape crisis center; volunteer to help others. If no organization exists, create one. Organize a support group. Engage in social media. Write an article or a book. Join a political campaign. Donate to a worthy cause. We must step forward; the Afro-American proverb "each one, teach one" is a model for future actions. The opportunities are available. If you don't know how to organize, then ask!

A direct engagement with established organizations, such as rape crisis centers, is the foundation of the movement. There are local, regional, and national organizations that address your abuse.

When movement leaders engage with politicians to advance new laws, they benefit by having a strong social and political movement standing with them. Social power is political power; political power compels legislative action.

Consent education, sex-positive education, and sexual abuse prevention are needed in schools and other organizations serving kids. How do we create new models of equality, empathy, and respect for boundaries?

An important focus of the movement in recent years has been increasing diversity, equity, and inclusion both in the movement itself and in organizations as a method of reducing exploitation, spreading the awareness and practice of consent, youth sex-positive education, and expanding awareness of the diversity of sexual/gender identities and orientations.

Now is the time to take action, volunteer, donate, and engage. The previous chapters highlighted campaigns, organizations, coalitions, and resources. The important point is to step forward; one step can lead to another. Your action, no matter how small, would benefit every organization, association, and social entity.

- a kind note of support for a victim on social media
- a letter to the editor or a letter to a politician
- a donation to a survivor organization
- participation in a public event, press conference, or organizational meeting
- signing a petition for legislative reform
- if you see a need, then initiate an action, form an organization, start a social media entity, start a petition, or organize your friends and community
- join an activist organization

I want the reader to step forward, knowing they are not alone. Seek out the dozens of organizations pointed to in the previous chapters. I also want the reader to understand that the issue is not someone else's problem; rather, we must see abuse as a social problem requiring action from every community. Each step we take to address the issue gives hope to many who have no hope.

This book celebrates the many heroes and victories of those actively engaging in advocacy and activism. Every one of us can be an organizer. Poet Marge Piercy celebrates those who stand up for justice: "The people I love the best, jump into work head first, without dallying in the shallows. . . ."[802]

Many Tributaries, One River

The power of the mighty Mississippi River exists due to the combination of dozens of contributory rivers, including the Missouri, Ohio, and Red Rivers, among others. As an analogy, our movement exists due to hundreds of organizations' combined advocacy and activism. All contribute, large and small, to the total effort of the movement.

The growing power of this movement has shifted public opinion and compelled dramatic social, political, and cultural change. First and foremost, it gives victims the power to fight back. Second, the increased strength of the movement creates more influence and power to compel stronger laws and more penalties on predators, enabling safer communities. Third, it compels accountability from the most powerful institutions in the world. As a social movement, it gives hope to all harmed, knowing they are not alone.

Society has changed because survivors have taken action. Courageous victims step forward and declare themselves survivors who have redefined interpersonal relationships and power dynamics, and new understandings of consent and coercive control. Survivors are no longer alone, afraid, and silent. They form vibrant, dynamic, and diverse organizations. Their advocacy and social activism are the foundation of the emerging Survivors Movement.

We are here, and we are not going away!

CHAPTER 16

CELEBRATING THE FUTURE

Our Survivors Movement is not the result of one leader, organization, or coalition; it is a collaboration of shared interests, objectives, and goals that thrives as the community of organizations and coalitions. This book serves as a resource to inform and guide advocacy. German playwright and poet Bertolt Brecht's sentiments highlight the collective power of survivor voices who engage daily and intervene to change the world.

> *Art is not a mirror with which to reflect reality*
> *but a hammer with which to shape it.*
>
> —Bertolt Brecht

Survivors have been at the forefront of every positive action addressing sexual abuse in all sectors of society. Building solidarity between and among organizations continues to expand in all areas of survivors' work, sponsoring support groups, forming healing circles, initiating social media interventions to raise awareness, and fostering personal connections.

Our Journey

Survivors have organized, mobilized, and rallied through collective action, challenging the centuries-long epidemic that has scorched our collective experience. As the movement matures, the old ways of siloed agendas and actions, where organizations worked individually within their given mission and program, have fallen away.

Our Movement interweaves diverse organizations, initiatives, associations, coalitions, and individuals to create a decisive and consequential shift in social consciousness, cultural identity, and political actions. As collaboration knits together hundreds of organizations, it addresses unique audiences, missions, objectives, and modalities of change. It is blessed with an army of passionate advocates and a rainbow of missions. The dramatic growth of activism, collective organizing, legislative initiatives, and cultural awareness demonstrates the growing political power. The hundreds of national organizations, the dozens of national associations and coalitions, and the thousands of social media entities are evidence of a new movement as it redefines the language, molds the culture, enriches social connections, and changes the laws we live under.

The formation of our movement did not appear in a single moment; rather, it has gained momentum to become a powerhouse that has risen from survivors' courage to demand truth, accountability, transparency, and justice. We have grabbed the microphone away from the misogynists, politicians, and shaming cultural commentators; survivors now dominate the conversation, create and control the message. We shape public opinion, push legislators, and change the laws. There is a dramatic shift in political power, cultural expression, and social consciousness. Our Movement challenges the previous ideologies of exploitation, such as misogyny, male supremacy, and subordination. We are winning.

There is Work Ahead

Poet Marge Piercy captures the work yet ahead as we work for respect and dignity. This stanza honors the advocates working for social justice in her poem "To Be of Use":

I love people who harness themselves, as an ox to a heavy cart,
who pull like water buffalo, with massive patience,
who strained in the mud and muck to move things forward,
who do what has to be done, again and again [803]

There is work to be done. Survivor leaders shoulder past burdens of abuse to step forward to help others. Throughout this book, I mention dozens of survivor leaders who committed to building this Survivors' Movement, empowering us with tools, initiatives, and organizations. While we are winning, there is work ahead worldwide in all sectors of society and all spheres of social life. The scope of abuse documented earlier continues to alarm, as the ubiquity of sexual violence has not been reduced.

We Are the Ones We Have Been Waiting For

We embrace the solidarity we have forged. The courage of survivor voices compelled change; the tide has turned in favor of respect and dignity. Our Movement continues to grow in number and cohesion. We continue to intervene in the great social and political issues of the day. Survivors step forward, into the light, and are no longer victims alone, silent, and in the dark. We no longer accept silence. Survivors step up and speak out.

AFTERWORD

Note 1

I call on the leaders of the diverse communities within our Survivors Movement to write their own books to share their histories, challenges, and successes within their respective sectors. *Stand Up Speak Up* serves as a starting point for dozens of related publications, reflecting the diversity of organizations, missions, and strategies. While this book examines the movement as a whole, it is just one resource. There needs to be, and will be, books addressing every sector of society that has been briefly touched on in this work.

Every leader is invited and encouraged to write a book that advances their work, background, and mission, including those from Boy Scouts, Jehovah's Witnesses, the military, Baptists, universities, elementary and middle schools, government institutions, corporations, sports teams, Native Americans, farmworkers, LGBTQ+ communities, and other sectors. We need shelves of books to address the breadth and depth of the Survivors Movement in all the sectors mentioned. Please give me a call if you need support with writing a book about your community.

I invited readers to step forward and join the Survivors Movement. That is a great first step, but it is not yet complete. I want the reader to take action. If there is no existing organization to join that addresses the needs of you and your community, I encourage you to consider establishing one—*organize*.

Note 2

My book devotes significant attention to the Catholic Church, frequently drawing on my thirty years of advocacy within Catholic communities, both as a survivor and a world leader. While doing so, I have actively supported survivors from Baptist communities, the Boy Scouts, gymnasts, athletes, and others. Tragically, abuse happens everywhere; survivor actions have arisen in every company, school, workplace, religious institution, college, and social organization in America.

While the sector of abuse varies, the challenges that survivors face are common. The vast diversity of communities all face similar challenges that I faced with the institutional church. Offending companies and institutions employ similar tools to protect notable individuals and conceal the institution's offenses (for example, see chapter six—"Playbook of the Powerful"). Abuse happens in every community and points to harm everywhere. There needs to be a corresponding intervention and response by survivors everywhere.

Note 3

The central focus of this book on sexual violence overlaps several areas of related abuses and social ills, such as domestic violence, physical child abuse, child labor, trafficking, discrimination, immigration status, exploitation of people with disabilities, and other vulnerabilities. Each of these elements intersect and sometimes overlaps with sexual abuse in all communities. The listed social ills are important to examine; however, my book has a specific focus, and other crimes fall outside its scope and are not addressed.

Note 4

Another area that is not addressed in the book is the international context of sexual abuse. Investigations must be initiated, and a series of books must follow. At every point, every nation must expose the scope of abuse within each country.

There have been international investigations, for instance, by the UN Committee on the Rights of the Child, the UN Committee on Torture, and reports from the International Criminal Court, as well as in other world jurisdictions. Both the Brave Movement and the "MeToo. Movement International" have established coalitions and actions on the world stage. Their work needs to be recognized and expanded. However, in this book, the focus and scope address sexual abuse in the USA.

Appendices Available on the Website

Stand Up Speak Up Website: https://standupspeakup.org/

Appendix I   *Database of 240 Allies & Sister Organizations*

Appendix II   *Timeline of Events*

Appendix III   *Timeline of Organizations' Founding*

Appendix IV   *Bibliography* (60 pages)

Appendix V   *Spreadsheet of my 160 local, national, and international media interviews*

Appendix VI   *Links to Databases of Predators.*

The catalog of databases compiled by the following organizations and media publicly outed predators: BishopAccountability, Baptist Accountability, Mennonite MAP List, ProPublic, Boy Scouts' "Perversion Files," AP List, Vox 262 Hollywood Predators, and Abuse in Mormonism.

Appendix VII *List of Sixty Leaders Who Stood Up and Spoke Out.* The significant leaders in our movement who work in the field include victims, leaders, attorneys, politicians, and media investigators. Engage with these wonderful leaders.

Tim Lennon
tim@StandupSpeakup.org

ENDNOTES

[1] Clericalism is a deformation of religious calling when a priest places himself between God and parishioners as evidence of higher authority. Therefore, he acts as God's representative on earth to do unspeakable acts. This authority given to the priest leads to demanding the faithful to defer and acquiesce to the priest to the detriment of the parishioners.

[2] "Fr. George B. McFadden," BishopAccountability, accessed April 24, 2025, https://www.bishop-accountability.org/?mo=mcfadden&post_type=accused&s=&order=ASC&orderby=post_name.

[3] See chapter 6, Playbook.

[4] The technique is still usable, but the decline of newspapers has less reach.

[5] Assignments in Iowa, St. Mary Parish, Danbury; Assumption Parish in Emmetsburg; Sacred Heart Parish in Fort Dodge; St. Michael Parish in Whittemore; and Blessed Sacrament Parish in Sioux City.

[6] Joshua Kendall, "The False Memory Syndrome at 30: How Flawed Science Turned into Conventional Wisdom," Mad in America, February 7, 2021, https://www.madinamerica.com/2021/02/false-memory-syndrome/; Jennifer J. Freyd, *Betrayal Trauma: The Logic of Forgetting Childhood Abuse* (Harvard University Press, 1996); Shaoni Bhattacharya, "The Lifelong Cost of Burying Our Traumatic Experiences," November 5, 2014, https://www.newscientist.com/article/mg22429941-200-the-lifelong-cost-of-burying-our-traumatic-experiences/.

[7] "My Story," Stand Up Speak Up, https://standupspeakup.org/my-story/. I was mistaken in the 1996 letter to the Diocese of Sioux City; the records show I was twelve years old in 1959 and probably in the seventh or eighth grade—not fifth.

[8] "Current Laws for Child Protection," CHILD USA, last accessed April 24, 2025. https://childusa.org/law/. The average age at which a child abuse victim steps forward is 52 years old.

[9] "My Story—Visit to Sioux City Diocese to Meet with the Bishop: Fiona's Letter to Nickless." Stand Up Speak Up, January 26, 2022, https://standupspeakup.org/my-story/.

[10] "Fr. Peter Brendan Murphy," BishopAccountability, last accessed April 24, 2024, https://www.bishop-accountability.org/accused/murphy-peter-brendan-1955/.

[11] "EMDR Therapy, Eye Movement Desensitization and Reprocessing," Cleveland Clinic, last updated March 29, 2022, https://my.clevelandclinic.org/health/treatments/22641-emdr-therapy.

[12] See chapter 7, "Legacies of Oppression."

[13] See chapter 4, "Scope of Abuse."

[14] Edward Walsh, "Study Finds Link Between Incarceration, Prior Abuse," *The Washington Post*, April 12, 1999, https://www.washingtonpost.com/archive/politics/1999/04/12/study-finds-link-between-incarceration-prior-abuse/9797338b-5d3b-491f-a065-e7f43752f54f/.

[15] Volunteering at the national SNAP office in Chicago, 2010 to 2018.

[16] "Resources and Links," Stand Up Speak Up, https://standupspeakup.org/resources-and-links/: Fact sheet and statistics, including spreadsheets on 240 allies, timeline of events, and media interviews.

[17] The Lily News, "Barbara Blaine, Advocate for Victims of Sex Abuse By Catholic Clergy, Dies At 61," *Medium* (story adapted from Harrison Smith's *Washington Post*, September 25, 2017), September 26, 2017, https://medium.com/the-lily/barbara-blaine-advocate-for-victims-of-sex-abuse-by-catholic-clergy-dies-at-61-dd08b0a1764c.

[18] Jason Berry, "The Tragedy of Gilbert Gauthe," *The Times of Acadiana*, May 23, 1985, https://www.bishop-accountability.org/news/1985_05_23_Berry_TheTragedy.htm. First reporting on clerical sex abuse.

[19] Bill Frogameni, "Toledo Native Barbara Blaine Crusades against Sexual Abuse in the Catholic Church," *Toledo City Paper*, April 29, 2004, https://www.bishop-accountability.org/news/2004_04_29_Frogameni_ToledoNative.htm.

[20] Laurie Goodstein, "Barbara Blaine, Who Championed Victims of Priests' Abuse, Dies at 61," *New York Times*, September 25, 2017, https://www.nytimes.com/2017/09/25/us/barbara-ann-blaine-dead-founded-sex-abuse-survivors-network.html.

[21] Frogameni, "Toledo Native Barbara Blaine."

[22] Bill Frogameni, "Barbara Blaine, Founder of Sex Abuse Survivor Group SNAP, Dies," *National Catholic Reporter*, September 25, 2017, https://www.ncronline.org/news/barbara-blaine-founder-sex-abuse-survivor-group-snap-dies.

[23] Frogameni, "Barbara Blaine, Founder."

[24] Defrocked means that a priest is stripped of his ability to say mass or present himself as a priest. In this case, Warren continued to serve as a priest with all the authority and status of a priest.

[25] "Survivor Support, Locations," SNAP Network," https://www.snapnetwork.org/snap_locations. List of worldwide support groups by location and identity.

[26] Phil Saviano, "What Took You So Long?" speech, Voice of the Faithful Conference, Boston, July 20, 2002, https://www.snapnetwork.org/survivors_voice/phil_saviano_votfspeech.htm.

27 Mike Miller, "The Incredible Story of *Spotlight's* Phil Saviano: The Child Sex Abuse Survivor Who Refused to Be Silenced by the Catholic Church," *People Magazine*, February 5, 2016, https://people.com/movies/the-incredible-story-of-spotlights-phil-saviano/.

28 Joseph P. Kahn and Mike Damiano, 'They knew and they let it happen': Uncovering child abuse in the Catholic Church," September 22, 2021, The Boston Globe, https://www.bostonglobe.com/2021/09/22/magazine/they-knew-they-let-it-happen-uncovering-child-abuse-catholic-church/?event=event12

29 Saviano, "What Took You So Long."

30 Crux Staff, "Pope to New Cardinals, You're Not Called to Be 'Princes of the Church,'" Crux, June 28, 2017, https://cruxnow.com/vatican/2017/06/pope-new-cardinals-youre-not-called-princes-church.

31 *ABC News*, "Cardinal Law, Bishops Subpoenaed," *ABC News*, December 12, 2002, https://abcnews.go.com/US/story?id=90980&page=1; Stephanie Kirchgaessner and Amanda Holpuch, "How Cardinal Disgraced in Boston Child Abuse Scandal Found a Vatican Haven," *Guardian*, November 6, 2015, https://www.theguardian.com/world/2015/nov/06/cardinal-bernard-law-disgraced-boston-child-abuse-scandal-vatican-haven-spotlight.

32 Al Baker, "Cardinal Law Given Post in Rome," *New York Times*, May 28, 2004, https://www.nytimes.com/2004/05/28/us/cardinal-law-given-post-in-rome.html; Cardinal Law fled to the sanctuary of Rome days before he was scheduled to give testimony to a grand jury about his complicity in cover-ups. He evaded this civic responsibility and fled the country.

33 Ramon Antonio Vargas, "US Archbishop Secretly Backed a Bid to Free Priest Convicted of Raping Child," *Guardian*, December 18, 2023, https://www.theguardian.com/us-news/2023/dec/18/new-orleans-archbishop-gregory-aymond-robert-melancon-catholic-church; Gina Christian, "Sacramento Diocese to File for Bankruptcy Amid More than 250 Abuse Lawsuits," *National Catholic Reporter*, December 13, 2023, https://www.ncronline.org/news/sacramento-diocese-file-bankruptcy-amid-more-250-abuse-lawsuits; "Take Action," Stand Up Speak Up, https://standupspeakup.org/take-action/: See analysis of bankruptcy plans and how they are used as a device to cover up crimes, especially to hide from the parishioners the scope of abuse; BishopAccountability, News Archive, https://www.bishop-accountability.org/news/list/: See 2025.

34 Ramon Antonio Vargas, "It Wasn't a Big Deal: Secret Deposition Reveals How a Child Molester Priest Was Shielded by His Church," *Guardian*, May 9, 2024, https://www.theguardian.com/us-news/ng-interactive/2024/may/09/new-orleans-catholic-church-abuse.

35 Vargas, "It Wasn't a Big Deal."

36 Vargas, "'It Wasn't a Big Deal.'"

37 Office of the Attorney General, *Pennsylvania*: See page 120 of the grand jury report for Bishop's chart of payouts to victims of sexual violence by clergy.

[38] Chapter 8, "Playbook of the Powerful," looks at the significant contributions by NGOs and civil society in addition to government agencies and media investigations.
[39] Daniel Burke, "Catholics Are Losing Faith in Clergy and Church After Sexual Abuse Scandal, Gallup Survey Says," *CNN*, January 11, 2019, https://www.cnn.com/2019/01/11/us/catholic-gallup-survey/index.html.
[40] "What Are SBC 'Good Guys?'" Together We Heal, December 5, 2023, https://togetherweheal.net/author/togetherweheal/.
[41] Christa Brown, "This Little Light of Mine . . . I'm Gonna Let It Shine," Stop Baptist Predators, September 30, 2010, http://stopbaptistpredators.org/index.htm.
[42] Christa Brown, *Baptistland: A Memoir of Abuse, Betrayal, and Transformation* (Lake Drive Books, 2024); Stop Baptist Predators, blog, http://stopbaptistpredators.blogspot.com/.
[43] Christa Brown, "About Me," Web Archive, October 1, 2015, https://web.archive.org/web/20230529060132/https://christabrown.me/about-me/.
[44] Brown, *Baptistland*, Kindle, 292.
[45] Correspondence with Brown, February 11, 2025; Robert Downen et al., "Abuse of Faith," Six-Part Series, *Houston Chronicle*, February 10 –August 27, 2019, https://www.houstonchronicle.com/news/houston-texas/houston/article/Abuse-of-Faith-Survivors-of-Baptist-sexual-abuse-13938643.php.
[46] Robert Downen et al., "20 Years, 700 Victims: Southern Baptist Sexual Abuse Spreads as Leaders Resist Reforms," *Houston Chronicle*, February 10, 2019, updated January 31, 2022, https://www.houstonchronicle.com/news/investigations/article/Southern-Baptist-sexual-abuse-spreads-as-leaders-13588038.php.
[47] Rohypnol® is a trade name for flunitrazepam, also known as a "roofie."
[48] Andrea Constand, interview by Timothy Lennon, January 27, 2022.
[49] Constand, interview.
[50] Ed Pilkington, "Cosby Release Shows How Prosecutors Hinder Sexual Assault Victims, Advocates Say," *Guardian*, July 2, 2021, https://www.theguardian.com/world/2021/jul/02/bill-cosby-bruce-castor-prosecutors-sexual-assault-victims.
[51] Andrea Constand, *The Moment: Standing Up to Bill Cosby, Speaking Up for Women* (Penguin Random House, 2021).
[52] Constand, *Moment*.
[53] Constand, *Moment*.
[54] Constand, interview
[55] Constand, interview.
[56] Constand, interview.
[57] The complete report was not released until August 2018 due to challenges by a dozen accused clergy predators who wanted their names removed from the report.
[58] Rachael Denhollander, "Read Rachael Denhollander's Full Victim Impact Statement about Larry Nassar," *CNN*, January 30, 2018, https://www.cnn.com/2018/01/24/us/rachael-denhollander-full-statement/index.html: Here's what Denhollander said to Judge Rosemarie Aquilina and to Nassar shortly before Nassar was sentenced Wednesday.

59 Tim Evans, Mark Alesia, and Marisa Kwiatkowski, "Former USA Gymnastics Doctor Accused of Abuse," *IndyStar*, September 12, 2016, https://www.indystar.com/story/news/2016/09/12/former-usa-gymnastics-doctor-accused-abuse/89995734/.

60 Juliet Macur, "Nassar Abuse Survivors Reach a $380 Million Settlement: More than 500 Girls and Women Abused by Lawrence G. Nassar, the Former National Gymnastics Team Doctor, or Someone Else in the Sport Will Be Compensated," *The New York Times*, December 13, 2021, https://www.nytimes.com/2021/12/13/sports/olympics/nassar-abuse-gymnasts-settlement.html.

61 Rachael Denhollander, "In Her Own Words: Nassar Victim's Emotional Statement," *Detroit News*, January 24, 2018, https://www.detroitnews.com/story/news/local/michigan/2018/01/24/rachael-denhollander-larry-nassar-statement/109781984/.

62 Alanna Durkin Richer and Eric Tucker, "Justice Department Watchdog Finds Failures in FBI's Handling of Child Sex Abuse Cases," *AP News*, August 29, 2024, https://apnews.com/article/fbi-child-sexual-abuse-inspector-general-investigation-e99e729147421fe166f92ca23eefc4e5.

63 Josh Peter and Tom Schad, "US to Pay $100 Million to Survivors of Nassar's Abuse. FBI Waited Months to Investigate," *USA Today*, April 17, 2024, https://www.usatoday.com/story/sports/olympics/2024/04/17/survivors-larry-nassar-sexual-abuse-100-million/73357079007/.

64 "Policy Agenda—Policy Priority Agenda: 118th Congress," The Army of Survivors, July 1, 2021, https://thearmyofsurvivors.org/.

65 See chapter 6, "Playbook of the Powerful": The corruptive and corrosive plays of the "playbook" are explored in chapter 6.

66 Sarah Klein is an attorney, advocate, and former gymnast. She was the first known victim of Larry Nassar, the predator doctor for Michigan State University. She is a member of the board of directors of CHILD USA Advocacy, an organization formed to protect children and keep children safe.

67 Julie Miller, "Inside the Powerful ESPYs Moment When Aly Raisman and Over 100 Athletes Accepted the Arthur Ashe Courage Award," *Vanity Fair Magazine*, July 18, 2018, https://www.vanityfair.com/style/2018/07/espys-women-gymnastics-arthur-ashe-courage-award?srsltid=AfmBOopGCmli6PIMQYNDvgyFhzs-2gr_uCFPU-ncJPjbN47HdTP9Rh3af.

68 Miller, "Inside."

69 Beth Harris, "Larry Nassar Sex-Abuse Victims Join Hands, Accept Courage Award at ESPYs," *AP News*, July 19, 2018, https://www.nbcnews.com/news/us-news/larry-nassar-sex-abuse-victims-join-hands-accept-courage-award-n892651.

70 Sarah Klein, interview by Timothy Lennon, April 2022.

71 Klein, interview.

72 Klein, interview.

73 Klein, interview.

[74] Eric Levensen, "Larry Nassar Sentenced Up to 175 Years in Prison for Decades of Sexual Abuse." *CNN*, January 4, 2018, https://www.cnn.com/2018/01/24/us/larry-nassar-sentencing.

[75] Steve Gardner and Nancy Armour, "Ex-USA Gymnastics Doctor Larry Nassar Stabbed in Prison. What We Know," *USA Today*, July 10, 2023, https://www.usatoday.com/story/sports/2023/07/10/larry-nassar-disgraced-ex-usa-gymnastics-doctor-stabbed-in-prison/70397013007/.

[76] Klein, interview.

[77] Sarah Klein, "Bar Fights," Apple Podcasts, https://podcasts.apple.com/us/podcast/bar-fights/id1581899928: "Insightful conversation will be the undercard and real change (or justice) will be the main event."

[78] Klein, interview.

[79] Klein, interview.

[80] For more information about Nomi Abadi, see The Female Composer Safety League, https://www.femalecomposersafetyleague.org/.

[81] Nomi Abadi, interview by Timothy Lennon, February 20, 2022.

[82] Abadi, interview.

[83] Abadi, interview.

[84] Abadi, interview.

[85] Abadi, interview.

[86] Abadi, interview.

[87] Daniel Sanchez, "A List of Every Musician and Music Executive Facing Abuse Allegations in 2018," *Digital Music News*, December 2018, https://www.digitalmusicnews.com/2018/12/26/musicians-music-executives-abuse-allegations/: Note: this is just a one-year list, 2018; April Baer, "Classical Music World Reckoning with Revelations of Sexual Abuse, Harassment," *The Columbian*, January 2019, https://www.columbian.com/news/2019/jan/06/classical-music-world-reckoning-with-revelations-of-sexual-abuse-harassment/.

[88] Andrea Domanick, "The Dollars and Desperation Silencing #MeToo in Music," *VICE Media*, March 5, 2018, https://www.vice.com/en/article/9kzex7/inside-music-industry-sexual-misconduct-harassment-problem-and-metoo.

[89] Domanick, "Dollars."

[90] Domanick, "Dollars."

[91] Lift Our Voices, The Female Composer Safety League, The Punk Rock Therapist, The Representation Project, "Sound Off: Make Music Safe Report," The Representation Project, February 27, 2024, https://therepproject.org/wp-content/uploads/2024/02/SOUND-OFF-Make-the-Music-Industry-Safe-Report-February-2024.pdf: "This Comprehensive Report Chronicles the Scathing History and Financial Impact of Decades of Sexual Abuse and Coverups, from the 1950s to the Present."

[92] AFP, "R Kelly, The R&B Star Who Sold Over 75 Mn Records Globally, on Trial for Sex Crimes," *Economic Times*, last updated August 6, 2021, https://tinyurl.com/4e8ym9vu.

93 "RAINN's National Sexual Assault Hotline Experiences Nearly 50% Increase in Calls After Lifetime Airs Surviving R. Kelly: The Final Chapter," RAINN, January 13, 2023, https://www.rainn.org/news/rainn%E2%80%99s-national-sexual-assault-hotline-experiences-nearly-50-increase-calls-after-lifetime.

94 Troy Closson, "R. Kelly's Last Criminal Trial Was in 2008. The World Has Changed Since," *The New York Times*, August 17, 2021, https://www.nytimes.com/2021/08/17/nyregion/r-kelly-trial-allegations.html.

95 Sonia Moghe and Dakin Andone, "R. Kelly Sentenced to 30 Years in Prison for Federal Racketeering and Sex Trafficking Charges," *CNN*, June 30, 2022, https://www.cnn.com/2022/06/29/us/r-kelly-sentencing-racketeering-sex-trafficking.

96 Lizzette Martinez and Keelin MacGregor, *Jane Doe, #9* (WildBlue Press, 2021).

97 Lizzie Martinez, interview by Timothy Lennon, March 2022.

98 Michelle Francis-Smith, interview by Timothy Lennon, February 2022.

99 Francis-Smith, interview.

100 Francis-Smith, interview.

101 Francis-Smith, interview.

102 Anonymous interviewee.

103 Anonymous interviewee.

104 Anonymous interviewee.

105 "Incest Effects," Incest AWARE, November 18, 2020, https://www.incestaware.org/incest-effects.

106 Mia Fontaine, "America Has an Incest Problem," *Atlantic Magazine*, 2013, https://www.theatlantic.com/national/archive/2013/01/america-has-an-incest-problem/272459/.

107 Jaclyn Friedman and Jessica Valenti, editors, *Yes Means Yes, Visions of Female Sexual Power & a World without Rape* (Seal Press, March 2019), 105; "About UNBUNTU," I Am Because We Are, January 16, 2007, https://iambecauseweare.wordpress.com/.

108 "The Cost of Rape," National Sexual Violence Resource Center (NSVRC), December 4, 2018, https://www.nsvrc.org/blogs/cost-rape.

109 "Statistics About Sexual Violence," NSVRC. https://www.nsvrc.org/sites/default/files/publications_nsvrc_factsheet_media-packet_statistics-about-sexual-violence_0.pdf

110 Fontaine, "America Has an Incest Problem."

111 "Scope of the Problem: Statistics," June 8, 2010, RAINN, https://www.rainn.org/statistics/scope-problem.

112 "Scope," RAINN.

113 "Statistics," NSVRC.

114 Holly Kearl, *The Facts Behind the #Metoo Movement: A National Study on Sexual Harassment and Assault* (Stop Street Harassment, February 2018), https://www.nsvrc.org/sites/default/files/2021-04/full-report-2018-national-study-on-sexual-harassment-and-assault.pdf.

[115] Tony Gonzalez, "Study: Sexual Assaults Greatly Underreported," *USA Today*, November 19, 2013, https://www.usatoday.com/story/news/nation/2013/11/19/study-sexual-assaults-greatly-underreported-/3648197/; Department of Justice, "National Crime Victimization Survey, 2015–2019," Office of Justice Programs, Bureau of Justice Statistics, (2020), as quoted by "The Criminal Justice System: Statistics," RAINN, September 9, 2008, https://www.rainn.org/statistics/criminal-justice-system: Council reports 80% of sexual assaults go unreported; "Sexual Misconduct in Schools," The American Association of University Women (AAUW), https://www.aauw.org/issues/education/sexual-misconduct/. Eighty-nine percent of colleges do not report any instance of rape!;

[116] "The Criminal Justice System," RAINN; Regina J. Johnson et al, "Prevalence of Childhood Sexual Abuse Among Incarcerated Males in County Jail," *Child Abuse and Neglect* 30, no. 1 (January 2006), 75–86, https://pubmed.ncbi.nlm.nih.gov/16412506/.

[117] Susan Brownmiller, *Against Our Will: Men, Women and Rape* (Ballantine Books, 1975); Sasha Cohen, "How a Book Changed the Way We Talk About Rape," *TIME*, October 7, 2015, https://time.com/4062637/against-our-will-40/.

[118] Cohen, "Book."

[119] Cora Peterson et al., "The Economic Burden of Child Maltreatment in the United States, 2015," *Child Abuse and Neglect* 86 (December 2018): 178—83, https://www.sciencedirect.com/science/article/abs/pii/S0145213418303867; John Hopkins Bloomberg School of Public Health, "One Year's Losses for Child Sexual Abuse in US Top $9 Billion, New Study Suggests," Science Daily, May 21, 2018, https://www.sciencedaily.com/releases/2018/05/180521131552.htm.

[120] Dean C. Kilpatrick et al., "Rape in America: A Report to the Nation." National Victim Center, Crime Victims Research and Treatment Center, Arlington, VA, 1992.

[121] "Effects of Sexual Assault and Rape," The Joyful Heart Foundation, https://www.joyfulheartfoundation.org/learn/sexual-assault-rape/effects-sexual-assault-and-rape: Thanks to why we call ourselves survivors—we survived suicide, mental illness, and emotional destruction.

[122] "Post Traumatic Stress Disorder (PTSD)," Mayo Clinic, August 16, 2024, https://www.mayoclinic.org/diseases-conditions/post-traumatic-stress-disorder/symptoms-causes/syc-20355967.

[123] David S. Riggs, "A Prospective Examination of Post-Traumatic Stress Disorder in Rape Victims," *Journal of Traumatic Stress* 5, no. 3 (1992): 455–75, https://doi.org/10.1002/jts.2490050309; Jonathan R. T. Davidson and Edna B. Foa, "Posttraumatic Stress Disorder: DSM-IV and Beyond." (American Psychiatric Press, 1993), 23–36; Kilpatrick et al., *Rape in America*; Lynn Langton and Jennifer Truman, "Socio-Emotional Impact of Violent Crime," Washington, DC: US Department of Justice, Office of Justice Programs, Bureau of Justice Statistics, September 23, 2014, https://bjs.ojp.gov/library/publications/socio-emotional-impact-violent-crime: All articles in this footnote were quoted by "Sexual Violence Can Have Long-Term Effects on Victims," RAINN, n.d., https://www.rainn.org/statistics/victims-sexual-violence.

124 "Preventing Child Sexual Abuse Through Education & Action," Darkness to Light, May 20, 2025, https://www.d2l.org/.

125 Xiangming Fang et al., "The Economic Burden of Child Maltreatment in the United States and Implications for Prevent. *Child Abuse & Neglect* 36, no. 2, (2012): 156–65, http://doi.org/10.1016/j.chiabu.2011.10.006, as quoted by Johnson County Children's Advocacy Center, https://cacjctx.org/2017/03/10/fighting-for-our-children/.

126 "Whether You Realize It or Not, Child Sexual Abuse Affects All of Us— The Economic Impact." Johnson County Children's Advocacy Center The Impact Is Tremendous," May 1, 2020, https://cacjctx.org/2017/03/10/fighting-for-our-children/.

127 Peterson et al., "Economic Burden."

128 Fang et al., "Economic Burden."

129 Nichole T. Buchanan and Louise F. Fitzgerald, "Effects of Racial and Sexual Harassment on Work and the Psychological Well-Being of African American Women," *Journal of Occupational Health Psychology* 13, no. 2 (2008): 137–51, https://pubmed.ncbi.nlm.nih.gov/18393583/.

130 Sara Kominers, *Working in Fear, Sexual Violence Against Women Farmworkers in the USA: A Literature Review*, (Oxfam, April 16, 2015), https://www.oxfamamerica.org/explore/research-publications/working-in-fear-sexual-violence-against-women-farmworkers-in-the-united-states-a-literature-review/.

131 "Statistics & Research," Incest AWARE, https://www.incestaware.org/statistics-research; Sabrina Gentlewarrior and Kim Fountain, "Culturally Competent Service Provision to Lesbian, Gay, Bisexual and Transgender Survivors of Sexual Violence." National Online Resource Center on Violence Against Women, 2009, https://vawnet.org/sites/default/files/materials/files/2016-09/AR_LGBTSexualViolence.pdf, as quoted on Incest AWARE; Jameta Nicole Barlow, "Black Women, the Forgotten Survivors of Sexual Assault," *American Psychological Association*, February 1, 2020, https://www.apa.org/topics/sexual-assault-harassment/black-women-sexual-violence, as quoted on Incest AWARE.

132 "Sexual Violence in the LGBTQ+ Community," Care Campus Resources & Education UC Merced, June 13, 2017, https://care.ucmerced.edu/sites/care.ucmerced.edu/files/page/documents/sexual_violence_in_lgbt_community_1.pdf :

133 David M. Lawson, "Understanding and Treating Survivors of Incest," *Counseling Today*, March 2018, https://www.counseling.org/publications/counseling-today-magazine/article-archive/article/legacy/understanding-treating-survivors-incest.

134 Fontaine, "America."

135 "Statistics," NSVRC: Comprehensive statistics on the scope of abuse—700k victims of rape in one year!

136 Nick Anderson et al., "Survey Finds Evidence of Widespread Sexual Violence at 33 Universities," *Washington Post*, October 15, 2019, https://www.washingtonpost.com/local/education/survey-finds-evidence-of-widespread-sexual-violence-at-33-universities/2019/10/14/bd75dcde-ee82-11e9-b648-76bcf86eb67e_story.html.

[137] "What Is Title IX?" Advocates for Youth, December 27, 2020, https://www.advocatesforyouth.org/what-is-title-ix/

[138] Caroline Kitchener and Alia Wong, "The Moral Catastrophe at Michigan State," *Atlantic*, September 12, 2018, https://www.theatlantic.com/education/archive/2018/09/the-moral-catastrophe-at-michigan-state/569776/.

[139] David Cantor et al., *Report on the AAU Campus Climate Survey on Sexual Assault and Sexual Misconduct* (Rockville, MD: Westat, September 21, 2015), https://www.aau.edu/sites/default/files/%40%20Files/Climate%20Survey/AAU_Campus_Climate_Survey_12_14_15.pdf: See Table 4.1.

[140] "What Consent Looks Like," RAINN, https://www.rainn.org/articles/what-is-consent.

[141] Cantor et al., *Report*.

[142] "Sexual Misconduct in Schools," AAUW.

[143] Shawn Hubler et al., "U.S.C. Agrees to Pay $1.1 Billion to Patients of Gynecologist Accused of Abuse," *The New York Times*, March 25, 2021, https://www.nytimes.com/2021/03/25/us/usc-settlement-george-tyndall.html; Rick Maese, "Ohio State Team Doctor Sexually Abused 177 Students over Decades, Report Finds," *The Washington Post*, May 17, 2019, https://www.washingtonpost.com/sports/2019/05/17/ohio-state-team-doctor-sexually-abused-students-over-decades-report-finds/.

[144] Christopher P. Krebs et al., *The Campus Sexual Assault (CSA) Study, Final Report*, (National Institute of Justice, October 2007), https://www.ojp.gov/pdffiles1/nij/grants/221153.pdf

[145] "Summary of the Jeanne Clery Act," Clery Center, accessed June 11, 2025, https://www.clerycenter.org/the-clery-act.

[146] Melinda Wenner Moyer, "'A Poison in the System': The Epidemic of Military Sexual Assault," *The New York Times Magazine*, last updated October 11, 2021, https://www.nytimes.com/2021/08/03/magazine/military-sexual-assault.html.

[147] "Facts on Military Sexual Trauma and Statistics," Hill and Ponton, last updated June 29, 2023, https://www.hillandponton.com/facts-on-military-sexual-trauma-and-statistics: An excellent review of history, facts, statistics, and resources.

[148] Martin R. Huecker et al., "Domestic Violence-Statpearls-NCBI Bookshelf." National Library of Medicine, 2023, https://www.ncbi.nlm.nih.gov/books/NBK499891/; Rebecca Blais et al., "Higher Depression Severity Mediates the Association of Assault Military Sexual Trauma and Sexual Function in Partnered Female Service Members/Veterans," *Journal of Affective Disorders* 261 (2020): 238–44, https://www.sciencedirect.com/science/article/abs/pii/S0165032719310237?via%3Dihub: Study shows 48% of women service members have been sexually harassed, 34% assaulted, and only 17% reported no assault.

[149] "Facts," Hill and Ponton.

[150] James Griffith, "The Sexual Harassment–Suicide Connection in the U.S. Military: Contextual Effects of Hostile Work Environment and Trusted Unit Leaders," *Suicide and Life-Threatening Behavior* 49, no. 1 (February 2019): 41–53. https://pubmed.ncbi.nlm.nih.gov/28972302/.

[151] Griffith, "Sexual Harassment"; *Facts on United States Military Sexual Violence*, MSA Fact Sheet, (Protect Our Defenders, May 2021), https://www.protectourdefenders.com/wp-content/uploads/2021/05/MSA-Fact-Sheet-2021.pdf: Statistics from the 2016–2020 DoD SAPRO Reports and their appendices/annexes, unless otherwise noted, https://www.sapr.mil/reports Updated May 2021

[152] Emily Cochrane and Jennifer Steinhauer, "Senator Martha McSally Says Superior Officer in the Air Force Raped Her," *The New York Times*, March 6, 2019, https://www.nytimes.com/2019/03/06/us/politics/martha-mcsally-sexual-assault.html.

[153] "The 1 in 6 Statistic," 1in6.org, December 15, 2018, https://1in6.org/statistic/.

[154] "The 1 in 6 Statistic," 1in6.org; Shanta R. Dube et al., "Long-Term Consequences of Childhood Sexual Abuse By Gender of Victim," *American Journal of Preventive Medicine 28*, (2005), 430–38, https://doi.org/10.1016/j.amepre.2005.02.010.

[155] Doug Stanglin, "Ex-Penn State Coach Jerry Sandusky Appears in Court; Resentenced to 30 to 60 Years." *USA Today*, November 22, 2019, https://www.usatoday.com/story/news/nation/2019/11/22/jerry-sandusky-ex-penn-state-coach-sex-abuse-re-sentencing-hearing/4269271002/.

[156] Howard N. Snyder, *Sexual Assault of Young Children as Reported to Law Enforcement: Victim, Incident, and Offender Characteristics*, (National Center for Juvenile Justice, July 2020), https://bjs.ojp.gov/content/pub/pdf/saycrle.pdf: Overall, 6% of the offenders who sexually assaulted juveniles were female, compared with just 1% of the female offenders who sexually assaulted adults.

[157] Karen G. Weiss, "Male Sexual Victimization: Examining Men's Experiences of Rape and Sexual Assault," *Men and Masculinities* 12, no. 3 (August 8, 2008), https://doi.org/10.1177/1097184X08322632; Hanna Rosin, "When Men Are Raped, A New Study Reveals that Men Are Often the Victims of Sexual Assault, and Women Are Often the Perpetrators," *Slate Magazine*, April 29, 2014, https://slate.com/human-interest/2014/04/male-rape-in-america-a-new-study-reveals-that-men-are-sexually-assaulted-almost-as-often-as-women.html.

[158] Rosin, "Men."

[159] Brook Sadler, "The Bad Optics of Bad Representation at the Kavanaugh Hearings," *MS.*, October 3, 2018, https://msmagazine.com/2018/10/03/bad-optics-bad-representation-kavanaugh-hearings/.

[160] Emma Brown, "California Professor, Writer of Confidential Brett Kavanaugh Letter, Speaks Out About Her Allegation of Sexual Assault," *The Washington Post*, September 16, 2018, https://tinyurl.com/2snne5z5.

[161] Andy Campbell, "Donald Trump Goes After Kavanaugh Accuser, Asks Why She Didn't Call Cops After Alleged Assault," *HuffPost*, September 21, 2018, https://www.huffpost.com/entry/trump-christine-blasey-ford-sexual-assault_n_5ba4f0a1e4b0375f8f9c3f83.

[162] Emily Birnbaum, "#WhyIDidntReport Hashtag Takes Off on Twitter," *The Hill*, September 22, 2018, https://thehill.com/blogs/blog-briefing-room/news/407804-whyididntreport-hashtag-takes-off-on-twitter/.

163 Emily Birnbaum, "#WhyIDidntReport: Hundreds of Thousands Confide Their Stories of Rape, Abuse," *CBS News*, September 24, 2018, https://www.cbsnews.com/news/whyididntreport-hundreds-of-thousands-confide-their-stories-of-rape-abuse/.
164 Jon Swaine, "Christine Blasey Ford Faces Unsettling Future," *The Guardian*, October 10, 2018, https://www.theguardian.com/us-news/2018/oct/10/christine-blasey-ford-faces-unsettling-future.
165 Ezra Klein, "The Ford-Kavanaugh Sexual Assault Hearings, Explained," *Vox*, September 28, 2018, https://www.vox.com/explainers/2018/9/27/17909782/brett-kavanaugh-christine-ford-supreme-court-senate-sexual-assault-testimony.
166 Sharon Zhang, "FBI Admits It Got 4,500 Tips on Kavanaugh But Didn't Investigate Them," Truthout, July 23, 2021, https://truthout.org/articles/fbi-admits-it-got-4500-tips-on-kavanaugh-but-didnt-investigate-them/.
167 Gonzalez, "Study."
168 Gonzales, "Study."
169 Jeanine P.D. Guidry et al., "#WhyIDidntReport: Women speak out about sexual assault on Twitter," *Journal of Forensic Nursing* 17, no. 3 (2021): 129–39, https://doi.org/10.1097/jfn.0000000000000335.
170 Laurie Goodstein, "After Abuse Settlement, an Apology to Victims," *The New York Times*, July 16, 2007, https://www.nytimes.com/2007/07/16/us/16abuse.html.
171 Goodstein, "After Abuse."
172 Amna Nawaz, "How Chanel Miller Took Her Story Back After Her Rapist's Lenient Sentence Left Her Feeling 'Invisible,'" *PBS NewsHour*, September 24, 2019, https://www.pbs.org/newshour/show/how-chanel-miller-took-her-story-back-after-her-rapists-lenient-sentence-left-her-feeling-invisible.
173 Harvard Law Review, "California Judge Recalled for Sentence in Sexual Assault Case," *Harvard Law Review* 132, no. 4, February 2019, https://harvardlawreview.org/print/vol-132/california-judge-recalled-for-sentence-in-sexual-assault-case/.
174 Erica Schwiegershausen, "How Many Jeffrey Epstein Victims Are There?" *The Cut*, July 19, 2019, https://www.thecut.com/2019/07/how-many-jeffrey-epstein-victims-are-there.html; Liam Quinn, "Transcripts Show Jeffrey Epstein Abuse Allegations Were Known to Prosecutors Years Before Plea Deal," *People*, July 2, 2024, https://people.com/jeffrey-epstein-abuse-allegations-known-prosecutors-years-before-lenient-plea-deal-transcripts-8672759.
175 United States Attorney's Office, Southern District of New York, "Jeffrey Epstein Charged in Manhattan Federal Court with Sex Trafficking of Minors," U.S. Department of Justice, July 8, 2019, https://www.justice.gov/usao-sdny/pr/jeffrey-epstein-charged-manhattan-federal-court-sex-trafficking-minors; Dan Mangan and Kevin Breuninger, "Billionaire Jeffrey Epstein Arrested on Sex Trafficking Charges," CNBC, July 7, 2019, https://www.cnbc.com/2019/07/07/billionaire-jeffrey-epstein-arrested-on-sex-trafficking-charges.html.
176 Associated Press Staff, "Justice Department Investigates Jeffrey Epstein's Attorneys," *The Guardian*, February 6, 2019, https://www.theguardian.com/us-news/2019/feb/06/justice-department-jeffrey-epstein-attorneys-investigation.

177 Jason B. Whiting et al., "Trauma, Social Media, and #WhyIDidntReport: An Analysis of Twitter Posts About Reluctance to Report Sexual Assault," *Journal of Marital and Family Therapy* 47, no. 3 (2021), 749–66, https://onlinelibrary.wiley.com/doi/epdf/10.1111/jmft.12470.

178 "The Criminal Justice System: Statistics, RAINN.

179 Maryland Coalition Against Sexual Assault, "Statistics on Sexual Violence Against Black & African American Women," MCASA, November 8, 2023, https://mcasa.org/assets/files/Sexual_Violence_Against_Black__AA_Women_Fact_Sheet_2023.pdf;

180 National Center on Violence Against Women in the Black Community, "For Every Black Woman Who Reports Rape, at Least 15 Do Not," SASC: The Center At 909, https://www.thecenterat909.org/africanamerican.

181 Department of Justice, Office of Justice Programs, Bureau of Justice Statistics, *Female Victims of Sexual Violence, 1994–2010* (2013), Revised May 31, 2016, https://bjs.ojp.gov/content/pub/pdf/fvsv9410.pdf, as quoted by "The Criminal Justice System: Statistics," RAINN.

182 Alanna Vagianos, "When the Criminal Legal System Doesn't Believe 'Imperfect Victims,'" *HuffPost*, January 31, 2023, https://tinyurl.com/bdfktz2d.

183 Vagianos, "When the Criminal."

184 *Boston Globe Spotlight* Team, "Church Allowed Abuse by Priest for Years," *The Boston Globe*, January 6, 2002, https://cache.boston.com/globe/spotlight/abuse/extras/coverups_archive.htm.

185 *Spotlight* Team, "Church Allowed Abuse."

186 Lisa Desjardins, "Congress Passes Law Banning Non-Disclosure Agreements in Sexual Harassment Cases," *PBS NewsHour*, November 23, 2022, https://www.pbs.org/newshour/show/congress-passes-law-banning-non-disclosure-agreements-in-sexual-harassment-cases.

187 Whiting et al. "Trauma, Social Media."

188 Lisa Jervis, "An Old Enemy in a New Outfit: How Date Rape Became Gray Rape and Why It Matters," in *Yes Means Yes*, 163–77.

189 Jervis, "An Old Enemy," 163–77.

190 Jervis, "An Old Enemy," 163–77.

191 Cass R. Sunstein, "#MeToo as a Revolutionary Cascade," in *The Routledge Handbook of the Politics of the #MeToo Movement* (Routledge, 2020), 34–41: Timur Kuran, who introduced the concept of preference falsification, has used the concept to explain the pre-#MeToo silence around sexual harassment and assault, drawing comparisons to the fear-induced preference falsification that preserved communist rule for decades; Jennifer Schmidt et al., *The Psychological Forces Behind a Cultural Reckoning: Understanding #MeToo*, *NPR*: "Hidden Brain Radio Broadcast,", Feb. 5, 2018, 52 min., https://www.npr.org/2018/02/05/582698111/the-psychological-forces-behind-a-cultural-reckoning-understanding-metoo.

192 Ashley Olivine, "Stockholm Syndrome in Relationships: Symptoms of Abuse," Verywell Health, last updated September 26, 2024, https://www.verywellhealth.com/stockholm-syndrome-7973977.

[193] Olivine, "Stockholm."
[194] "The Criminal Justice System: Statistics," RAINN.
[195] Cara Kulwicki, "Real Sex Education," in *Yes Means Yes*, 305–12.
[196] Kulwicki, "Real Sex Education."
[197] Anita Hill, *Believing: Our Thirty-year Journey to End Gender Violence* (Penguin Random House, 2021), 39.
[198] Halle Golden, "US Indigenous Women Face High Rates of Sexual Violence—with Little Recourse," *The Guardian*, May 17, 2022, https://www.theguardian.com/world/2022/may/17/sexual-violence-against-native-indigenous-women.
[199] Golden, "US Indigenous Women."
[200] Golden, "US Indigenous Women."
[201] Laura Palumbo, "Seeing the Whole Survivor: Why It's Necessary to Talk About Identity for Survivors as Individuals and in Groups," NSVRC—National Sexual Violence Resource Center, February 25, 2019, https://www.nsvrc.org/blogs/seeing-whole-survivor-why-its-necessary-talk-about-identity-survivors-individuals-and-groups; Judy Woodruff et al., "Sex Abuse Against People with Disabilities Is Widespread," *PBS NewsHour*, January 17, 2018, https://www.pbs.org/newshour/show/sex-abuse-against-people-with-disabilities-is-widespread-and-hard-to-uncover; *Sexual Violence & Transgender/Non-Binary Communities*," NSVRC—National Sexual Violence Resource Center, February 2019, https://www.nsvrc.org/sites/default/files/publications/2019-02/Transgender_infographic_508_0.pdf; "Demographics and Domestic Violence," Domestic Shelters, January 7, 2015, https://www.domesticshelters.org/resources/statistics/demographics-and-domestic-violence; Maren Machles et al., "1 in 3 American Indian and Alaska Native Women Will Be Raped," *USA Today*, October 18, 2019, https://www.usatoday.com/story/news/nation/2019/10/18/native-american-women-sexual-assault-justice-issue-tribe-lands/3996873002/.
[202] Shirley Davis, "Incest: The Secret No One Should Keep," CPTSD Programs, April 25, 2022, https://cptsdfoundation.org/2022/04/25/incest-the-secret-no-one-should-keep/.
[203] "Fact Sheet: Window Legislation for Child Sex Abuse Statutes of Limitations," CHILD USA, March 31, 2020, https://childusa.org/wp-content/uploads/2020/03/SOLFactSheet2019.pdf
[204] *The Issue of Child Sexual Abuse*, Darkness to Light, March 15, 2023, https://www.d2l.org/wp-content/uploads/2023/03/Child-Sexual-Abuse-Statistics_The-Issue.pdf.
[205] Margaret C. Cutajar et al., "Suicide and Fatal Drug Overdose in Child Sexual Abuse Victims: A Historical Cohort Study," *Medical Journal of Australia* 192, no. 4 (2010), 184–87, https://pubmed.ncbi.nlm.nih.gov/20170453/.
[206] Michael Bassett, "Child Abuse Linked to Increased Odds of Suicide Attempts, Ideation," *Physician's Weekly*, Aug 7, 2020, https://www.physiciansweekly.com/child-abuse-linked-to-increased-odds-of-suicide-attempts-ideation/.
[207] "Child Sexual Abuse Statistics: The Magnitude of the Problem," Darkness to Light, December 22, 2015, (previously cited, but no longer available in official publications): Jessica White, "Sexual Trauma & Mental Health," LinkedIn, May 13, 2020, https://www.linkedin.com/pulse/sexual-trauma-mental-health-jessica-t-white-m-s-/.

[208] "Why Child Abuse Victims Don't Tell," La Casa Center, July 15, 2020, https://lacasacenter.org/why-child-abuse-victims-dont-tell/: Reposted by permission from Nicole Matthews-Creech and Robin L. O'Grady, "Why Victims Don't Tell: Sandusky Case Sheds Light on Complexities of Sexual Abuse," *The Livingston Post*, June 26, 2012, https://thelivingstonpost.com/why-victims-dont-tell-sandusky-case-sheds-light-on-complexities-of-sexual-abuse/.

[209] Toni Tails, "This Is Why I Kept Sexual Abuse a Secret for 20 Years," (blog), *Medium*, November 19, 2019, https://medium.com/survivors/this-is-why-i-kept-sexual-abuse-secrets-for-20-years-59c71cc6b20d.

[210] "Child Sexual Abuse Statistics," Darkness to Light; Dafna Tener and Sharon B. Murphy, "Adult Disclosure of Child Sexual Abuse: A Literature Review." *Trauma, Violence, & Abuse* 16, no. 4 (2015), 391–400, https://doi.org/10.1177/1524838014537906; Bette L. Bottoms et al., "Abuse Characteristics and Individual Differences Related to Disclosing Childhood Sexual, Physical, and Emotional Abuse and Witnessed Domestic Violence." *Journal of Interpersonal Violence* 31, no. 7 (2016): 1308–339, https://doi.org/10.1177/0886260514564155.

[211] Isabel Fay et al., "Disclosure, Twitter, and the Power of #WhyIDidntReport: Applying French and Raven's Bases of Power to Tweets from Victims of Sexual Violence," *The Journal of Social Media in Society* 10, no. 2 (2021): 402–22, https://thejsms.org/index.php/JSMS/article/view/1001.

[212] I used his full name Peter Brendan Murphy. My parish knew him as Fr. Peter Murphy. Later, I assume, to escape discovery and accountability, he took the name Fr. Brendan Murphy. Other clergy predators used similar devices, such as using initials as well as middle names to hide identity.

[213] "Diocese of Sioux City IA," BishopAccountability, February 26, 2021, https://www.bishop-accountability.org/dioceses/usa-ia-sioux-city/: A database of Catholic Clergy sexual predators, over 7,000 are listed.

[214] Excerpt from Msgr. Mark Duchaine, *Living Stones: Priests in the Sioux City Diocese, 1856–2004* (Diocese of Sioux City, 2004), 182–3, https://www.bishop-accountability.org/news5/2004_Duchaine_Living_Stones_re_Peter_Brendan_Murphy.pdf.

[215] Office of the Attorney General, *Report I*: describes the intentional destruction of documents by the diocese.

[216] Mike Argento, "Lies and Cover-Ups: Catholic Church in Pa. Had 'Playbook' to Keep Priest Abuse Secret," *York Daily Record*, August 16, 2018, https://www.ydr.com/story/news/watchdog/2018/08/16/pa-priest-abuse-how-catholic-church-covered-up-widespread-clergy-abuse-grand-jury-report-ag/1002107002/.

[217] Argento, "Lies."

[218] Argento, "Lies."

[219] "Reports of Attorneys General, Grand Juries, Individuals, Commissions, and Organizations," BishopAccountability, 2004, https://www.bishop-accountability.org/AtAGlance/reports.htm: A database of hundreds of reports, commissions, investigations, and grand juries.

[220] I use predator in the singular here, but this identifier is equally true for all complicit institutions that perpetuate sexual violence, including covering up or engaging in activities (bribing politicians, intimidation, etc.) that allow predators and complicit institutions to escape justice.

[221] "Child Sex Abuse Facts: Facts and Stats on Child Sexual Abuse," Lauren's Kids, January 8, 2020, https://laurenskids.org/awareness/about-faqs/facts-and-stats/: "A typical pedophile will commit 117 sexual crimes in a lifetime."

[222] Ryan Foley, "Catholic Diocese in Iowa Covered Up Priest's Abuse of 50 Boys," *Des Moines Register*, October 31, 2018, https://www.desmoinesregister.com/story/news/2018/10/31/catholic-priest-abuse-sioux-city-iowa-diocese-jerome-coyle/1833317002/.

[223] In Catholic Canon Law, a confessor, in this case the bishop, is forbidden to disclose confessions.

[224] Brit McCandless Farmer, "60 Minutes Overtime: Why Bishop Malone's Assistant Became a Whistleblower," *CBS News*, 60 Minutes Overtime, *CBS News* October 28, 2018, https://www.cbsnews.com/news/why-bishop-malones-assistant-became-a-whistleblower-60-minutes/.

[225] Charlie Specht, "Buffalo Catholic Whistleblower Came Forward Because of Victims, 'Allegiance to the Common Good,'" WBKW, October 28, 2018, https://www.wkbw.com/news/i-team/buffalo-catholic-whistleblower-came-forward-because-of-victims-allegiance-to-the-common-good. Exposed massive cover-up of sex abuse allegations.

[226] "Diocese of Buffalo NY," BishopAccountability, February 26, 2021, https://www.bishop-accountability.org/dioceses/usa-ny-buffalo/.

[227] Amanda Sakuma, "Top Cardinal Admits the Catholic Church Destroyed Files to Hide Sex Abuse," *Vox Reporting*, February 23, 2019, https://www.vox.com/2019/2/23/18237702/catholic-church-sex-abuse-summit-destroyed-documents.

[228] Ralph Cipriano, "Grand Jury Findings," *National Catholic Reporter*, October 7, 2005, https://natcath.org/NCR_Online/archives2/2005d/100705/100705a.php; Jon Hurdle, "Philadelphia Priests Accused by Grand Jury of Sexual Abuse and Cover-Up," *The New York Times*, February 11, 2011, https://www.nytimes.com/2011/02/11/us/11priest.html?scp=4&sq=philadelphia%20catholic%20sexual%20abuse&st=cse; Jan Murphy, "Read the Grand Jury Report on Sexual Abuse of Children by Priests (Warning, Graphic Content)," *PennLive*, March 1, 2016, http://www.pennlive.com/news/2016/03/altoona_diocese_catholic_clerg_1.html.

[229] Office of the Attorney General, *Pennsylvania Grand Jury Report*, (Harrisburg, PA: March 1, 2016), http://www.bishop-accountability.org/reports/2016_03_01_Pennsylvania_Grand_Jury_Report_on_Diocese_of_Altoona_Johnstown.pdf.

[230] Office of the Attorney General, *Pennsylvania Grand Jury Report*.

[231] Office of the Attorney General, *Report I of the 40th Investigating Grand Jury*, 230.

[232] Murphy, "Read."

[233] Laurie Mason Schroeder and Steve Esack, "Pennsylvania Catholic Diocese Covered up Decades Worth of Child Abuse, Grand Jury Says," *The Morning Call*, March 2, 2016, https://www.mcall.com/2016/03/02/pennsylvania-catholic-diocese-covered-up-decades-worth-of-child-abuse-grand-jury-says/.

234 Annysa Johnson, "Newly Appointed Bishop Destroyed Sex Abuse Records," *Milwaukee Sentinel Journal*, December 17, 2013, https://archive.jsonline.com/news/religion/vatican-chooses-green-bay-diocesan-official-to-be-marquette-bishop-b99166024z1-236250991.html/.

235 Candy Woodall and Brandie Kessler, "Feds Put Catholic Church Across the Nation on Notice: Don't Destroy Any Evidence of Abuse," *York Daily Record*, October 26, 2018, https://www.ydr.com/story/news/2018/10/26/catholic-priest-abuse-all-us-dioceses-now-included-federal-investigation/1779082002/.

236 Woodall and Kessler, "Feds."

237 Johnson, "Newly Appointed Bishop."

238 No action was taken. Conclusion: priests cover for priests, and bishops cover for priests—the end result is the predator priest remains in ministry to abuse other children.

239 David W. Wahl, "The Dangers of Sexual Gaslighting," *Psychology Today*, July 23, 2021, https://www.psychologytoday.com/us/blog/sexual-self/202107/the-dangers-sexual-gaslighting.

240 Wahl, "Dangers."

241 Robin Stern and Marc Brackett, "Gaslighting Is Emotional Abuse. Here's How to Recognize and Stop It," *The Washington Post*, June 2, 2023, https://www.washingtonpost.com/wellness/2023/06/02/gaslighting-signs-strategies/.

242 Stacey Benson, "Gaslighting—When Abusers Distort Reality," Jeff Anderson & Associates, December 16, 2023, https://www.andersonadvocates.com/blog/gaslighting-when-abusers-distort-reality/.

243 Conversation with Frank at SNAP Convention, 2012.

244 Benson, "Gaslighting."

245 Kevin Scott Wing, "Fr. Miles Riley, Class of 1993," *National Academy of Television Arts and Sciences, Northern California Chapter*, November 2010, https://emmysf.tv/files/2016/09/SC-Profile-Riley-Miles-1110.pdf.

246 "CA Victims Want Accused Priest Discipline," SNAP, December 5, 2013, https://www.snapnetwork.org/victims_want_accused_priest_disciplined: A "victim assistant coordinator" had the responsibility to control and manage victims/survivors who came forward to complain of clergy sexual abuse, while the "administrator's job," they became the gatekeeper of the diocese, approving or denying support for those harmed.

247 *Psychology Today* Staff, "Gaslighting, *Psychology Today*, May 10, 2023, https://www.psychologytoday.com/us/basics/gaslighting; Patrick Hamilton, *Gas Light*, (London: Constable and Company Ltd., 1939).

248 J. J. Freyd, "Violations of Power, Adaptive Blindness, and Betrayal Trauma Theory," *Feminism & Psychology* 7, no. 1 (1997): 22–32. https://psycnet.apa.org/record/1997-07734-003; Eric Patterson, "DARVO: Deny, Attack, Reverse Victim & Offender," *Choosing Therapy*, February 8, 2023, https://www.choosingtherapy.com/darvo/.

249 Ben Zimmer, "'Casting Couch': The Origins of a Pernicious Hollywood Cliché," *Atlantic Magazine*, October 16, 2017, https://www.theatlantic.com/entertainment/archive/2017/10/casting-couch-the-origins-of-a-pernicious-hollywood-cliche/543000/.

250 Patricia Hurtado, "Weinstein Prosecutors Build Case That Casting Couch Was Trap," *Bloomberg*, January 29, 2020, https://www.bloomberg.com/news/articles/2020-01-29/weinstein-casting-couch-could-save-him-or-send-him-to-prison.

251 Hurtado, "Weinstein."

252 "262 Celebrities, Politicians, CEOs, and Others Who Have Been Accused of Sexual Misconduct Since April 2017," *Vox Media*, Update: July 16, 2021, https://www.vox.com/a/sexual-harassment-assault-allegations-list/.

253 Ronan Farrow, "From Aggressive Overtures to Sexual Assault: Harvey Weinstein's Accusers Tell Their Stories," *New Yorker*, October 10, 2017, https://www.newyorker.com/news/news-desk/from-aggressive-overtures-to-sexual-assault-harvey-weinsteins-accusers-tell-their-stories.

254 Refer to the case of Bishop Malone of Buffalo Diocese hiding accusations and documents on page 83.

255 Office of the Attorney General, *Report I of the 40th Investigating Grand Jury*.

256 Anne Bachle Fifer, "Should Christian Organizations Use NDAs?" Anne Bachle Fifer Blog, December 11, 2021, https://abfifer.com/blog/2021/12/should-christian-organizations-use-ndas/.

257 Fifer, "Christian Organizations."

258 *Spotlight* Team, "Church Allowed Abuse."

259 "Scandals in the Church: The Bishops' Decisions; The Bishops' Charter for the Protection of Children and Young People," *The New York Times*, June 15, 2002, https://www.nytimes.com/2002/06/15/us/scandals-church-bishops-decisions-bishops-charter-for-protection-children-young.html.

260 Christa Brown, et at., "Letter to Southern Baptist Convention," SNAP, September 26, 2006, https://www.snapnetwork.org/snap_letters/2006_letters/092606_southern_baptist.htm.

261 Brown et al., "Letter."

262 Miguel Prats et al., "Statement Regarding Secret File of Clergy Predators," SNAP, September 20, 2006, https://www.snapnetwork.org/snap_statements/2006_statements/022006_baptist_convention_texas.htm.

263 Christa Brown, "The SBC's Sexual Abuse Hotline: Who Does It Serve?" blog post, SubStack, February 23, 2025, https://christabrown.substack.com/p/the-sbcs-sexual-abuse-hotline-who; Bob Smietana, "Southern Baptist Leaders Remain Undaunted as Legal Bills from Abuse Investigation Mount," Religion News Service, February 18, 2025, https://religionnews.com/2025/02/18/southern-baptist-leaders-remain-undaunted-as-legal-bills-from-abuse-investigation-mount/.

264 Bob Allen, "Southern Baptist Leaders Challenged to Get Tough on Sex Abuse by Clergy," SNAP Network, September 27, 2006, https://www.snapnetwork.org/news/baptist/baptist_leaders_challenged.htm.

[265] Steve Rabey, "Thou Shalt Not Disclose: How Churches and Ministries Use Legal Agreements to Silence Victims and Conceal Sin," MinistryWatch, February 6, 2020, https://ministrywatch.com/thou-shalt-not-disclose-how-churches-and-ministries-use-legal-agreements-to-silence-victims-and-conceal-sin/; Farrow, "Aggressive Overtures"; Rebecca Keegan, "The Secret Sources for 'Bombshell': Why Ex-Fox News Staffers Broke Their NDAs for Filmmakers," *The Hollywood Reporter*, October 29, 2019, https://www.hollywoodreporter.com/news/general-news/secret-sources-bombshell-why-fox-news-staffers-broke-ndas-filmmakers-1250668/.

[266] Kim Elsesser, "Congress Passes Law Restoring Victims' Voices, Banning NDAs In Sexual Harassment Cases," *Forbes Magazine*, November 16, 2022, https://www.forbes.com/sites/kimelsesser/2022/11/16/congress-passes-law-restoring-victims-voices-banning-ndas-in-sexual-harassment-cases/?sh=60fdec847b30.

[267] "Should Churches Use NDAs? It Depends," National Association of Evangelicals, online post, January 5, 2022, https://www.nae.org/churches-use-ndas/: Fifty-four percent of Evangelical leaders surveyed said, "It depends."

[268] John Manly, "Lawyer for Olympic Gymnasts: NDAs Allow Sexual Abuse to Fester," *TIME* magazine, October 31, 2017, https://time.com/5003827/non-disclosure-agreements-sexual-assault/.

[269] Manly, "Lawyer."

[270] Manly, "Lawyer."

[271] Emily Steel and Michael S. Schmidt, "Bill O'Reilly Settled New Harassment Claim, Then *Fox* Renewed His Contract," *The New York Times,* October 21, 2017, https://www.nytimes.com/2017/10/21/business/media/bill-oreilly-sexual-harassment.html.

[272] Steel and Schmidt, "Bill O'Reilly."

[273] Steel and Schmidt, "Bill O'Reilly."

[274] Keegan, "Bombshell."

[275] "The Criminal Justice System: Statistics," RAINN.

[276] Kitchener and Wong, "The Moral Catastrophe."

[277] Sarah Pulliam Bailey, "Southern Baptist Leaders Covered up Sex Abuse, Kept Secret Database, Report Says," *The Washington Post*, May 22, 2022, https://www.washingtonpost.com/religion/2022/05/22/southern-baptist-sex-abuse-report/.

[278] Mary Curtis, "How the Southern Baptist Convention Became a Safe Haven for Abusers, Sexual assault within the denomination has been rampant for years," article, Slate, August 24, 2022

[279] Bailey, "Baptist Leaders."

[280] Mary Curtis, "Sexual Assault within the Denomination Has Been Rampant for Years," *Slate*, August 24, 2022, https://slate.com/human-interest/2022/08/southern-baptist-convention-sexual-abuse-investigation-justice-department.html.

[281] Ailsa Chang et al., "What's Next for Southern Baptists After Sex Abuse Scandal," *NPR*, May 24, 2022, https://www.nprillinois.org/2022-05-24/whats-next-for-southern-baptists-after-sex-abuse-scandal.

²⁸² Sarah Stankorb, "The Southern Baptist Church Ignored Its Abuse Crisis. She Exposed It." *Vice News*, January 4, 2023, https://www.vice.com/en/article/the-southern-baptist-church-ignored-its-abuse-crisis-she-exposed-it/.

²⁸³ Robert Downen et al., "Abuse of Faith": Ms. Brown created the Stop Baptist Predators website—provides a wealth of information on sexual abuse in the SBC and Baptist community. www.stopbaptistpredators.org/index.htm: Christa Brown, an advocate for survivors of sexual abuse in the Baptist communities for over twenty years, has led efforts to raise awareness and hold predators accountable: See Stankorb, "Baptist Church."

²⁸⁴ Robert Downen, interview by Terry Gross "All Things Considered," *NPR*, June 2, 2022, https://www.npr.org/2022/06/02/1102621352/how-the-southern-baptist-convention-covered-up-its-widespread-sexual-abuse-scand.

²⁸⁵ Stop Baptist Predators, http://stopbaptistpredators.org/index.htm; Christa Brown, *Baptistland*.

²⁸⁶ "Highly Confidential: Released to Guidepost Solutions, Sunny Lee": Southern Baptist Conference List of Accused Predators, February 28, 2022, https://sbcec.s3.amazonaws.com/FINAL+-+List+of+Alleged+Abusers+-+SBC+REDACTED.pdf.

²⁸⁷ Liam Adams and Katherine Burgess, "Southern Baptist Convention Leaders Publish Long-Secret List of Accused Ministers," *The Tennessean*, May 26, 2022, https://www.tennessean.com/story/news/religion/2022/05/26/southern-baptist-convention-list-accused-abusers-released/9915284002/.

²⁸⁸ Stankorb, "Baptist Church."

²⁸⁹ Michelle Boorstein, "Justice Dept. Investigating Southern Baptist Convention Handling of Sex Abuse," *The Washington Post*, August 12, 2022, https://www.washingtonpost.com/religion/2022/08/12/fbi-southern-baptist-sexual-abuse/.

²⁹⁰ Baptist Accountability, a database of predator ministers in the Baptist community, https://baptistaccountability.org/; "A Documentary History of the Crisis," BishopAccountability, last updated September 12, 2007, https://www.bishop-accountability.org/AtAGlance/timeline.htm.

²⁹¹ Stop Baptist Predators, http://stopbaptistpredators.org/index.htm.

²⁹² Bailey et al., "Southern Baptist Leaders."

²⁹³ Robert Downen et al., "Abuse of Faith": Part two of a six-part investigation of the SBC.

²⁹⁴ Curtis, "How the Southern Baptist Convention."

²⁹⁵ For victims of sexual abuse or for those who suspect sexual abuse by a pastor, staff member, or member of an SBC church or entity. Hotline: 202-864-5378 or SBChotline@guidepostsolutions.com.

²⁹⁶ Bob Smietana, "SBC Abuse Reform Task Force Ends Its Work with No Names on Database and No Long-Term Plan," *Religion News Service*, June 4, 2024, https://religionnews.com/2024/06/04/sbc-abuse-reform-task-force-ends-its-work-with-no-names-on-database-and-no-long-term-future-plan/.

²⁹⁷ Smietana, "Abuse."

298 Christa Brown et al., "Please, No More Hollow Words on Sexual Abuse Reform," opinion, *Baptist News Global*, February 8, 2025, https://baptistnews.com/article/please-no-more-hollow-words-on-sexual-abuse-reform/.

299 *Los Angeles Times* Staff, "Inside the 'Perversion Files' Tracking Decades of Allegations in the Boy Scouts," October 18, 2012, *Los Angeles Times*, https://spreadsheets.latimes.com/boyscouts-cases/.

300 Marisa Kwiatkowski and John Kelly, "The Catholic Church and Boy Scouts are Lobbying Against Child Abuse Statutes. This Is Their Playbook," *USA Today*, April 2020, https://www.usatoday.com/in-depth/news/investigations/2019/10/02/catholic-church-boy-scouts-fight-child-sex-abuse-statutes/2345778001/.

301 Kwiatkowski and Kelly, "Catholic Church."

302 Hill, *Believing*.

303 Hill, *Believing*.

304 Hill, *Believing*.

305 Monica Hesse, "Anita Hill's Testimony Compelled America to Look Closely at Sexual Harassment," *The Washington Post*, April 13, 2016, https://www.washingtonpost.com/lifestyle/style/anita-hills-testimony-compelled-america-to-look-closely-at-sexual-harassment/2016/04/13/36999612-ea2e-11e5-bc08-3e03a5b41910_story.html.

306 Hesse, "Anita Hill."

307 Glenn Collins, "Patriarchy: Is It Invention or Inevitable?" *New York*, April 1986 https://www.nytimes.com/1986/04/28/style/patriarchy-is-it-invention-or-inevitable.html.

308 Charles Darwin, *The Descent of Man, and Selection in Relation to Sex* (John Murray, 1871): Darwin did not believe men and women were equal.

309 Darwin, *Descent*.

310 Spencer Greenberg and Holly Muir, "Men Aren't from Mars, nor Are Women from Venus," *Scientific American*, June 31, 2022, https://www.scientificamerican.com/article/most-of-us-combine-personality-traits-from-different-genders/.

311 Lucien Carr, *Reports of the Peabody Museum of American Archaeology and Ethnology, Vol. 3.*, (John Wilson and Son, 1887).

312 Evelyn Reed, *Women's Evolution, from Matriarchal Clan to Patriarchal Family* (Pathfinder Press, 1975).

313 Lewis Henry Morgan, *Ancient Society; Or, Researches in the Lines of Human Progress from Savagery to Civilization* (Forgotten Books, 1877); Eleanor Leacock, *Myths of Male Dominance: Collected Articles on Women Cross-Culturally* (Haymarket Books, 1981).

314 Reed, *Woman's Evolution*.

315 Brownmiller, *Against Our Will*.

316 Steven Mintz, "Placing Childhood Sexual Abuse in Historical Perspective," The Immanent Frame, July 13, 2012, https://tif.ssrc.org/2012/07/13/placing-childhood-sexual-abuse-in-historical-perspective/.

317 Mary Ann Mason, *From Father's Property to Children's Rights: The History of Child Custody in the United States* (Columbia University Press, 1996).

[318] Reid Maki, "Timeline of Child Labor Developments in the United States," The Child Labor Coalition, October 20, 2010, https://laborcenter.uiowa.edu/special-projects/child-labor-public-education-project/about-child-labor/child-labor-us-history; Catherine A. Paul, "National Child Labor Committee (NCLC): Founded April 25, 1904," National Child Labor Committee," https://socialwelfare.library.vcu.edu/programs/child-welfarechild-labor/national-child-labor-committee/.

[319] New York Society for the Prevention of Cruelty to Children (NYSPCC), https://nyspcc.org/. The first child protection agency in the world.

[320] Mintz, "Historical Perspective."

[321] "About Us: History of the APSCA," American Society for the Protection of Animals, https://www.aspca.org/about-us/history-of-the-aspca.

[322] Kriste Lindenmeyer, "Children's Bureau," Virginia Commonwealth University, https://socialwelfare.library.vcu.edu/programs/child-welfarechild-labor/childrens-bureau/.

[323] Michael Schuman, "History of Child Labor in the United States—Part 1: Little Children Working." U.S. Bureau of Labor Statistics, *Monthly Labor Review*, January 2017, https://www.bls.gov/opub/mlr/2017/article/history-of-child-labor-in-the-united-states-part-1.htm.

[324] Stephen J. Pfohl, "The 'Discovery' of Child Abuse," *Social Problems* 24, no. 3, (February 1977): 310–22, https://www.jstor.org/stable/800083.

[325] John Caffey, "Multiple Fractures in Long Bones of Infant Suffering from Chronic Subdural Haematoma." *American Journal of Roentgenology* 187, no. 6 (1946): 163–73, https://doi.org/10.2214/AJR.06.0418.

[326] C. Henry Kempe, "The Battered Child-Syndrome," *Journal of the American Medical Association* 181, no. 1 (1962), 17–24, https://jamanetwork.com/journals/jama/article-abstract/327895.

[327] Andrew L. Yarrow, "History of U.S. Children's Policy, 1900–Present," First Focus, April 2009, https://firstfocus.org/wp-content/uploads/2014/06/Childrens-Policy-History.pdf.

[328] John B. Myers, "A Short History of Child Protection in America," *Family Law Quarterly* 42, no. 3 (2008): 449–63. https://www.jstor.org/stable/25740668.

[329] Vincent De Francis, *Protecting the Child Victim of Sex Crimes Committed by Adults. Final Report*, (American Humane Association, Children's Division, 1969), https://eric.ed.gov/?id=ED055645.

[330] De Francis, *Protecting the Child*.

[331] Marci Hamilton, *Justice Denied, What America Must Do to Protect Its Children* (Cambridge University Press, 2008).

[332] "A History of Hope and Healing," Childhelp, March 24, 2025, https://www.childhelp.org/our-history/.

[333] Call the Childhelp National Child Abuse Hotline 24/7. (1-800) 4-A-Child or (1-800) 422-4453.

[334] Joanne Stevelos, "Child Sexual Abuse Declared an Epidemic: World Health Organization Publishes CSA Guidelines," *Psychology Today*, November 29,

2017, https://www.psychologytoday.com/us/blog/children-at-the-table/201711/child-sexual-abuse-declared-an-epidemic.

[335] David Finkelhor, "Sexually Victimized Children (1979)," in *Violence Against Women: Classic Papers*, ed. R. K. Bergen et al. (Pearson Education New Zealand, 2005), 42–56

[336] Simon David Finkelhor, *Sourcebook on Child Sexual Abuse* (Sage Publications, Inc, 1986).

[337] *State of Missouri v. Celia, a Slave* (Mo. 1855), Wikipedia, https://en.wikipedia.org/wiki/State_of_Missouri_v._Celia,_a_Slave.

[338] *Missouri v. Celia*,

[339] Brownmiller, *Against Our Will*.

[340] Amanda Taub, "Rape Culture Isn't a Myth. It's Real, and It's Dangerous," *Vox*, December 15, 2014, https://www.vox.com/2014/12/15/7371737/rape-culture-definition.

[341] "Criminal Law—Rape—Cautionary Instruction in Sex Offense Trial Relating Prosecutrix's Credibility to the Nature of the Crime Charged Is No Longer Mandatory; Discretionary Use Is Disapproved," *Fordham Urban Law Journal* 4, no. 2 (1976), https://ir.lawnet.fordham.edu/ulj/vol4/iss2/10/.

[342] Deborah C. England, *The History of Marital Rape Laws*, https://www.criminaldefenselawyer.com/resources/criminal-defense/crime-penalties/marital-rape.htm [this link/page doesn't match the author or title and I can't find the England article online]

[343] Danielle McGuire, *At the Dark End of the Street: Black Women, Rape, and Resistance--A New History of the Civil Rights Movement from Rosa Parks to the Rise of Black Power* (Vintage, 2010): Read this book!

[344] Kathie Sarachild, *Consciousness-Raising: A Radical Weapon*, 1973, comments from the First National Women's Liberation Conference outside Chicago, November 27, 1968, https://www.rapereliefshelter.bc.ca/wp-content/uploads/2021/03/Feminist-Revolution-Consciousness-Raising-A-Radical-Weapon-Kathie-Sarachild.pdf.

[345] WBAI radio, "New York Radical Feminists' Talk about the 1971 Rape Speakout," audio recording, WBAI, https://avplayer.lib.berkeley.edu/Pacifica/b23305850.

[346] Stacey Cowley, "Anne Forer Pyne, a Feminist Who Opened Eyes, Dies at 72," *The New York Times*, https://www.nytimes.com/2018/03/30/obituaries/anne-forer-pyne-a-feminist-who-opened-eyes-dies-at-72.html: "Feminist activist and writer whose use of the phrase 'consciousness raising' helped make it a foundational principle of the women's rights movement."

[347] Gillian Greensite, "History of the Rape Crisis Movement." Washington Coalition of Sexual Assault Programs. WCSAP. Last accessed April 22, 2025, https://www.wcsap.org/sites/default/files/uploads/resources_publications/outside_authors/History_of_the_Rape_Crisis_Movement.pdf.

[348] "International History of TBTN," Take Back the Night, March 14, 2019, https://takebackthenight.org/history/.

[349] "What Is Title IX?" Advocates.

350 "NAESV Applauds the President's Budget," National Alliance to End Sexual Violence, May 28, 2021, https://endsexualviolence.org/wp-content/uploads/2021/05/PresidentBidenBudgetStatement-FINAL-PDF.pdf.

351 "Building a future where Black Women and Girls Are Safe, Respected, and Thriving," Ujima: The National Center on Violence Against Women in the Black Community, October 2018, https://ujimacommunity.org/wp-content/uploads/2018/12/Ujima-Womens-Violence-Stats-v7.4-1.pdf.

352 "Building a Future," The National Center.

353 Barlow, "Black Women."

354 McGuire, *At the Dark End of the Street*: Hundreds of documented cases, with 90 pages of notes and bibliography, provocative narrative, read this book!

355 Raquel Kennedy Bergen and Elizabeth Barnhill, "Marital Rape: New Research and Directions," National Resource Center on Domestic Violence, February 2006, https://vawnet.org/material/marital-rape-new-research-and-directions.

356 Sewell Chan, "Recy Taylor, Who Fought for Justice After 1944 Rape," *The New York Times*, December 29, 2017, http://www.nytimes.com/2017/12/29/obituaries/recy-taylor-alabama-rape-victim-dead.html.

357 Samhita Mukhopadhyay, "Trial by Media: Black Female Lasciviousness and the Question of Consent," in *Yes Means Yes*, 161–172.

358 Laura Palumbo, "Survivor Identity, Race, Immigrant Status, etc., Abuse Statistics Higher for Disabled, Transgender, Black and Multi-Racial, Native Americans," National Sexual Violence Resource Center, February 25, 2019, https://www.nsvrc.org/blogs/seeing-whole-survivor-why-its-necessary-talk-about-identity-survivors-individuals-and-groups; Joseph Shapiro, "The Sexual Assault Epidemic No One Talks About," *NPR*, January 8, 2018, https://www.npr.org/2018/01/08/570224090/the-sexual-assault-epidemic-no-one-talks-about; "Sexual Violence," NSVRC; Sandy E. James et al., "The Report of the 2015 U.S. Transgender Survey." Resource Center for Minority Data, May 22, 2019, https://doi.org/10.3886/ICPSR37229.v1; "An Overview of Intimate Partner Violence in the United States—2010 Findings," NISVS—National Intimate Partnerand Sexual Violence Survey, February 26, 2014, https://www.wvdhhr.org/wvhomevisitation/pdf/IntimatePartnerViolenc_FactSheet.pdf; Palumbo, "Seeing."

359 Jody Jessup-Anger et al., "History of Sexual Violence in Higher Education," *New Direction for Student Services* 514, no. 161 (Spring 2015), https://epublications.marquette.edu/edu_fac/514/.

360 Brownmiller, *Against Our Will*.

361 Cohen, "How a Book."

362 Susan Griffiths, "Rape: The All-American Crime," in Alix Kates Shulman and Honor Moore, eds., *Women's Liberation! Feminist Writings That Inspired a Revolution & Still Can* (Library of America, 2021), 26–35.

363 Shulman and Moore, *Women's Liberation*!

364 National Sexual Violence Resource Center, Directory of Organizations, March 13, 2009, https://www.nsvrc.org/organizations.

365 Conversation with the victim, whose name has been changed. Bishop Nickless of the Diocese of Sioux City refuses to add nuns to the list of "credibly accused" clergy. He refuses to name nuns, even though they are abusers and clergy.

366 Marci Hamilton, "Listen Up: There Is a Solution to the Sex Abuse and Harassment Epidemic Unfolding Before Your Eyes—And You Will Be Surprised at Who Must Step Up to Succeed," *Verdict*, November 22, 2017, https://verdict.justia.com/2017/11/22/listen-solution-sex-abuse-harassment-epidemic-unfolding-eyes-will-surprised-must-step-succeed.

367 "31 Accused in this Diocese," BishopAccountability, Gallup Diocese, New Mexico, February 26, 2021, https://www.bishop-accountability.org/dioceses/usa-nm-gallup/: Fr. James Schlaffer assaulted a young woman while she was in traction in a hospital.

368 Glenn Bunting, "Lawsuit Ends Silence on Abuse at Jesuit Retreat," *Los Angeles Times*, March 24, 2002, https://www.latimes.com/archives/la-xpm-2002-mar-24-mn-34467-story.html.

369 Rape Crisis Information Pathfinder, "Multiple Victimization of Rape Victims: What Is the explanation?" ibiblio, last accessed May 1, 2025, http://www.ibiblio.org/rcip/mvrv.html; Farahnaz Mohammed, "The Repetition Compulsion: Why Rape Victims Are More Likely to Be Assaulted Again," Girls' Globe, August 4, 2015, https://www.girlsglobe.org/2015/08/04/the-repetition-compulsion-why-rape-victims-are-more-likely-to-be-assaulted-again/.

370 Hamilton, *Justice*: Path-breaking exposure of how statute of limitation laws harms victims of abuse.

371 Hamilton, *Justice*.

372 Anthony J. Machcinski, "Priests Used Gold Crosses to ID Kids as Abuse Targets and Other Horrors from Pa. Report," *York Daily Record*, August 15, 2018, https://www.ydr.com/story/news/2018/08/15/pa-grand-jury-report-catholic-priest-abuse-most-shocking-cases-clergy-sexual-abuse/995904002/.

373 Machinski, "Priests."

374 *CNN* Editorial Research, "Penn State Scandal Fast Facts," *CNN*, October 28, 2013, https://www.cnn.com/2013/10/28/us/penn-state-scandal-fast-facts.

375 Maureen Dowd, "Personal Fowl at Penn State," *The New York Times*, November 8, 2011, https://www.nytimes.com/2011/11/09/opinion/dowd-personal-foul-at-penn.html.

376 Stanglin, "Ex-Penn State Coach."

377 Jennifer Smola Shaffer, "What to Know about Ohio State University Athletic Doctor Richard Strauss' Career, Abuse, and Death," *The Columbus Dispatch*, https://www.dispatch.com/story/news/education/2021/03/10/osu-sex-abuse-scandal-richard-strauss-career-abuse-death/6947149002/.

378 Jordan Laird, "OSU Trying to Block Strauss Abuse Victims from Using Independent Report in Court," *The Columbus Dispatch*, February 9, 2024, https://www.dispatch.com/story/news/education/2024/02/09/ohio-state-university-seeks-to-block-dr-richard-strauss-abuse-report-from-court/72538150007/.

379 Shaffer, "What to Know."

[380] Lauren Reichart Smith and Ann Pegoraro "Media Framing of Larry Nassar and the USA Gymnastics Child Sex Abuse Scandal," *Journal of Child Sexual Abuse* 29, no. 4 (2020): 373–92, https://pubmed.ncbi.nlm.nih.gov/32040384/.

[381] Smith and Pegoraro, "Media Framing."

[382] Data Desk Staff, "Inside the 'Perversion Files,'" *Los Angeles Times*, October 18, 2012, https://documents.latimes.com/boy-scouts-paper-trail-of-abuse-documents/.

[383] Kim Christensen, "Boy Scouts Sex Abuse Victims Vote on $1.9-Billion Settlement Plan," October 15, 2021, https://www.latimes.com/world-nation/story/2021-10-15/boy-scouts-sex-abuse-victims-vote-on-1-9-billion-settlement-plan; Dietrich Knauth, "US Supreme Court Lets $2.46 Billion Boy Scouts Sex Abuse Settlement Proceed," Reuters, February 22, 2024, https://www.reuters.com/legal/us-supreme-court-lets-246-billion-boy-scouts-sex-abuse-settlement-proceed-2024-02-22/.

[384] Laurie Goodstein, "Deal Accepted in Los Angeles Abuse Cases," *The New York Times*, July 16, 2007, https://www.nytimes.com/2007/07/16/us/16cnd-abuse.html: Attorney John Manly led the legal team in securing a $660 million settlement against the L.A. Archdiocese in one of the largest clergy abuse cases in U.S. history in the case against L.A. Archdiocese.

[385] "CA—Psychiatrist Accused of Sexual Abuse," SNAP Network, December 5, 2014, https://www.snapnetwork.org/ca_psychiatrist_accused_of_sexual_abuse.

[386] Eric Kurhi, "Mountain View: Advocates for Those Molested by Priests Want Psychiatrist out of El Camino Hospital," *The Mercury News,* December 5, 2014, https://www.mercurynews.com/2014/12/05/mountain-view-advocates-for-those-molested-by-priests-want-psychiatrist-out-of-el-camino-hospital/.

[387] Jeff Gottlieb, "Priest-Psychiatrist's Offer to Settle Sex Suit Is Rejected," *San Jose Mercury News*: The original link is no longer available. The screenshot is taken from Havel's personnel file in the court case, https://www.bishop-accountability.org/docs/marianists/Havel_Rev_Thomas_E/Havel_Rev_Thomas_E.pdf

[388] It is bad form for one doctor to criticize another doctor, as all are expected to extend "professional courtesy" to fellow doctors; in other words, to look the other way. I refer to "insular oversight" as the accepted practice of the state "medical boards" operating as an "old boys club" that dismisses valid complaints. It is beyond the scope of this book, but serious investigation and reform must be taken for justice in these professions.

[389] Conversation with author—name changed.

[390] BishopAccountability.org, https://www.bishop-accountability.org/: Documents from public sources of over 7,000 accused clergy predators.

[391] Anna Orso, "'Passing the Trash': Pa. Teachers Slip Through the Cracks by Quitting Amid Allegations," *PennLive*, September 3, 2014, https://www.pennlive.com/midstate/2014/09/passing_the_trash_teachers_acr.html.

[392] Diana E. H. Russell, "Politicizing Sexual Violence: A Voice in the Wilderness," revised May 6, 1995, https://www.dianarussell.com/politicizing_sexual_violence.html.

[393] Diana E. H. Russell, *Sexual Exploitation: Rape, Child Sexual Abuse, and Workplace Harassment* (Sage Publishers, 1984).

[394] Hill, *Believing*.
[395] Stephanie Zacharek et al., "Person of the Year 2017: The Silence Breakers," *TIME*, November 10, 2017, https://time.com/time-person-of-the-year-2017-silence-breakers/.
[396] Rebecca Keegan, "She Wrote the Memo That Helped Take Down Harvey Weinstein. She's Finally Ready to Talk," *Hollywood Reporter*, December 8, 2022, https://www.hollywoodreporter.com/movies/movie-features/harvey-weinstein-whistleblower-interview-lauren-oconnor-1235276169/.
[397] Justin Rohrlich and Kate Briquelet, "38 Women Accuse 'Predator' Filmmaker of Using 12-Step Playbook to Lure and Abuse," *Daily Beast,* December 5, 2022, https://www.thedailybeast.com/sexual-predator-james-toback-abused-actresses-at-his-moms-house-bombshell-lawsuit-claims.
[398] Glenn Whipp, "395: The Number of Women Who Have Contacted the *Times* with Allegations of Sexual Harassment Against James Toback," *Los Angeles Times*, January 7, 2018, https://www.latimes.com/entertainment/la-et-mn-james-toback-women-sexual-harassment-breaking-silence-20180107-story.html.
[399] Glenn Whipp, "Jury Awards $1.68 Billion to 40 Women in James Toback Sexual Misconduct Lawsuit," *Los Angeles Times*, April 9, 2025, https://www.latimes.com/entertainment-arts/story/2025-04-09/james-toback-lawsuit-sexual-misconduct-verdict.
[400] Statute of limitation laws are examined fully in chapter 6: Playbook of the Powerful.
[401] "Adult Survivors Act," New York State Academy of Trial Lawyers, October 4, 2024, https://trialacademy.org/?pg=adult-survivors-act.
[402] "38 Women Accuse James Toback of Sexual Misconduct in Lawsuit," Associated Press, December 6, 2022, https://apnews.com/article/new-york-lawsuits-sexual-abuse-statutes-1d036352a3df05ee442071a5c358b18e.
[403] Whipp, "395."
[404] Palumbo, "Seeing": Survivor identity, race, immigrant status, etc., abuse statistics higher for disabled, transgender, Black and multi-racial, Native Americans.
[405] "Building a Future," The National Center.
[406] Pennsylvania Coalition Against Rape, "Racism & Sexual Violence: What's the Connection?" Technical Assistance Bulletin (TAB), 2017, https://pcar.org/sites/default/files/resource-pdfs/tab_2017_racismsexual_violence_connections-508d.pdf.
[407] Cecily Hilleary, "For Native American Clergy Sex Abuse Survivors, Justice Is Elusive," *VOA News*, September 27, 2018, https://www.voanews.com/a/native-americans-forgotten-survivors-of-clergy-abuse-church-coverup/4589535.html.
[408] 9littlegirls, Facebook, https://www.facebook.com/9littlegirls.
[409] Patrick Anderson, "Native American Victims of Sex Abuse at Catholic Boarding Schools Fight for Justice," Argus Leader, May 16, 2019, https://www.argusleader.com/story/news/2019/05/16/native-american-sex-abuse-victims-catholic-boarding-schools-south-dakota/1158590001/.
[410] 9littlegirls, Facebook.

411 Andreas Wiseman, "Leonardo DiCaprio & Appian Way Join 'Nine Little Indians' about Abuse at American Indian Boarding School," Deadline, March 26, 2025, https://deadline.com/2025/03/leonardo-dicaprio-nine-little-indians-boarding-school-abuse-1236351067/.
412 Robin Whyatt, "Violence Against Native Women Has Colonial Roots," Progressive, March 2, 2023, https://progressive.org/magazine/violence-against-native-women-has-colonial-roots-whyatt/.
413 Whyatt, "Violence."
414 Daniel Imwalle, "Trauma and Truth: Native American Boarding Schools," Franciscan Media, June 2024, https://www.franciscanmedia.org/st-anthony-messenger/trauma-and-truth-native-american-boarding-schools/; Lisa Desjardins et al., "Sexual Abuse of Native American Children at Boarding Schools Exposed in New Report," *PBS NewsHour*, May 29, 2024, https://www.pbs.org/newshour/show/sexual-abuse-of-native-american-children-at-boarding-schools-exposed-in-new-report; Red Lake Nation News, "'In the Name of God': Native American Children Endured Years of Sexual Abuse at Boarding Schools," *Red Lake Nation News*, May 30, 2024, https://www.redlakenationnews.com/story/2024/05/30/features/in-the-name-of-god-native-american-children-endured-years-of-sexual-abuse-at-boarding-schools/122754.html.
415 "'Kill the Indian, Save the Man:' An Introduction to the History of Boarding Schools," August 3, 2020, National Native American Boarding School Healing Coalition, https://boardingschoolhealing.org/kill-the-indian-save-the-man-an-introduction-to-the-history-of-boarding-schools/.
416 David Kirton, "Sask. Residential School Survivors Share Experiences," Prince Albert Now, June 16, 2012, https://panow.com/2012/01/16/sask-residential-school-survivors-share-experiences/.
417 "Native Abuse," BishopAccountability, May 28, 2021, https://www.bishop-accountability.org/native-abuse/: Online bibliography of hundreds of media articles about the sexual abuse on Indian reservations. The topic deserves a major, nationwide investigation of these criminal actions that were perpetrated over historical times of many decades and systematic in all Indian reservations. Books need to be written to document this tragic abuse.
418 "Native Abuse," BishopAccountability
419 Sarah Ransome, "I Survived Epstein and Maxwell's Sex Ring, and Then . . ." July 19, 2022, *The Washington Post*, https://www.washingtonpost.com/opinions/2022/07/19/i-survived-jeffrey-epstein-ghislaine-maxwell-sex-trafficking-ring/.
420 Matt Zapotosky and Beth Reinhard, "Justice Dept. Faults Former Epstein Prosecutor for 'Poor Judgment' But Finds No Misconduct," *The Washington Post*, November 12, 2020, https://www.nytimes.com/2020/11/12/us/politics/jeffrey-epstein-justice-department-miami.html; Eliza Relman and Azmi Haroun, "The 26 Women Who Have Accused Trump of Sexual Misconduct," *Business Insider*, May 9, 2023, https://www.businessinsider.com/women-accused-trump-sexual-misconduct-list-2017-12; Jennifer Savin, "A Timeline of Donald Trump's Many (Alleged) Crimes and Convictions," *Cosmopolitan Magazine*, November 6, 2024, https://www.cosmopolitan.com/uk/reports/a62831426/trump-allegations-timeline/.

421 "The Criminal Justice System: Statistics," RAINN.
422 Beth LeBlanc, "Police Seize Misconduct Records from Michigan's Catholic Diocese," *Detroit News*, October 3, 2018, https://www.detroitnews.com/story/news/religion/2018/10/03/police-serve-search-warrants-michigans-catholic-dioceses/1513938002/.
423 David Tarrant et al., "Missing and Incomplete Sex Abuse Files Spark Dallas Police Raid of Catholic Diocese Storage Facility," *Dallas News*, May 15, 2019, https://www.dallasnews.com/news/2019/05/15/missing-and-incomplete-sex-abuse-files-spark-dallas-police-raid-of-catholic-diocese-storage-facility/.
424 Marjorie Owens and Tanya Eiserer, "Here's What Police Seized During the Catholic Diocese of Dallas Raid," TV ABC 8, May 29, 2019, https://www.wfaa.com/article/news/heres-what-police-seized-during-the-catholic-of-diocese-dallas-raid/287-2e103131-90df-462c-a62f-ab586e7eebee.
425 Rachel de Leon, "If the Police Don't Believe You, They Might Prosecute You': How Officers Turn Victims of Sexual Assault into Suspects," *Reveal News*, September 25, 2023, https://revealnews.org/article/if-the-police-dont-believe-you-they-might-prosecute-you-how-officers-turn-victims-of-sexual-assault-into-suspects/; Joseph A. Reaves and Kelly Ettenborough, "Inheriting a Legacy of Secrecy, Scandal," BishopAccountability, May 4, 2003, https://www.bishop-accountability.org/news2003_01_06/2003_05_04_Reaves_InheritingA.htm.
426 Eloise Barry, "Who's Paying Prince Andrew's $16 Million Settlement to Virginia Giuffre? What to Know About Royal Finances," *TIME* magazine, February 17, 2022, https://time.com/6149123/prince-andrew-settlement-virginia-giuffre-royal-finances/; Sarah Ransome, "I Survived Epstein and Maxwell's Sex Ring. Then the Gaslighting Began," *The Washington Post*, July 19, 2022, https://www.washingtonpost.com/opinions/2022/07/19/i-survived-jeffrey-epstein-ghislaine-maxwell-sex-trafficking-ring/: Sarah Ransome is the author of *Silenced No More* about her ordeal in Jeffrey Epstein and Ghislaine Maxwell's sex trafficking operation.
427 "200 Men Step Forward to Speak about Childhood Sexual Abuse," *Oprah Winfrey Show*, [video] November 5, 2010, https://www.oprah.com/own-oprahshow/full-episode-200-adult-men-who-were-molested-come-forward-video.
428 "200 Men," *Oprah Winfrey Show*.
429 "Male Sexual Abuse Survivors Stand Together," *Oprah Winfrey Show*, November 5, 2010, https://www.oprah.com/oprahshow/male-sexual-abuse-survivors-stand-together/all.
430 "200 Men," *Oprah Winfrey Show*.
431 Chan, "Recy Taylor,"
432 Chan, "Recy Taylor."
433 McGuire, *At the Dark End of the Street*: Highlights sexual violence in the broader context of racial injustice and the fight for freedom. Excellent review and telling of rape and fightback of women from 1940 to 1975.
434 Brownmiller, *Against Our Will*, 162–3.
435 Friedman and Valenti, *Yes*.

[436] Friedman and Valenti, *Yes*.
[437] Friedman and Valenti, *Yes*.
[438] Sophie Gilbert and Tori Latham, "Oprah Winfrey's Speech at the Golden Globes," *Atlantic*, January 8, 2018, https://www.theatlantic.com/entertainment/archive/2018/01/full-transcript-oprah-winfreys-speech-at-the-golden-globes/549905/.
[439] Danielle McGuire, "Landmark 1959 Rape Case in Tallahassee, Florida Was Central to the Civil Rights Movement," March 1, 2018, https://daniellemcguire.com/2018/03/01/landmark-1959-tallahassee-rape-case-central-to-civil-rights-movement/.
[440] McGuire, *At the Dark End of the Street*.
[441] Berry, "The Tragedy of Gilbert Gauthe": Msgr. Richard Mouton, the Abbeville Louisiana pastor, shortly after Gauthe's removal, gave a sermon saying that Gauthe left the parish because of "serious moral indiscretions."
[442] Jason Berry, *Lead Us Not into Temptation* (University of Illinois Press, 1992). An investigation into clergy abuse in Louisiana.
[443] "Join Us in Our Mission to Protect Athletes & End Sexual Violence in Sports." The Army of Survivors, July 1, 2021, https://thearmyofsurvivors.org/.
[444] Phil Saviano, "1993 Phil Donahue Show - 'Catholic Priest Sex Abuse' Part One," YouTube, March 1993, https://www.youtube.com/watch?v=zQu3K-BAMLlI; "1993 Pt. 5 – PHIL DONAHUE SHOW: Catholic Priest Sexual Abuse of Children and Adolescents," BishopAccountability.org, April 2012, https://www.bishop-accountability.org/2012/04/1993-pt-5-phil-donahue-show-catholic-priest-sexual-abuse-of-children-and-adolescents/; Mark Pattison, "Legendary Talk Show Host Phil Donahue Highlighted Clergy Abuse Crisis," *National Catholic Reporter*, August 20, 2024, https://www.ncronline.org/news/legendary-talk-show-host-phil-donahue-highlighted-clergy-abuse-crisis.
[445] David Clohessy, "Phil Donahue Gave Support to Clergy Sex Abuse Survivors Like Us," *National Catholic Reporter*, August 26, 2024, https://www.ncronline.org/opinion/guest-voices/phil-donahue-gave-support-clergy-sex-abuse-survivors-us.
[446] Clohessy, "Phil Donahue."
[447] "1993 Pt. 5 – PHIL DONAHUE," BishopAccountability.
[448] "Male Sexual Abuse Survivors Stand Together," *Oprah Winfrey Show*, November 5, 2010, https://www.oprah.com/oprahshow/male-sexual-abuse-survivors-stand-together/all; Clohessy, "Phil Donahue."
[449] Personal communication with the author.
[450] "Fact Sheet: Window Legislation," CHILD USA.
[451] Ian Richardson, "Sioux City Diocese Asks for Information on Children Victimized by Clergy," *Sioux City Journal* July 3, 2016, https://siouxcityjournal.com/news/sioux-city-diocese-asks-for-information-on-children-victimized-by-article_637c9fa3-991c-5272-8aad-8af79dac55f2.html.
[452] Tim Evans et al., "Former USA Gymnastics Doctor."
[453] "What Is the Connection between Media, Sexual Violence, and Systems of Oppression?" National Sexual Violence Resource Center (NSVRC), March 8, 2023, https://www.nsvrc.org/blogs/saam/what-connection-between-media-and-sexual-violence-and-systems-oppression.

454 Joseph P. Kahn and Mike Damiano, "They Knew and They Let It Happen': Uncovering Child Abuse in the Catholic Church," *Boston Globe*, Updated September 22, 2021, https://www.bostonglobe.com/2021/09/22/magazine/they-knew-they-let-it-happen-uncovering-child-abuse-catholic-church/.

455 "60 Minutes," "60 Rewind: Before *Spotlight*: 60 Minutes on Priest Sex Abuse," *CBS News*, https://www.cbsnews.com/news/before-spotlight-60-minutes-on-priest-sex-abuse/.

456 Ray Sanchez and Julian Cummings, "Former Penn State President Spanier Gets Jail Time in Sandusky Case," *CNN*, June 2, 2017, https://www.cnn.com/2017/06/02/us/penn-state-administrators-sentenced/index.html.

457 Sara Ganim, "Penn State Scandal: A Timeline of Events," *CNN*, November 10, 2011, https://www.cnn.com/2011/11/10/us/pennsylvania-penn-state-scandal-timeline/index.html.

458 Shawn Hubler et al., "U.S.C."

459 Hubler et al., "U.S.C."

460 Mark Alesia et al., "Larry Nassar's Downfall Started with an Email to IndyStar," *IndyStar*, December 7, 2017, https://www.indystar.com/story/news/2017/12/07/larry-nassars-downfall-started-email-indystar/922774001/.

461 Peter and Schad, "US to Pay $."

462 Smith and Pegoraro, "Media Framing."

463 Peter and Schad, "US to Pay," 8–10.

464 *Los Angeles Times* Staff, "Inside the 'Perversion Files.'"

465 "WATCH: McKayla Maroney Says FBI Made Up Statements She Never Said to Protect Larry Nassar," *PBS NewsHour*, September 15, 2021, https://www.youtube.com/watch?v=Vv1Wcq3zBm4.

466 Smith and Pegoraro, "Media Framing," 373–92.

467 Laurie Goodstein and Sharon Otterman, "Catholic Priests Abused 1,000 Children in Pennsylvania, Report Says," *The New York Times*, August 14, 2018, https://www.nytimes.com/2018/08/14/us/catholic-church-sex-abuse-pennsylvania.html.

468 "Reports of Attorneys General," BishopAccountability.

469 Contact author for information, August 2018.

470 Robert Downen et al., "20 years, 700 victims."

471 Nicole Chavez, "Texas Megachurch Faces Exodus of Worshippers After a Sex Abuse Scandal Set off a Summer of Turmoil," *CNN*, August 30, 2024, https://www.cnn.com/2024/08/29/us/gateway-church-scandal-texas/index.html.

472 "Reporting on Sexual Violence," Dart Center for Journalism and Trauma, July 15, 2011, https://dartcenter.org/content/reporting-on-sexual-violence#.VA8sM_ldXHs: The Dart Center is a project of the Columbia University Graduate School of Journalism and is a guide for reporters of sexual violence.

473 David Don Guttenplan, "The Media Monopoly Crisis," *The Nation*, December 11, 2023, https://www.thenation.com/article/society/media-consolidation-monopoly-big-5/.

474 Barlow, "Black Women."

475 Williams Institute, "LGBT People Nearly Four Times More Likely than Non-LGBT People to Be Victims of Violent Crime," UCLA School of Law, October 2, 2020, https://williamsinstitute.law.ucla.edu/press/ncvs-lgbt-violence-press-release/.
476 "Native Abuse," BishopAccountability; *Maze of Injustice, the Failure to Protect Native Women from Sexual Violence in the USA*, (Amnesty International, Spring 2008), https://www.amnestyusa.org/wp-content/uploads/2017/05/MazeOfInjustice_1yr.pdf; Sari Horwitz et al., "In the Name of God," *The Washington Post*, May 29, 2024, https://www.washingtonpost.com/investigations/interactive/2024/sexual-abuse-native-american-boarding-schools/: Important attention to Indian suffering at the hands of the Catholic Church.
477 Palumbo, "Seeing,"
478 "Lincoln Man Sentenced After Carrying on Sexual Relationship with 15-Year-Old Girl," KOLN TV, February 28, 2024, https://www.wowt.com/video/2024/02/29/lincoln-man-sentenced-after-carrying-sexual-relationship-with-15-year-old-girl/.
479 "Case by Case: News Coverage of Child Sexual Abuse," *Berkely Media Studies Group* May 19, 2011, https://www.bmsg.org/resources/publications/issue-19-case-by-case-news-coverage-of-child-sexual-abuse/.
480 "Sexual Violence: A Guide for Journalists," Minnesota Coalition Against Sexual Assault, 2017, https://yourcallmn.org/wp-content/uploads/2020/11/MNCASA_Media_Manual_2017.pdf: An updated guide for reporters of sexual violence.
481 Natalie Yahr, "Mandatory Reporting: What Journalists Get Wrong When They Cover Child Abuse, and How to Get it Right," Center for Journalism Ethics, May 17, 2021, https://ethics.journalism.wisc.edu/2021/05/17/mandatory-reporting-what-journalists-get-wrong-when-they-cover-child-abuse-and-how-to-get-it-right/.
482 Horwitz et al., "Name of God."
483 "News Platform Fact Sheet," Pew Research Center, November 15, 2023, https://www.pewresearch.org/journalism/fact-sheet/news-platform-fact-sheet/.
484 Siva Vaidhyanathan, "The New Nightmare Scenario for the Media," *Slate*, May 21, 2021, https://slate.com/business/2021/05/att-warnermedia-discovery-hbo-media-concentration-facebook-google.html.
485 Roxane Gay, *Not That Bad: Dispatches from Rape Culture* (New York: HarperCollins, 2018).
486 Jodi Kantor and Meghan Twohey, "Harvey Weinstein Paid Off Sexual Harassment Accusers for Decades," *The New York Times*, October 5, 2017, https://www.nytimes.com/2017/10/05/us/harvey-weinstein-harassment-allegations.html.
487 Farrow, "Aggressive Overtures."
488 Farrow, "Aggressive Overtures."
489 Dalvin Brown, "19 Million Tweets Later: A Look at #MeToo a Year After the Hashtag Went Viral," *USA Today*, October 13, 2018, https://www.usatoday.com/story/news/2018/10/13/metoo-impact-hashtag-made-online/1633570002/.
490 Debra Birnnbaum, "Alyssa Milano on #MeToo Campaign: 'I Wanted to Take the Focus Off the Predator,'" October 17, 2017, *Variety*, https://variety.com/2017/biz/news/metoo-alyssa-milano-harvey-weinstein-1202592308/.

[491] Janice Williams, "Harvey Weinstein Accusers: Over 80 Women Now Claim Producer Sexually Assaulted or Harassed Them," *Newsweek Magazine*, October 30, 2017, https://www.newsweek.com/harvey-weinstein-accusers-sexual-assault-harassment-696485.

[492] Anna North et al., "262 Celebrities, Politicians, CEOs, and Others Who Have Been Accused of Sexual Misconduct Since April 2017," *Vox*, updated July 16, 2021, https://www.vox.com/a/sexual-harassment-assault-allegations-list/.

[493] Jacey Fortin, "The Women Who Have Accused Harvey Weinstein," *The New York Times*, October 10, 2017, https://www.nytimes.com/2017/10/10/us/harvey-weinstein-accusations.html.

[494] Alyssa Edes and Mary Louise Kelly, "Arquette: After Rejecting Weinstein, 'I Had A Completely Different Career,'" *National Public Radio*: "All Things Considered," May 31, 2018, https://www.npr.org/2018/05/31/615911004/arquette-after-rejecting-weinstein-i-had-a-completely-different-career.

[495] Ryan Smith, "Rosanna Arquette Slams Weinstein's Attorney's 'Transactional Sex' Defense," *Newsweek*, October 26, 2022, https://www.newsweek.com/rosanna-arquette-slams-harvey-weinstein-defense-rape-trial-1754814; Janice Williams, "A Complete List of All the Women Accusing Harvey Weinstein, from Rose McGowan to Kate Beckinsale," *Newsweek*, October 12, 2017, https://www.newsweek.com/harvey-weinstein-sexual-harassment-assault-683675.

[496] Paula Cocozza, "Rosanna Arquette: 'They said I was a pain in the ass. It's not true,'" *Guardian*, August 26, 2019, https://www.theguardian.com/film/2019/aug/26/rosanna-arquette-they-said-i-was-a-pain-in-the-ass-its-not-true.

[497] Cocozza, "Rosanna."

[498] Farrow, "Aggressive Overtures."

[499] Farrow, "Aggressive Overtures."

[500] Kantor and Twohey, "Harvey Weinstein."

[501] Farrow, "Aggressive Overtures."

[502] Kantor and Twohey, "Harvey Weinstein."

[503] Beth Winegarner, "Weinstein Isn't the Only One: Screen Celebs Who Abuse Women or Children," *Medium*, April 15, 2017, https://bethwinegarner.medium.com/weinstein-isnt-the-only-one-screen-celebs-who-abuse-women-or-children-c5732e15cf92.

[504] me too. International, Inc. https://metoomvmt.org/.

[505] Ronan Farrow, *Catch and Kill* (Little, Brown and Company, 2019).

[506] Aaron Katersky and Peter Charalambous, "Timeline: Manhattan DA's Stormy Daniels Hush Money Case Against Donald Trump," *ABC News*, January 10, 2025, https://abcnews.go.com/Politics/timeline-manhattan-district-attorney-case-donald-trump/story?id=98389444.

[507] Stefan Becket, "Timeline: Donald Trump, Stormy Daniels and the $130,000 Payment to Buy Her Silence," *CBS News*, last updated April 15, 2024, https://www.cbsnews.com/news/donald-trump-stormy-daniels-indictment-investigation-timeline-manhattan-district-attorney/.

508 Associated Press, "Harvey Weinstein Will Return to Court for Hearing Ahead of Sex Crime Retrial," *The Guardian*, October 23, 2024, https://www.theguardian.com/world/2024/oct/23/harvey-weinstein-return-court-retrial: Uncertainty in the application of justice. "The former movie mogul was facing retrial on two sex crime charges after the state's highest court overturned his 2020 conviction earlier this year. Then in September, he was hit with a new charge accusing him of another assault. He has pleaded not guilty. Weinstein was convicted on charges that he forcibly performed oral sex on a TV and film production assistant in 2006, and rape in the third degree for an attack on an aspiring actor in 2013. In the new charge, prosecutors say he forced oral sex on a different woman in a Manhattan hotel in the spring of 2006." Weinstein also has a conviction in California, he remains in jail.

509 Aaron Katersky, "Harvey Weinstein Appears in Court Days before New Trial," *ABC News*, April 9, 2025, https://abcnews.go.com/US/harvey-weinstein-appears-court-days-new-trial/story?id=120646315.

510 Amy J. Binder and Jeffrey L. Kidder, *The Channels of Student Activism: How the Left and Right Are Winning (and Losing) in Campus Politics Today* (University of Chicago Press, 2022), 117–18; - Kathleen Doyle, "The Queen Mary Psalter," in *The Book by Design: The Remarkable Story of the World's Greatest Invention*, ed. P. J. M. Marks and Stephen Parkin (University of Chicago Press, 2023), 64; John J. Mearsheimer and Stephen M. Walt, *The Israel Lobby and U.S. Foreign Policy* (New York: Farrar, Straus and Giroux, 2007), 203.

511 Winegarner, "Weinstein."

512 Steel and Schmidt, "Bill O'Reilly."

513 Steel and Schmidt, "Bill O'Reilly."

514 Jodi Kantor and Megan Twohey, *She Said* (Penguin Random House, 2019), 22.

515 Winegarner, "Weinstein."

516 Gianna Melillo, "Five Years After It Took Off, Around Half of Americans Support the #MeToo Movement," *The Hill*, October 3, 2022, https://tinyurl.com/ywu9x3rf

517 Audrey Carlsen et al., "#MeToo Brought Down 201 Powerful Men. Nearly Half of Their Replacements Are Women," *The New York Times*, October 13, 2018, Updated October 29, 2018, https://www.nytimes.com/interactive/2018/10/23/us/metoo-replacements.html.

518 Carlsen et al., "Powerful Men."

519 Carlsen et al., "Powerful Men."

520 Gonzalez, "Study: "80 percent of sexual assaults go unreported."

521 Melillo, "Five Years."

522 The Editors of ProCon, "ProCon—Social Media: Is Social Media Good for Society?" *Britannica*, May 24, 2024, https://socialnetworking.procon.org/history-of-social-media/.

523 Facebook, Instagram, X (Twitter), WhatsApp, YouTube, TikTok and a dozen others.

524 See StandupSpeakup website for organizations. StandupSpeakup, https://standupspeakup.org/survivors-movement-emerges/.

[525] Mitch Smith and Anemona Hartocollis, "Michigan State's $500 Million for Nassar Victims Dwarfs Other Settlements," *The New York Times*, May 16, 2018, https://www.nytimes.com/2018/05/16/us/larry-nassar-michigan-state-settlement.html; Hubler et al., "U.S.C. Agrees to Pay."

[526] H.K. Wilson, "Jeff Anderson & Associates: From Pioneer to Powerhouse," *Attorney at Law*, June 4, 2021, https://attorneyatlawmagazine.com/stories/law-firm-feature/jeff-anderson-associates.

[527] Jeff Anderson, *Revealing the Truth: The First Clergy Abuse Lawsuit in America* (Jeff Anderson & Associates, 1983): This case marked a turning point in survivor advocacy, challenging institutional silence and setting legal precedents.

[528] Wilson, "Jeff Anderson."

[529] Dan Gilgoff, "One Lawyer Behind Many Allegations of Catholic Church Abuse," *CNN*, April 26, 2010, http://www.cnn.com/2010/US/04/26/church.abuse.victims.lawyer/index.html.

[530] Wilson, "Jeff Anderson."

[531] Chapter 9, "Media Sounds the Alarm," examines in-depth the *Spotlight* investigative series and popular movie—later adapted to the award-winning movie, *Spotlight*.

[532] Ronald Claiborne, "Mitchell Garabedian: The Lawyer Who Helped Expose the Boston Priest Scandal," BishopAccountability, May 23, 2023, https://www.bishop-accountability.org/2023/05/mitchell-garabedian-the-lawyer-who-helped-expose-the-boston-priest-scandal/.

[533] Claiborne, "Mitchell Garabedian."

[534] Claiborne, "Mitchell Garabedian."

[535] Ross Farrow, "Stockton Diocese Accused of Cover-up in Michael Kelly Case," Lodinews, April 13, 2012, https://www.lodinews.com/news/article_2cc84273-73fd-5ac3-9452-f1d6fe4902da.html.

[536] "Stockton Diocese Agrees To Pay $3.75 Million To Settle Sex Abuse Case," *CBS* Channel 13, April 20, 2012, https://www.cbsnews.com/sacramento/news/stockton-diocese-agrees-to-pay-3-75-million-to-settle-sex-abuse-case/.

[537] Timothy Lennon, "Why Did the Stockton Diocese Pay $3.75 Million to Settle Clergy Abuse of Children?" *The Bay Citizen*, April 22, 2012, https://www.bishop-accountability.org/news2012/03_04/2012_04_22_Lennon_WhyDid.htm.

[538] Jean Casarez et al., "Larry Nassar Victims Reach $380 Million Settlement with USA Gymnastics, US Olympic Committee and Insurers," *CNN*, December 13, 2021, https://www.cnn.com/2021/12/13/us/larry-nassar-gymnastics-settlement/index.html.

[539] Hubler et al., "U.S.C. Agrees to Pay."

[540] Richard Winton, "UC Pays Record $700 Million to Women Who Accused UCLA Gynecologist of Sexual Abuse," *LA Times*, May 24, 2022, https://www.latimes.com/california/story/2022-05-24/heaps-settlement-312-patients-takes-cost-of-his-abuse-to-700-million.

[541] Doha Madani, "USC Agrees to $1.1 Billion in Settlement with Hundreds of Women Alleging Abuse by Gynecologist," NCB, March 25, 2021, https://www.nbcnews.com/news/us-news/usc-agrees-1-1-billion-settlement-hundreds-women-alleging-abuse-n1262075.

542 United Nations Committee on the Rights of the Child, *Concluding Observations on the Second Periodic Report of the Holy See*, CRC/C/VAT/CO/2 (February 5, 2014), https://www.bishop-accountability.org/UN/CRC/2014_02_05_CRC_Concluding_Observations.pdf; UN Committee Against Torture: "Church Obstructing Justice for Clerical Child Abuse, Say UN Experts," Justice Info, November 17, 2021, https://www.justiceinfo.net/en/80002-church-obstructing-justice-for-clerical-child-abuse-say-un-experts.html; John R. Morss, "The International Legal Status of the Vatican/Holy See Complex," *European Journal of International Law* 26, no. 4 (2015): 927–46, https://academic.oup.com/ejil/article/26/4/927/2599610.

543 "Summary of the History of Rape Crisis Centers," Offices of Victims of Crime, Training and Technical Assistance, https://www.ovcttac.gov/downloads/SAACT/files/summ_of_history.pdf.

544 Polly Poskin, "A Brief History of the Anti-Rape Movement, Resource Sharing Project," Illinois Coalition Against Sexual Assault, October 2006, http://resourcesharingproject.org/wp-content/uploads/2021/11/History_of_the_Movement.pdf: "The anti-rape movement of the 1970s did not materialize from thin air."

545 See the Stand Up Speak Up website for listing: https://standupspeakup.org/survivors-movement-emerges/.

546 Rape Abuse Incest National Network (RAINN), https://rainn.org/.

547 Incest AWARE, https://www.incestaware.org/; Prompting Awareness, Victim Empowerment (PAVE), https://www.shatteringthesilence.org/.

548 A corollary development is the emergence of thousands of local and regional organizations, including tens of thousands of Facebook pages, Instagram posts, and Twitter accounts that are not included in this list.

549 Every organization and NGO begins with a unique mission addressing a specific sector, e.g., school, church, workplace, military, and sports. Early on, this mission focus sometimes limited its viewpoint, but over time solidarity and mutual support set the stage for a social movement.

550 There is an extensive review and analysis of the role of media in disclosing sexual abuse in chapter 9, "Media Sounds the Alarm."

551 "The Criminal Justice System: Statistics, (RAINN).

552 Thomas Doyle and Ray Mouton, "The Problem of Sexual Molestation by Roman Catholic Clergy: Meeting the Problem in a Comprehensive and Responsible Manner," BishopAccountability, 1985, https://www.bishop-accountability.org/reports/1985_06_09_Doyle_Manual/: The *first* challenge to the Catholic Clergy and Bishops about sexual abuse by clergy.

553 "Notes on the Manual," BishopAccountability, June 9, 1985, https://www.bishop-accountability.org/reports/1985_06_09_Doyle_Manual/notes.htm.

554 Canon Law is the legal system of the Catholic Church; Thomas Doyle, "Canon Law: What Is It?" February 2006, http://www.awrsipe.com/doyle/2006/2006-02-Canon_Law-What_Is_It.pdf.

555 Richard Sipe, "Celibacy, Sex & Catholic Church: Thomas Patrick Doyle," http://awrsipe.com/Doyle/index.html: Listing of significant articles by Thomas Doyle; Thomas Doyle, "Clergy Sexual Abuse: Bibliography of Selected Sources Related to Clergy Sexual Abuse, Ecclesiastical Politics, Theology, and Church History," June 20, 2021, http://awrsipe.com/Doyle/2021/Doyle-Bibliography-08-12-2021.pdf.

556 Voice of the Faithful, "Keep the Faith, Change the Church, 2025, https://www.votf.org/content/in-2022-voice-of-the-faithful-marks-20-years-of-keeping-the-faith-changing-the-church/.

557 BishopAccountability, https://www.bishop-accountability.org/.

558 "Voice for Clergy Accountability," Stop Baptist Predators, November 12, 2016, http://stopbaptistpredators.org/index.htm; Mennonite Abuse Prevention, "Home Page," April 16, 2024, https://mennoniteabuseprevention.org/; "BSA Perversion Files: List of Confirmed BSA Abusers," Abused in Scouting, n.d., https://abusedinscouting.com/list-of-confirmed-bsa-abusers/.

559 "Who We Are," BishopAccountability, Jan. 19, 2004, https://www.bishop-accountability.org/who-we-are/.

560 "Who We Are," BishopAccountability.

561 BishopAccountability.org: end-of-year email citing their support of civil authorities.

562 See chapter 8, "Privilege of Power and Complicit Institutions."

563 "A Documentary History of the Crisis—Timeline of Events, Documents, Reporting, and Commentary," BishopAccountability, last updated on September 12, 2007, https://www.bishop-accountability.org/AtAGlance/timeline.htm.

564 "Assignment History—Rev. Peter B. Murphy," BishopAccountability, March 4, 2016, https://www.bishop-accountability.org/assign/Murphy_Peter_B.htm.

565 "Abuse Tracker," BishopAccountability, May 15, 2025, https://www.bishop-accountability.org/category/news-archive/abusetracker/: Calendar of media reports of predators in Catholic Church.

566 Included in this list are 240 national advocacy organizations and a thousand local and regional organizations, including tens of thousands of Facebook pages, Instagram posts, Twitter, and social media accounts.

567 June Jordan, "Poem for South African Women" in *Directed by Desire: The Collected Poems of June Jordan, 2005* (Copper Canyon Press, 2005). Commemoration of the 40,000 women and children who, August 9, 1956, presented themselves in bodily protest against the "dompass" in the capital of apartheid. Presented at The United Nations, August 9, 1978.

568 Take Back the Night Foundation, https://takebackthenight.org/.

569 "Survivor's Movement," StandupSpeakup, https://standupspeakup.org/survivors-movement-emerges/: A working database of 240 survivor organizations, allies, and sister organizations, 2024.

570 "About Rain," RAINN, June 7, 2010, https://rainn.org/about-rainn.

571 "Rape, Abuse & Incest National Network," Wikipedia, last modified June 3, 2025, https://en.wikipedia.org/wiki/Rape,_Abuse_%26_Incest_National_Network.

572 "About RAINN," RAINN.

573 "Programs and Expertise," RAINN, December 23, 2016, https://rainn.org/programs-and-expertise.
574 "You Are Not Alone," me too., October 28, 2017, https://metoomvmt.org/.
575 "Vision & Theory of Change," me too. July 23, 2020, https://metoomvmt.org/get-to-know-us/vision-theory-of-change/.
576 "Our Mission," Survivors' Agenda, June 25, 2020, https://survivorsagenda.org/about-page/.
577 Darkness to Light, "Our Story," February 4, 2025, https://www.d2l.org/our story/.
578 "Home," Darkness to Light," May 20, 2025, https://www.d2l.org/ "Illumination and Prevention: Darkness to Light Reduces Stigma and Protects Children by Educating Adults," PIR, accessed June 6, 2025: Darkness to Light's Advocacy and Training Programs.
579 "Stewards of Children," Darkness to Light, May 22, 2017, https://www.d2l.org/training-catalog/stewards-of-children/.
580 "Reflecting on Our Impact in 2024," Darkness to Light, December 18, 2024, https://www.d2l.org/our-impact-2024/.
581 "Our Story," Darkness to Light, February 4, 2025, https://www.d2l25.org/our-story.
582 Talk Hong Kong, "Darkness to Light: Make Your Own Family Code of Conduct," July 27, 2020, https://www.talkhongkong.org/2020/07/darkness-to-light-make-your-own-family-code-of-conduct/.
583 "Prevent 360°: A Comprehensive Approach to Prevent Child Abuse," Monique Burr Foundation for Children, accessed June 6, 2025, https://mbfpreventioneducation.org/monique-burr-foundation-for-children-partners-with-darkness-to-light-launching-prevent-360-a-comprehensive-approach-to-prevent-child-abuse/.
584 "Honest Conversations," Darkness to Light, March 7, 2021, https://www.d2l.org/honest-conversations/.
585 "Prevent Now!" Darkness to Light, January 17, 2014, https://www.childsafehouse.org/wp-content/uploads/prevent-now.pdf.
586 "About Us," CHILD USA, October 23, 2024, https://childusa.org/about-us/.
587 Hamilton, *Justice Denied*.
588 "Current Laws for Child Protection," CHILD USA, December 6, 2016, https://childusa.org/law/.
589 "Contact Us," CHILD USA, September 4, 2016, https://childusa.org/about-us/.
590 Survivors Network of those Abused by Priests June 4, 2025, SNAP, https://www.snapnetwork.org/.
591 "Clergy Victims File International Criminal Court Complaint: Case Charges Vatican Officials with 'Crimes Against Humanity,'" Center for Constitutional Rights, September 13, 2011, https://ccrjustice.org/icc-vatican-prosecution.

592 "SNAP and CCR Livestream Report Back After the Holy See Review by the UN Committee on the Rights of the Child," Center for Constitutional Rights, January 16, 2014, https://ccrjustice.org/home/get-involved/events/snap-and-ccr-livestream-reportback-after-holy-see-review-un-committee; "The Vatican answers to the UN Committee Against Torture: CCR and SNAP Reportback," Center for Constitutional Rights, May 6, 2014, https://ccrjustice.org/home/get-involved/events/vatican-answers-un-committee-against-torture-ccr-and-snap-report-back.

593 "Support Groups," Survivors Network of those Abused by Priests, SNAP, September 20, 2011, https://www.snapnetwork.org/events.

594 "Victims of Sexual Violence, Statistics," Rape, Abuse & Incest National Network (RAINN), https://rainn.org/statistics/victims-sexual-violence.

595 "Scope," RAINNE

596 Childhelp Hotline, https://www.childhelphotline.org/. Live chat, phone call, or text available: 800-422-4453.

597 Childhelp Speak Up Be Safe, Childhelp, February 11, 2025, https://www.childhelp.org/speakupbesafe/.

598 "Home Page," Together for Girls, October 31, 2024, https://www.togetherforgirls.org/en.

599 "Home Page," Speak Out to Stop Child Sex Abuse, April 22, 2025, https://soscsa.org/; "Surviving Boy Scouts Child Sexual Abuse—SOSCSA" Survivor Scouting, February 18, 2024, https://survivingscouting.org/.

600 "Will You Help Protect Childhood Joy?" Thorn, July 13, 2018, https://www.thorn.org/.

601 "Safe Spaces of Healing," Empower Survivors, September 17, 2016, https://www.empowersurvivors.net/.

602 To find out more about Elizabeth Sullivan and Empower Survivors, see her YouTube channel, https://www.youtube.com/channel/UCH6z5SuGVIvMPL6uVjpwSrQ.

603 Rights4Girls, accessed June 11, 2025, https://www.facebook.com/rights4girls/: Their organization site is here: https://rights4girls.org/.

604 "Get the Latest Updates from NCMEC," National Center for Missing and Exploited Children, October 22, 2003, https://www.missingkids.org/home; "The CyberTipline Is the Place to Report Child Sexual Exploitation," National Center for Missing and Exploited Children, July 16, 2022, https://report.cybertip.org/

605 Promoting Awareness Victim Empowerment (PAVE), https://www.shatteringthesilence.org/; "Shattering the Red Zone," Promoting Awareness Victim Empowerment, August 15, 2023, https://www.shatteringthesilence.org/red-zone; "Arts for Awareness," Promoting Awareness Victim Empowerment, Accessed June 7, 2023, https://www.shatteringthesilence.org/blog/4z30ixillfbwwgfyya8ie5ebxxn5tx; "2025 Toolkit Teen Dating Violence Awareness & Prevention Month," Promoting Awareness Victim Empowerment, January 29, 2025, https://humanoptions.org/wp-content/uploads/2025/01/TDVAPM-2025-Toolkit.pdf; "Resources and Hotlines," Promoting Awareness Victim Empowerment, June 6, 2020, https://www.shatteringthesilence.org/hotlines: There are many hotlines listed here.

606 "You Are Not Alone," Survivors, May 1, 2025, https://www.survivors.org/; "Home—Helping Survivors," Survivors, November 14, 2019, https://www.survivors.org.

607 "Our Mission," Survivors Assault Advocacy Network, December 2, 2024, https://www.saancommunity.org/.

608 "Be the Change," Zero Abuse Project, September 3, 2023, https://zeroabuseproject.org/.

609 "About Jacob Wetterling Resource Center," Zero Abuse Project, February 10, 2020, https://zeroabuseproject.org/victim-assistance/jwrc/.

610 "Vision & Mission," Echo Training, October 15, 2021, https://www.echotraining.org/vision-mission/.

611 "Ending Clergy Abuse Global Justice Project" May 9, 2025, Ending Clergy Abuse https://www.ecaglobal.org/.

612 "Home," Godly Response to Abuse in Christian Environment, accessed June 7, 2025, https://www.netgrace.org/.

613 "For Parishes—About Us," Awake, May 7, 2024, https://www.awakecommunity.org/.

614 "Home," Mennonite Abuse Prevention, April 16, 2024, https://www.themaplist.org/.

615 "Mission Statement," Silent Lambs, August 20, 2020, https://silentlambs.org/.

616 "About Us," Female Composers Safety League, October 16, 2023, https://www.femalecomposersafetyleague.org/.

617 Jeff Anderson, "Nomi Abadi Speaks Out Against the Music Industry," July 20, 2023, Jeff Anderson and Associates PA, https://www.andersonadvocates.com/news/nomi-abadi-speaks-out-against-the-music-industry/.

618 "Home," Hire Hollywood Survivors, accessed June 7, 2025, https://hiresurvivorshollywood.org/.

619 Elizabeth Wagmeister, "After Weinstein Retaliation, Sarah Ann Masse Is Urging Hollywood to Work With Sexual Harassment Survivors," Variety, December 21, 2021, https://variety.com/2021/film/news/hire-survivors-hollywood-sarah-ann-masse-1235139743/.

620 "About," Maestra, March 15, 2020, https://maestramusic.org/about/; "Sexual Harassment Resources for Music Makers," Maestra, March 19, 2010, https://maestramusic.org/blog/sexual-harassment-resources-for-music-makers/.

621 End Rape on Campus, https://endrapeoncampus.org/.

622 "Home," Stop Educator Sexual Abuse Misconduct and Exploitation, January 22, 2023, https://www.sesamenet.org/.

623 "Join Our Mission," Protect All Children from Trafficking (PACT), Jun 23, 2023, https://www.wearepact.org/.

624 "Federal Criminals Records Relief," Polaris, October 21, 2022, https://polarisproject.org/.

625 "The National Human Trafficking Hotline," Polaris, January 15, 2020, https://polarisproject.org/national-human-trafficking-hotline/.

626 "Our Work," National Organization of Sisters of Color Ending Sexual Assault, August 5, 2008, https://sisterslead.org/ourwork/.

[627] "What We Do," Alianza Nacional de Campesinas, accessed June 7, 2025, https://www.alianzanacionaldecampesinas.org/.

[628] "The National Center on Violence Against Women," Ujima: The National Center on Violence Against Women in the Black Community, February 3, 2017, https://ujimacommunity.org/.

[629] "Our Practice: What We Do," National Organization of Asians and Pacific Islanders Ending Sexual Violence, October 18, 2019, https://www.napiesv.org/.

[630] "Resources," National Organization of Asians and Pacific Islanders Ending Sexual Violence, April 19, 2024, https://napiesv.org/resource/.

[631] "Resource Library: Missing and Murdered Indigenous Women" Native Hope, February 19, 2025, https://www.nativehope.org/missing-and-murdered-indigenous-women-mmiw.

[632] "Through Unity," Minnesota Indian Women's Sexual Assault Coalition, February 28, 2023, https://www.miwsac.org/.

[633] "Donate to SWIWC," Southwest Indigenous Women's Coalition, November 27, 2020, http://www.swiwc.org/.

[634] "Domestic and Sexual Violence Is Never Okay," StrongHearts Native Helpline, September 17, 2018, https://strongheartshelpline.org/.

[635] "About Male Survivor," Male Survivor, July 14, 2019, https://malesurvivor.org/.

[636] "The 1 in 6 Statistic," 1 in 6, December 16, 2018, https://1in6.org/.

[637] "Home," Protect Our Defenders, April 24, 2016, https://www.protectourdefenders.com/

[638] "About Us," Service Women Advocacy Project, accessed June 7, 2025, https://www.servicewomensactionnetwork.org/.

[639] "Home," Glass Soldier, June 4, 2024, https://www.glasssoldier.org/.

[640] "Our Values," Incest AWARE, April 11, 2024, https://www.incestaware.org/.

[641] "For Those in Other 12 Step Programs," Survivors of Incest Anonymous, January 2, 2020, https://siawso.org/.

[642] "M*OASIS: For People Supporting of Incest and Abuse," Mothers of Adult Survivors of Incest and Sexual Abuse, December 15, 2020, https://www.moasissupport.com/.

[643] 5Waves: Confronting and Healing Sibling Sexual Trauma, 5Waves, accessed June 7, 2025, https://www.5waves.org/.

[644] "Heal the Healers Fund," Joyful Heart Foundation, June 28, 2024, https://www.joyfulheartfoundation.org/programs/heal-healers-fund; End the Backlog, "Ending the Backlog of Unprocessed Rape Kits," Joyful Heart Foundation, March 24, 2020, https://www.joyfulheartfoundation.org/tags/end-backlog; "Our Story—Retreats for the Mind, Body, and Spirit," Joyful Heart Foundation, accessed June 7, 2025, https://www.joyfulheartfoundation.org/about-us/our-story.

[645] "Who We Are," Leila Grace Foundation, September 28, 2014, https://leilagrace-foundation.com/.

[646] "Child Sexual Abuse Is Preventable, Not Inevitable," Moore Center for the Prevention of Child Sexual Abuse, October 15, 2024, https://publichealth.jhu.edu/moore-center-for-the-prevention-of-child-sexual-abuse.

[647] "Healing Is a Human Right," Sanar Institute, June 17, 2022, https://sanar-institute.org/.

[648] "Values, Mission & History," Oak Foundation, March 15, 2018, https://oakfnd.org/.
[649] Marci Hamilton, "Prevent Child Sexual Abuse Programme / Partner story," March 19, 2024, https://oakfnd.org/reforming-statutes-of-limitations-justice-shouldnt-have-an-expiration-date/.
[650] "They Need You," A Breeze of Hope Foundation, March 11, 2021, https://abreezeofhope.org/.
[651] "Our Mission," Elizabeth Smart Foundation, April 14, 2020, https://www.elizabethsmartfoundation.org/our-mission.
[652] "Allies and Sister Organizations," Stand Up Speak Up, November 7, 2023, https://standupspeakup.org/survivors-movement-emerges/.
[653] "Directory of Organizations," National Sexual Violence Resource Center, March 13, 2009, https://www.nsvrc.org/organizations.
[654] "Our Team," Incest AWARE, October 20, 2020, https://www.incestaware.org/our-team.
[655] "Our Mission," SAAN.
[656] Suzanne Isaza, interview by Timothy Lennon, June 14, 2022:
[657] Keep Kids Safe, https://www.keep-kids-safe.org/ and Survivors' Agenda Initiative, https://survivorsagenda.org/ are two expressions of that emerging movement.
[658] For clarity and brevity, associations and alliances are included under coalition.
[659] "Promoting Federal Policies That," National Coalition for Child + Family Well-Being, accessed June 8, 2025, https://www.nccfwb.org/; "Members," National Coalition for Child + Family Well-Being, accessed June 8, 2025, https://www.nccfwb.org/members; "Policy Agenda," National Coalition for Child + Family Well-Being, Accessed June 8, 2025, https://www.nccfwb.org/policy-agenda.
[660] "Prevent Together," National Coalition to Prevent Child Sexual Abuse and Exploitation, March 18, 2021, http://www.preventtogether.org/.
[661] "Protect Kids Online," End Online Sexual Exploitation and Abuse of Children (OSEAC), March 22, 2025, https://endoseac.org/; "About: Members of the Coalition," End Online Sexual Exploitation and Abuse of Children, accessed June 7, 2025, https://endoseac.org/about/.
[662] "Home Page,' Alliance to End Slavery and Trafficking (ATEST), January 15, 2016, https://endslaveryandtrafficking.org/; "Who We Are," Alliance to End Slavery and Trafficking, November 15, 2024, https://endslaveryandtrafficking.org/who-we-are/.
[663] "Blog," Coalition to Abolish Slavery and Trafficking, Los Angles (CAST), May 20, 2020, https://www.castla.org/: "What We Do," Coalition to Abolish Slavery and Trafficking, accessed June 25, 2025, https://www.castla.org/what-we-do/.
[664] "Stand up for the Rights of all Women and Girls Everywhere," Coalition Against Trafficking in Women, accessed June 7, 2025, https://catwinternational.org/.
[665] "Who We Are," Coalition to Stop Violence Against Native Women, September 13, 2017, https://csvanw.org/.
[666] "Addressing Domestic And Sexual Violence In Indian Country And Alaska," Alliance of Tribal Coalitions to End Violence, accessed June 8, 2025, https://www.atcev.org/.

[667] "About Us: How We Started, " National Native American Boarding School Healing Coalition (NABS), July 21, 2017, https://boardingschoolhealing.org/; Olivia Waxman, "The History of Native American Boarding Schools Is Even More Complicated than a New Report Reveals," *TIME*, May 17, 2022, https://time.com/6177069/american-indian-boarding-schools-history/; The true scope of the crimes against Indian children in the United States has not yet been fully investigated and reported. Its horror approaches the documented crimes of abuse reported in Canada.

[668] "Home," National Organization of Asians and Pacific Islanders Ending Sexual Violence, August 27, 2019, http://www.napiesv.org/Monsoon Asians and Pacific Islanders in Solidarity, https://monsooniowa.org/.

[669] The cities are Philadelphia, PA; Washington, D.C.; Baltimore, MD; Chicago, IL; New York, NY; San Francisco, CA; Seattle, WA; Stillwater, MN; Phoenix, Groton, Norwich, CT; Richmond, VA; Los Angeles, CA; Lakewood, OH; Dubuque, IA; Seneca, SC; Louisville, KY; and Austin, TX; London, UK; Paris, France; Berlin, Germany; Toronto, Canada; Milan, Italy; Venice, Italy; Quito, Ecuador; Sydney, Australia; Kampala, Uganda; Warsaw, Poland; Vancouver, Canada; Osorno, Chile; Lausanne, Switzerland; Brussels, Belgium; and Helsinki, Finland.

[670] Coalition partners: The Army of Survivors, Childhelp, Darkness to Light, Together We Heal, Godly Response to Abuse in The Christian Environment, Joyful Heart Foundation, Ending Clergy Abuse, Empower Survivors, National Association of Adult Survivors of Child Abuse, Angel Heart Foundation, Stop Child Predators, and the Amends Project.

[671] Bob Allen, "'All Survivors Day' Piggybacks on All Saints' Day to raise awareness about sexual abuse," Baptist News Global, October 13, 2019, https://baptistnews.com/article/all-survivors-day-piggybacks-on-all-saints-day-to-raise-awareness-about-sexual-abuse/.

[672] Objectives: Shines a light on widespread sexual abuse and recognizes the scope of abuse, protects the vulnerable, and supports those harmed.

[673] "Welcome to the Keep Kids Safe Movement!" Keep Kids Safe, October 28, 2023, https://www.keepkidssafe.us/.

[674] "Keep Kids Safe Movement Launches Sweeping National Reform Blueprint," Monique Burr Foundation, https://mbfpreventioneducation.org/keep-kids-safe-national-blueprint-launch/.

[675] RAINN, www.rainn.org: The largest organization addressing sexual violence; SNAP, https://www.snapnetwork.org/: An international network of survivors supporting those harmed in religious communities; TAOS, https://www.thearmyofsurvivors.org: dedicated to ending sexual violence in sports; Together for Girls, https://www.togetherforgirls.org/: Works to end violence against children and adolescents; D2L works to prevent sexual violence, https://www.d2l.org/; CHILD USA, CHILDUSA.org: A nonprofit think tank for children devoted to ending child abuse and neglect; National Children's Alliance, https://www.nationalchildrensalliance.org/: Works to eradicate abuse and keep kids safe; Prevent Child Abuse America, https://preventchildabuse.org/: Works to prevent child abuse and neglect; Monique Burr Foundation for Children, https://mbfpreventioneducation.org/: Works to protect children from bullying, digital dangers, abuse, and exploitation.

676 "World Day for the Prevention of and Healing From Child Exploitation, Abuse, and Violence," United Nations, November 18, 2022, https://www.un.org/en/observances/child-sexual-exploitation-prevention-and-healing-day.
677 Senate Judiciary Committee U.S. Senate Judiciary Committee, "Durbin Meets with the Keep Kids Safe Coalition to Discuss Efforts to Protect Children from Exploitation," April 26, 2023, https://www.judiciary.senate.gov/press/dem/releases/durbin-meets-with-the-keep-kids-safe-coalition-to-discuss-efforts-to-protect-children-from-exploitation; "Keep Kids Safe," Darkness to Light, November 17, 2021, https://www.d2l.org/national-blueprint/; Together for Girls—Keep Kids Safe Movement Together for Girls, "Keep Kids Safe Movement," May 3, 2023, https://www.togetherforgirls.org/en/our-movements/keep-kids-safe.
678 "Read the Agenda," Survivors' Agenda, June 25, 2020, https://live-survivorsagendaorg.pantheonsite.io/agenda/; Jenna Ashendouek, "Survivors' Agenda Hosts Survivors' Summit September 24–26—With Anita Hill, Ayanna Pressley, Tarana Burke and More," Ms. Magazine, September 2, 2020, https://msmagazine.com/2020/09/02/survivors-agenda-metoo-leaders-amplify-voices-of-sexual-violence-survivors/.
679 "Our Mission," Survivors' Agenda: Forty-four community partners; "You Are Not Alone," "me too. International".
680 "Home," National Alliance to End Sexual Violence, accessed June 8, 2025, https://endsexualviolence.org/; National Alliance to End Sexual Violence (NAESV)," Safe Housing Partnerships accessed June 8, 2025, https://safehousingpartnerships.org/team/national-alliance-to-end-sexual-violence-naesv/.
681 "Home," National Center on Sexual Exploitation (NCOSE), February 26, 2022, https://endsexualexploitation.org/.
682 "The National Center on Sexual Exploitation," Ministry Watch, March 15, 2024, https://db.ministrywatch.com/ministry.php?ein=132608326.
683 "Sexual Violence Should Not Be a Part of the College Experience," Every Voice Coalition, June 17, 2020, https://www.everyvoicecoalition.org/.
684 "About: Overview," LinkedIn, accessed June 8, 2025, https://www.linkedin.com/company/everyvoicecoalition/about/.
685 "Survivors Movement," Stand Up Speak Up, accessed June 8, 2025, https://standupspeakup.org/survivors-movement-emerges.
686 "ME TOO. International's Social and Political Framework," me too., https://drive.google.com/file/d/1JvZpZgJ-fcy8FhBXXylWvE4-sKth9EeB/view.
687 Elena Ruíz et al., "Measuring the Economic Impact Of Covid-19 On Survivors of Color," me too., November 18, 2020, https://metoomvmt.org/wp-content/uploads/2020/11/MeTooFreeFrom_CovidImpactReport2020.pdf; "me too. Impact Report 2019," me too., January 20, 2020, https://metoomvmt.org/wp-content/uploads/2020/01/2019-12-09_MeToo_ImpactReport_VIEW_4.pdf;
688 The Global Network," me too. International, YouTube video, 53 sec., December 3, 2024, https://www.youtube.com/watch?v=R3NsjBV9qto.

[689] "Announcing 'me too.' Global," me too. International, me too. Movement, October 22, 2021, https://metoomvmt.org/global/; Stacy Jackson, "'Me too.' International Expands Its Reach With A Global Network To Fight Sexual Violence," Black Enterprise, September 19, 2024, https://www.blackenterprise.com/me-too-global-network-sexual-violence/.

[690] The Global Network," me too. International.

[691] "Together for Girls and The Brave Movement welcome the first-ever Global Ministerial Conference on Ending Violence Against Children Together for Girls," Together with Girls, May 15, 2024, https://www.togetherforgirls.org/en.

[692] "Survivors of Violence Against Children to Play Major Role in the First-Ever Global Ministerial Conference on the Issue," Brave Movement, August 5, 2024, https://www.bravemovement.org/press-releases/survivors-of-violence-against-children-to-play-major-role-in-the-first-ever-global-ministerial-conference-on-the-issue.

[693] CHILD GLOBAL is a project of CHILD USA; "Justice Unleashed: Ending Limitations, Protection Children," Brave Movement and Child Global, July 17, 2023, https://cdn.bravemovement.org/files/Justice-Unleashed-In-Europe.pdf.

[694] "Global Ministerial Conference on Ending Violence Against Children," End Violence Against Children Conference, https://endviolenceagainstchildrenconference.org/children-youth-survivors-and-csos/: The first time that all governments of the world will convene to commit to preventing violence against children: 1400 delegates, including representatives from 130 countries.

[695] "Survivors," Brave Movement.

[696] "Survivors," Brave Movement.

[697] "Survivors," Brave Movement.

[698] "A Vision To Zero: A Roadmap to Ending Childhood Sexual Violence," To Zero, January 2025, https://to-zero.org/our-vision/our-report.

[699] The age of majority refers to the age at which an individual will be legally considered an adult and subject to the full legal rights and responsibilities of an adult.

[700] The limitation for prosecution varied by state, some three years, some five years, some longer previous to 2000: See "SOL Rankings," CHILDUSA, https://childusa.org/sol-rankings/ and "2025 SOL Tracker," CHILD USA, https://childusa.org/2025-sol-tracker/ for detailed background on SOL laws.

[701] "Delayed Disclosure: CHILUSA 2024 Factsheet," CHILD USA, https://childusa.org/wp-content/uploads/2024/06/Delayed-Disclosure-2024.pdf.

[702] Ian Richardson and Stephen Gruber-Miller, "New Iowa Law Eliminates Statute of Limitations for Sex Crimes Committed Against Children," *Des Moines Register*, May 12, 2021, https://www.desmoinesregister.com/story/news/politics/2021/05/12/gov-kim-reynolds-new-iowa-law-statute-limitations-child-sex-crimes-abuse-human-trafficking/5062099001/.

[703] Other sectors also oppose SOL reforms: Boy Scouts, Mormons, athletic teams, etc.

[704] Brian Witte, "Maryland's Highest Court Upholds Ending Statute of Limitations on Child Sex Abuse Lawsuits," *ABC 7 News*, February 4, 2024, https://wjla.com/news/local/maryland-child-sex-abuse-baltimore-archdiocese-limitation-statute-legal-general-assembly-state-supreme-court-legislature-priests-abused-network-justice-trial-defendents

⁷⁰⁵ "2024 SOL Tracker," CHILD USA, https://childusa.org/2024sol/.
⁷⁰⁶ Mallory Simon and Erica Hill, "What These Victims Want the Pope to Know," *CNN*, August 23, 2018, https://www.cnn.com/2018/08/23/us/pennsylvania-abuse-victims-angry-at-pope/index.html.
⁷⁰⁷ "Child Sex Abuse Statute of Limitations Reform," CHILD USA, https://childusa.org/sol/.
⁷⁰⁸ Nancy Eve Cohen. "What Survivors, Advocates Know about Mass. AG's Inquiry into Child Sexual Abuse at Catholic Dioceses," New England Public Media/PBS/NPR, February 5, 2025, https://www.nepm.org/regional-news/2025-02-05/what-survivors-advocates-know-about-mass-ag-inquiry-into-child-sexul-abuse-at-catholic-dioceses.
⁷⁰⁹ Cohen, "What Survivors, Advocates Know."
⁷¹⁰ Hamilton, *Justice Denied*.
⁷¹¹ *40th Statewide Investigating Grand Jury REPORT 1 Interim—Redacted*, Grand Jury of Pennsylvania, 2018, https://www.attorneygeneral.gov/wp-content/uploads/2023/05/INVESTIGATING-GRAND-JURY-REPORT-NO.-1_FINAL_May-2023_Redacted.pdf.
⁷¹² *40th Statewide, Report 1*, Grand Jury.
⁷¹³ Deb Erdley, "Pennsylvania AG Shapiro: New information has surfaced since Catholic sex abuse report," Trib Live, September 27, 2018, https://triblive.com/local/westmoreland/14124858-74/pennsylvania-ag-shapiro-new-information-has-surfaced-since-catholic-sex-abuse-report: PA phones ringing off the hook—40 states AGs contact PA AG Shapiro
⁷¹⁴ Erdley, "Pennsylvania AG Shapiro."
⁷¹⁵ Ivey DeJesus, "Calls to Clergy Sex Abuse Hotline Continue to Surge," PennLive, August 22, 2018, https://www.pennlive.com/news/2018/08/calls_to_clergy_sex_abuse_hotl.html.
⁷¹⁶ (get Meltwater citation/report)
⁷¹⁷ "SNAP Calls for Action in Pennsylvania—Monday, Aug. 20th and Tuesday, Aug. 21st," SNAP, August 19, 2018, https://www.snapnetwork.org/snap_calls_for_action_in_pennsylvania.
⁷¹⁸ *Scranton Times-Tribune* Staff, "Abuse Survivors Group Discusses Diocese Grand Jury Report in Scranton," *Scranton Times-Tribune*, August 20, 2018, https://www.thetimes-tribune.com/2018/08/20/abuse-survivors-group-discusses-diocese-grand-jury-report-in-scranton/.
⁷¹⁹ "Survivors and Supporters Demand Investigations in Every State," SNAP, August 22, 2018, http://www.snapnetwork.org/survivors_and_supporters_urged_to_demand_investigations_in_every_state.
⁷²⁰ "Survivors," SNAP.
⁷²¹ "Reports of Attorneys General," BishopAccountability.
⁷²² *Report on Catholic Clergy—Child Sex Abuse in Illinois*, Office of the Illinois Attorney General (Chicago, IL: 2023), https://clergyreport.illinoisattorneygeneral.gov/download/report.pdf.
⁷²³ *Report*, Office of the Illinois Attorney General.

724 Jason DeRose, "Illinois Attorney General Finds Massive Cover-up of Clergy Sexual Abuse," *NPR*, May 23, 2023, https://www.npr.org/2023/05/23/1177773654/illinois-attorney-general-finds-massive-cover-up-of-clergy-sexual-abuse.

725 DeRose, "Illinois."

726 Beth LeBlanc, "Police Seize Misconduct Records from Michigan's Catholic Dioceses Michigan Raids," *The Detroit News*, October 3, 2018, https://www.detroitnews.com/story/news/religion/2018/10/03/police-serve-search-warrants-michigans-catholic-dioceses/1513938002/.

727 *Attorney General's Report on Child Sexual Abuse in the Archdiocese of Baltimore,* Office of the Attorney General (Baltimore, MD: September 2023), https://htv-prod-media.s3.amazonaws.com/files/aob-report-revised-redacted-interim-65131ba2b23b4.pdf.

728 Tommie Clark, "Survivors of Clergy Abuse Push for Results in AG Investigation into 2 Dioceses Serving Maryland," WBAL-TV, NBC-11, September 4, 2024, https://www.bishop-accountability.org/2024/09/survivors-of-clergy-abuse-push-for-results/.

729 Tarrant et al., "Missing and Incomplete."

730 "Survivors Do Not Believe that an Investigation Sponsored by the San Jose Diocese Will Be Completely Transparent," SNAP, September 14, 2018, https://www.snapnetwork.org/survivors_do_not_believe_that_an_investigation_sponsored_by_the_san_jose_diocese_will_be_completely_transparent.

731 Ruth Graham, "What the Latest Investigations into Catholic Church Sex Abuse Mean, about 20 State Attorneys General Have Mounted Investigations that Have Cataloged Decades of Abuse but Yielded Few Criminal Prosecutions," *The New York Times*, June 2, 2023, https://tinyurl.com/ybh4eedy.

732 "Active Investigations and Information Hotlines," SNAP, August 16, 2019, https://www.snapnetwork.org/ag_investigation_hotlines.

733 "Active Investigations," SNAP.

734 Timothy Lennon et al., "Demand for Investigation and Prosecution of High-level Officials in the Catholic Church for Widespread and Systemic Rape and Other Forms of Sexual Violence," letter, August 15, 2018, https://ccrjustice.org/sites/default/files/attach/2018/08/CCR%20SNAP%20ltr%20to%20DOJ%20w%20Exhibit%20Aug%2015%202018%20web%202.pdf.

735 Lennon et al., "Demand for Investigation."

736 Lennon et al., "Demand for Investigation."

737 "After PA Grand Jury Report, Survivors Renew Demand for Federal Investigation into Church Sexual Violence and Cover-Up," CCR and SNAP, August 15, 2018, https://ccrjustice.org/home/press-center/press-releases/after-pa-grand-jury-report-survivors-renew-demand-federal.

738 "Survivors Demand Federal Investigation into Church Sexual Violence and Cover-Up." SNAP, August 16, 2018, https://www.snapnetwork.org/after_pa_grand_jury_report_survivors_renew_demand_for_federal_investigation_into_church_sexual_violence_and_cover_up

739 Woodall and Kessler, "Feds."
740 Stankorb, "Southern Baptist Church."
741 Stankorb, "Southern Baptist Church."
742 Stankorb, "Southern Baptist Church."
743 Richer and Tucker, "Justice Department Watchdog."
744 Richer and Tucker, "Justice Department."
745 *Report of Investigation and Review of the FBI's Handling of Allegations of Sexual Abuse*, Department of Justice, Office of Inspector General July 14, 2021, https://oig.justice.gov/sites/default/files/2021-07/2021-07-14_0.pdf: by former USA Gymnastics Physician Lawrence Gerard Nassar.
746 *Report of Investigation*, Department of Justice.
747 "Victims of Crime Act," Rape, Abuse, Incest National Network (RAINN), June 7, 2016, https://www.rainn.org/articles/victims-crime-act.
748 "20 U.S.C. § 1092(f)—Institutional and Financial Assistance Information for Students," United States Code, 2015, https://www.govinfo.gov/app/details/USCODE-2015-title20/USCODE-2015-title20-chap28-subchapIV-partF-sec1092/summary.
749 "Clery Act Violators Number More than 300," Student Press Law Center, December 1, 2000, https://tinyurl.com/yvb7s7fk: The list of schools is available online at http://campussafety.org/publicpolicy/cleryact/violations.html.
750 David Jesse, "MSU Sets Record It Doesn't Want, Thanks to Nassar: Most Rapes Reported in One Year in Clery Report," *Detroit Free Press*, October 3, 2019, https://www.freep.com/story/news/education/2019/10/03/michigan-state-university-most-rapes-clery-report/3848219002/.
751 Jesse, "MSU."
752 Jesse, "MSU."
753 Tara Molina and Todd Feurer, "SNAP Asks Pope Leo XIV to Sign Cannon Law on Clergy Sex Abuse," CBS News, May 20, 2025, https://www.cbsnews.com/chicago/news/sexual-abuse-survivors-snap-allegations-pope-leo-xiv-peru/; SNAP v. the Pope, et al., Center for Constitutional Rights, August 18, 2018, https://ccrjustice.org/home/what-we-do/our-cases/snap-v-pope-et-al.
754 Lennon et al., "Demand for Investigation."
755 Lennon et al., "Demand for Investigation."
756 Mychael Schnell, "Bill Eliminating Statute of Limitations for Child Sex Abuse Civil Suits Heads to Biden's Desk," The Hill, September 13, 2022, https://thehill.com/homenews/house/3641319-bill-eliminating-statute-of-limitations-for-child-sex-abuse-civil-suits-heads-to-bidens-desk/; Gibson Dunn, "Biden Signs 'Speak Out Act' Limiting the Enforceability of Non-Disclosure and Non-Disparagement Clauses in Sexual Harassment Cases," December 9, 2022, https://www.gibsondunn.com/biden-signs-speak-out-act-limiting-the-enforceability-of-non-disclosure-and-non-disparagement-clauses-in-sexual-harassment-cases/.
757 "H.R.3355—103rd Congress (1993-1994): Violent Crime Control and Law Enforcement Act of 1994," Congress.gov., September 13, 1994. https://www.congress.gov/bill/103rd-congress/house-bill/3355.

758 "The 2022 Violence Against Women Act (VAWA) Reauthorization," Congressional Research Service, May 22, 2023, https://crsreports.congress.gov/product/pdf/R/R47570/2.
759 "VAWA Guide: Everything You Need to Know About VAWA," Gillman Immigration Law, January 29, 2024, https://gillmanimmigration.com/vawa-guide-everything-you-need-to-know-about-vawa/.
760 "All Info—S.4926—117th Congress (2021–2022): Respect for Child Survivors Act," Congress.gov., January 5, 2023, https://www.congress.gov/bill/117th-congress/senate-bill/4926/all-info.
761 "Respect for Child Survivors Act: Introduction to the New FBI MDT Law and What It Means for CACs," National Children's Alliance, February 29, 2020, https://learn.nationalchildrensalliance.org/products/respect-for-child-survivors-act-introduction-to-the-new-fbi-mdt-law-and-what-it-means-for-cacs: Link to law can be found at https://www.congress.gov/bill/117th-congress/senate-bill/4926/text.
762 Vargas, "US Archbishop."
763 Vargas, "US Archbishop."
764 Soma Biswas, "Bankruptcy Bill Would Weaken Protections for Organizations Facing Sex Abuse Claims," April 18, 2024, Deborah Ross, https://ross.house.gov/2024/4/bankruptcy-bill-would-weaken-protections-for-organizations-facing-sex-abuse-claims.
765 Dietrich Knauth, "US Boy Scouts Exits Chapter 11 Bankruptcy After Abuse Settlement," Reuters, April 19, 2023, https://www.reuters.com/legal/boy-scouts-emerges-chapter-11-bankruptcy-2023-04-19/.
766 Randi Love, "Lawmakers Seek Bankruptcy Law Changes for Child Sex Abuse Cases," Deborah Ross, April 18, 2024, https://ross.house.gov/2024/4/lawmakers-seek-bankruptcy-law-changes-for-child-sex-abuse-cases.
767 "Campus SaVE Act," RAINN, November 21, 2015, https://rainn.org/articles/campus-save-act.
768 "Since 2004, the Debbie Smith Act Has Been Helping to End the Backlog of Untested Rape Kits," RAINN, July 30, 2024, https://rainn.org/policy/debbie-smith-act.
769 Laurie Goodstein, "Abuse Victims Ask Court to Prosecute the Vatican," *The New York Times*, September 14, 2011, https://www.nytimes.com/2011/09/14/world/europe/14vatican.html?_r=1&hp.
770 Laurie Goodstein, "Hague Is Asked to Investigate Vatican Over Abuse," SNAP, September 13, 2011, https://www.snapnetwork.org/hague_is_asked_to_investigate_vatican_over_abuse.
771 Adam Klasfeld, "Priest-Abuse Victims Take Fight to The Hague," Court House News Service, September 13, 2011, https://www.courthousenews.com/priest-abuse-victims-take-fight-to-the-hague/#:~:text=MANHATTAN%20(CN)%20%2D%20A%20support,Vatican%20for%20crimes%20against%20humanity.
772 Klasfeld, "Priest-Abuse."

773 Laurie Goodstein, "Hague Court Declines Inquiry into Church Abuse Cover-Up," *The New York Times*, June 13, 2013, https://www.nytimes.com/2013/06/14/world/europe/hague-court-declines-inquiry-into-church-abuse-cover-up.html?_r=0.

774 "SNAP Legal Action," SNAP, June 6, 2025, https://www.snapnetwork.org/snap_legal_action: Landing page for all things related to the ICC complaint; "SNAP v. the Pope, et al., Center for Constitutional Rights": Timeline of complaints to ICC, UN Committee on the Rights of the Child, and the UN Committee on Torture.

775 Katherine Gallagher and Pam Spees, *Fighting for the Future, Adult Survivors Work to Protect Children & End the Culture of Clergy Sexual Abuse*, The Center for Constitutional Rights, (New York: February 2013), https://ccrjustice.org/sites/default/files/assets/SNAP%20Shadow%20Report%20to%20UN%20CRC.pdf.

776 "U.N. Expresses 'Deepest Concern' over Widespread Sexual Abuse by Clergy, Finding Vatican Failed to Protect Children," Center for Constitutional Rights, February 5, 2014, https://ccrjustice.org/home/press-center/press-releases/un-expresses-deepest-concern-over-widespread-sexual-abuse-clergy.

777 "Vatican Officials Questioned by Second UN Committee About Sexual Violence," Center for Constitutional Rights, May 5, 2014, https://ccrjustice.org/home/press-center/press-releases/vatican-officials-questioned-second-un-committee-about-sexual.

778 *Shadow Report: Prepared for 52nd Session of the UN Committee Against Torture in Connection with its Review of the Holy See*, Center for Constitutional Rights, April 2014, https://ccrjustice.org/sites/default/files/attach/2014/12/CCR_SNAP_Shadow_Report_apr2014.pdf.

779 press@ccrjustice.org, "Vatican Summoned to Report to UN Committee on Torture," Center for Constitutional Rights, April 14, 2014, https://ccrjustice.org/home/press-center/press-releases/vatican-summoned-report-un-committee-torture.

780 press@ccrjustice.org, "UN Committee Addresses Clergy Rape and Sexual Violence as Torture," Center for Constitutional Rights, May 23, 2014, https://ccrjustice.org/home/press-center/press-releases/un-committee-addresses-clergy-rape-and-sexual-violence-torture.

781 "United Nations Recommendations for Vatican Accountability for Sexual Violence in the Church," Center for Constitutional Rights, September 22, 2015, https://ccrjustice.org/UnitedNationsRecommendsVaticanAccountability.

782 Blaine stepped down as president of the SNAP Board in 2016 and passed away in 2017 due to a sudden injury. Many believe that her work helped save their lives—I do.

783 "Measuring Progress Towards a World Free of Child Sexual Violence," Out of the Shadows, September 19, 2022, https://outoftheshadows.global/.

784 "About the Global Index," Out of the Shadows, September 26, 2022, https://outoftheshadows.global/about-the-index.

785 "Global Index," Out of the Shadows.

786 "About the U.S. Pilot OOSI," Out of the Shadows, September 26, 2022, https://outoftheshadows.global/us-index-data.

[787] Tarana Burke, "Me Too Is a Movement, Not a Moment," TEDWomen 2018, 16.05 mins., November 2018, https://www.ted.com/talks/tarana_burke_me_too_is_a_movement_not_a_moment/transcript?language=en.
[788] Suzanne Isaza, interview by Timothy Lennon.
[789] Survivor's Movement is one name to call this new social movement. It can be called the Movement for Respect and Dignity, or another name. We are a Movement, no matter what the name is.
[790] "Child Sex Abuse Statute of Limitation Reform," CHILD USA, April 15, 2020, https://childusa.org/sol/: CHILD USA leads the SOL Reform Movement.
[791] "United States Child Marriage Problem: Study Findings (April 2021)" Unchained at Last, April 2021, https://www.unchainedatlast.org/united-states-child-marriage-problem-study-findings-april-2021/.
[792] Alaina Demopoulos, "'I Was Handed to a Complete Stranger': The Survivors Fighting to End Child Marriage in 37 US States—And the People Who Want to Keep It Legal," *The Guardian*, July 9, 2024, https://www.theguardian.com/society/article/2024/jul/09/child-marriage-laws.
[793] Marci Hamilton and Carina Nixon, *A National Overview of Child Marriage Data and Law*, CHILD USA, (Philadelphia, PA: March 14, 2024), https://childusa.org/wp-content/uploads/2024/03/FINAL-2023-CH-MARRIAGE-REPORT.pdf.
[794] Hamilton and Nixon, *Overview*.
[795] "The Criminal Justice System: Statistics," RAINN.
[796] Ruth Graham, "What the Latest Investigations into Catholic Church Sex Abuse Mean, about 20 State Attorneys General Have Mounted Investigations that Have Cataloged Decades of Abuse but Yielded Few Criminal Prosecutions," *The New York Times*, June 2, 2023, https://www.nytimes.com/2023/06/02/us/catholic-church-sex-abuse-investigations.html?fbclid=IwAR0c1LcJ9jpFiWfXgVJ-8JshRiKATNVfL0eOdosVtA1RYMM1JdNPhiE1poE.
[797] Deepa Bharath et al., "Report: Top Southern Baptists Stonewalled Sex Abuse Victims," AP News, May 23, 2022, https://apnews.com/article/baptist-religion-sexual-abuse-by-clergy-southern-convention-bfdbe64389790630488f854c3dae3fd5.
[798] See Bibliography, links to investigations by *Rolling Stone*, *The Washington Post*, AP News, *The New York Times*, *Variety*, *The New Yorker*, *Vice*, BBC, *The Guardian*, *Glamour*, *The Atlantic*, *Dallas Morning News*, *USA Today*, PennLive, *Detroit Free Press*, *Politico*, and dozens more.
[799] "Tech-Enabled Sexual Abuse," RAINN, March 16, 2025, https://rainn.org/education/online-sexual-abuse.
[800] "Tech-Enabled Sexual Abuse," RAINN.
[801] Luisa Blanchfield, *The United Nations Convention on the Rights of the Child*, Congressional Research Service, (Washington, DC: July 27, 2015), https://crsreports.congress.gov/product/pdf/R/R40484/25.
[802] Marge Piercy, *Circles on the Water: Selected Poems of Marge Piercy* (Knopf, 1982).
[803] Piercy, *Circles*.

ACKNOWLEDGMENTS

Family

My daughters, Fiona and Maya, have been my cheerleaders and supporters in countless ways over the past twenty-five years as I navigated the bumpy road of healing. Their unwavering support bolstered me along the path as I beat back the dark clouds of doubt and uncertainty in my writing journey. Like bright sunshine, they light my day and warm my heart.

I also want to acknowledge a loving Irish Catholic family of ten siblings, eight brothers and two sisters. They have walked with me on the path of justice and stood with me during all my challenges as a survivor over the last three decades. They have been my rock upon which I venture forward. Dan, Cathy, John, Mike, and Kelly made significant donations to ensure the publication of this book.

I honor the support I received from my ex, Lisa, who supported my healing with patience when memories first surfaced, and I suffered months of PTSD symptoms.

SNAP

When I came across a SNAP demonstration in front of the Cathedral in San Francisco in 1995, long-buried memories of child abuse emerged, hidden for the previous thirty-five years. That event sparked a journey of advocacy that continues to this day. SNAP leaders held my hand and lifted me out of the darkness.

When I first stepped forward as a victim, shaken and depressed by emerging buried memories, Terrie Light and Melanie Sakoda, SNAP leaders, were my first introduction to SNAP peer support groups in the San Francisco Bay Area. They helped me move from victim to survivor and survivor to advocate. Terrie and Melanie supported my healing, gave sage advice, and demonstrated spirited public activism.

The founder of SNAP, Barbara Blaine, who passed away in 2017, established SNAP in 1988, which now reaches around the world with tens of thousands of members. Her passion and vision in creating SNAP were the crucial elements of my healing. She lit a fire worldwide with her vision of peer support, which continues to shine brightly today with hundreds of local SNAP leaders throughout the USA and around the world. I would not be here without the support of the SNAP network and support groups. David Clohessy, the SNAP executive director for thirty years, inspired my public activism with his passionate advocacy. His leadership taught me the value of public advocacy; I learned to step forward and speak the truth publicly.

Snappers Here, There, Everywhere

During my thirty years of advocacy across the USA and worldwide, I had the great privilege of working with some amazing SNAP advocates and activists. Many have been mentioned in this book. Additionally, I would like to acknowledge the support of my Arizona SNAP co-leader, Vickie Jahaske. I also want to acknowledge the contributions of SNAP activists and leaders past and present who have been part of my healing: Phil Saviano, Mary Dispenza, Mary Caplan, Joey Piscitelli, Steve Theisen, Jeb Barrett, Judy Jones, David Lorenz, Peter Isley, Mark Crawford, Mary McKenna, Barbara Dorris, Christopher Longhurst from Aotearoa, New Zealand, and others. Please understand that this is a small list; there are hundreds more.

ACKNOWLEDGMENTS

Allies

I have been blessed to know and work with some amazing heroes who have become friends as we have collaborated over the decades. Not all were survivors; many were secular saints who recognized a problem and stepped in to support survivors and challenge the offenders. They could have stood aside when faced with violence in society, but these leaders stepped up to speak truth to power. I am so thankful for their advocacy and activism. I honor their contribution to our movement.

Those who lead that list are true heroes: Anne Barrett Doyle and Terry McKiernan from BishopAccountability. They have been warriors in the fight for justice and accountability since 2002. They have stormed the battlements of the Catholic Church's obstinance, obstruction, and obfuscation to expose the true scope of abuse in the church. Their courage breached the walls of systematic coverup, revealing the history of abuse and naming names. Their work has become a beacon for all victims: Here is the evidence—you are not alone. I am honored to be their friend.

Baptist leader Christa Brown and Mennonite leader Barbra Graber are leaders from religious communities who share the struggle for justice. For decades, these wonderful leaders have shown others the path forward with courage and determination.

A special shout-out is due to the advocacy of Tom Doyle, a Catholic Canon lawyer who first raised the issue of clergy abuse over three decades ago, in 1985. He is the very definition of the vanguard of our movement. He has supported survivors at every stage with his groundbreaking research, providing overwhelming evidence that highlights the church's failure to protect the vulnerable. His advocacy opened the door to the machinations of the Catholic hierarchy in covering up abuse. He has helped many. His research enriched much of this book.

Marci Hamilton, the dynamic founder of CHILD USA, continue to be at the forefront of advocacy for children's safety for two decades. She is a formidable champion who stands on the front line as an advocate with child abuse survivors, challenging the forces of darkness.

Attorneys have represented thousands of survivors with dignity, compassion, and heart. They are the champions of those harmed by sexual abuse. Three stand out for their spirited advocacy: Jeff Anderson of Minnesota, John Manly of Southern California, and Mitch Garabedian from Boston. There are dozens of attorneys deserving of praise. Here are a few of note: Tim Hale, Jeff Herman, Anthony DeMarco, Paul Mones, and Irwin Zalkin.

The media's reporting on sexual abuse in society took it from a local and individual problem to a national and society-wide problem. The reporter, Jason Berry from Louisiana, in the early 1980s, was the first to kick the issue into a national scandal. He exposed the cover-ups that the Catholic Church tried to hide, leading victims to understand they are not alone.

The *Boston Globe Spotlight* team in 2002 brought the problem of widespread sexual abuse in the Catholic Church to a nationwide audience. They exposed the scandal, naming names and holding the powerful accountable. All that had been hidden was exposed. That team of Michael Rezendes, Sacha Pfeiffer, Matt Carroll, and Walter "Robby" Robinson forever changed popular awareness of clergy sex abuse in the Catholic Church, not only in Boston but worldwide.

Readers

While writing this book, I benefited from the reviews, criticisms, and suggestions of about a dozen readers, including family, friends, Snappers, allies, and advocates. They pointed out the lacuna of discourse, challenged my assertions, and added context and background to the manuscript. They enriched my manuscript. I am so grateful for their contribution to this book!

Book Coach

Midway through the writing process, Robin Coleman helped me move from a collection of essays to developing a coherent book. He is an acquisition editor at Johns Hopkins University Press and the author coach of *Write Like an Expert,* a peer support group for writers. Robin provided sound counsel as I moved from an unformed manuscript, with a wealth of history, analysis, and facts, to becoming a book. He guided me in organizing the thicket of elements to plan, organize, and develop a book that provides history, heroes, and a call to action. And true to the definition, as my "author coach," he cheered me on when I faced challenges. If you are writing a nonfiction book, contact Robin.

In the beginning . . .

M. Maeve Eagan has been my editor since I began writing in 2021; I could not have published this book without her.

I enjoyed working with Maeve as my book editor and am grateful for her talent, creativity, and support. She was an outstanding editor, adviser, and guide who helped me develop coherence as I wrote about our growing Survivors Movement.

Her editorial expertise improved every sentence, paragraph, and chapter. Her extensive experience as a writer and ghostwriter provided a solid foundation for her professional guidance. Her support for the possibilities of my book encouraged me whenever I was challenged. I honor Maeve's contribution to completing my book; her contribution is valued and appreciated.

Maeve is a trauma-informed writing coach, collaborator, ghostwriter, and editor, as well as a host of writing workshops. I recommend her to other authors working on their manuscripts. Visit her website for more information: *Traumainformedwriter.com.*

INDEX

#
1 in 6, 185
5Waves, 187

A
Abadi, Nomi, 32–34, 39, 181
Acosta, Alexander, 125
Ailes, Rodger, 153
Alianza Nacional de Campesinas, 183
All Survivors Day, 14, 195–96, 234
Alliance of Tribal Coalitions to End Violence (ATCEV), 194
Alliance to End Slavery and Trafficking (ATEST), 193
American Medical Association (AMA), 101–2, 231
Anderson, Jeff, 159–60
Arizona, 14, 184
Arquette, Rosanna, 147, 149–50
Artificial Intelligence (AI), 231–32
Ashcroft, John, 211
Awake, 180

B
Baptists, 26–27, 87–94, 140, 167, 212–13, 231
Baselice, Arthur, 207
Benedict XVI, Pope, 220
Berkowitz, Scott, 172
Bernstein, Rachel Witlieb, 153
Berry, Jason, 19–20, 132–34, 144
Bevilacqua, Cardinal, 76
Biden, Joseph, 60, 80, 95–97
BishopAccountability (BA), 71, 75, 92, 119, 140, 166–68, 207–9
Black survivors. *See* people of color
Blaine, Barbara, 19–20, 132–33, 223–24
Blaire, Stephen Bishop, 161
Blasey Ford, Christine, 53–55, 80
Boston Globe exposé, 22, 59, 86, 92–93, 126, 133–38, 144, 160, 166–67, 210
Boy Scouts cases, 94–95, 117, 138, 143, 160, 167, 217–18, 225
Brave Movement, 201, 243
Brecht, Bertolt, 238
Breeze of Hope Foundation, 188
Brown, Christa, 26–27, 39, 87, 92–93, 212–13
Brown, Julie, 144
Brownmiller, Susan, 42, 104, 111, 130
Brunner, Lisa, 64
Burke, Tarana, 150–51, 173, 199–200, 225

C
California, 16–17, 80–81, 105, 118, 120, 137, 152, 161–63, 210, 226
Campus SaVE, 219
Carr, Lucien, 99
Castor, Bruce, 28
Catholic church: and abuse cover up, 5–13, 20–24, 56, 59, 71–91, 115–27, 132, 160–68, 209–18; power of, 23–24, 59–60, 126, 159, 163, 166, 204, 217; and the Pope, 14, 163, 207, 220
Catholic upbringing, 1–5, 62, 119–20
Center for Constitutional Rights (CCR), 217–22
Charbonneau-Dahlen, 122–23
Chicago, IL, 13, 19, 34
child abuse. *See* child welfare movement; childhood; molestation

303

CHILD GLOBAL, 201
Child Predators Act, 218
CHILD USA, 68–69, 135, 172, 174–75, 195, 229–30
child welfare movement, 101–4, 217–25, 230, 233–34, 239–40
Childhelp, 102–3, 176
childhood, 38, 100–104
civil rights movement, 100–109, 130–31, 159, 189, 204, 211, 234
Civil War era, 130
class privilege, 57, 60–64, 89–90, 99, 109, 119–26, 150
Clery Act, 214, 219
Clinton, Bill, 57
Clohessy, David, 9, 20–21, 93, 133–34
Coalition Against Trafficking in Women, 193
Coalition to Abolish Slavery and Trafficking (CASTLA), 193
Coalition to Stop Violence Against Native Women (CSVANW), 194
Cohen, Michael, 152
colleges/universities, 29–30, 48–49, 56–57, 110, 115–17, 136–39, 159, 162, 182, 187, 219–20
Committee for Equal Justice, 130
Constand, Andrea, 27–28, 36–37, 39
Cosby, Bill, 27–28, 85, 135, 152, 196
court cases. *See* lawsuits
coverups (general), 70–94, 116–17, 137, 233. *See also* Catholic church: coverup; family coverup
Covid-19 pandemic, 37, 200
Coyle, Jerome Father, 74–75
Cullen, Edward Bishop, 76

D

Daniels, Stormy, 152
Darkness to Light (D2L), 44–45, 68–69, 172–74
Darwin, Charles, 98
Davis, Shirley, 66

Debbie Smith Act, 219
DeFrancis, Vincent, 102
Denhollander, Rachael, 29–30, 39, 116–17, 137
Dershowitz, Alan, 125
Dhue, Laurie, 153
disabled victims, 65
Doerfler, John Francis Father, 76
Donahue, Phil, 133
Douglas, Gabby, 138
Dowd, Maureen, 116
Downen, Robert, 92
Doyle, Anne Barrett, 167
Doyle, Thomas Father, 165–66
Dunning, Dawn, 84
Durbin, Dick, 197

E

Echo Training, 179
Egan, Nicole Weisensee, 144
Elizabeth Smart Foundation, 189
Empower Survivors, 177–78
End Rape on Campus (EROC), 182
Ending Clergy Abuse (ECA), 179–80
Epstein, Jeffrey, 57–59, 125–27, 135, 213
Every Voice Coalition, 199

F

family coverups, 61–62, 66–67
family support, 10–12, 17. *See also* survivor support
Farrow, Ronan, 147, 151
Female Composer Safety League, 32–34, 181
Finaldi, Vince, 161
Finkelhor, David, 103
Firestone, Shulamith, 106
Five Waves. *See* 5Waves
Florida, 57, 125, 131
Fontaine, Mia, 40–41, 46
Francis-Smith, Michelle, 35–37
Friedman, Jaclyn, 39

G

Gallagher, Katherine, 215
Garabedian, Mitch, 159–62
gaslighting, 64–65, 77–82
Gauthe, Gilbert Father, 19, 132, 166
Gay, Roxane, 144
gender relations, 47–52, 57–60, 64, 95–101, 128, 177–78, 197
Geoghan, John Father, 160–61
Glass Soldier, 186
Godly Response to Abuse in Christian Environment (GRACE), 180
Gomez, Rebecca, 153
Goodmark, Leigh, 59–60
Greeley, Andrew Father, 133
Griffin, Susan, 112
Griffith, James, 50
grooming, 4, 35, 48, 66–67, 115–16
Guiterrez, Ambra Battilana, 147
gymnastics, 29–30, 48, 116–17, 132, 137–39, 162, 225

H

Hamilton, Marci, 113–15, 174–75, 195–96, 208
Haughton, Aaliyah Dana, 35
Havel, Thomas, 117–18
Hawkins, Tiffany, 35
Healing Circles, 37
healthcare costs, 43–45
Hecker, Lawrence, 23
Hesse, Monica, 96
Hill, Anita, 53, 64, 95, 120, 134
Hire Survivors Hollywood, 181
Hoffman, Bishop, 20
Holley, David, 21
Hollywood, 24, 28, 47, 72, 84–85, 118–21, 135, 147–56, 181–82. *See also* Harvey Weinstein
Hope, Healing, and Transformation, 37
Huddy, Juliet, 153
human rights, 46, 51, 178–84, 222–23, 233–34

I

Ianni, Becky, 140
Illinois, 13, 19, 34, 197, 209
immigrants, 46, 122
incarceration, 42
incest, 37–38, 40–41, 46, 66–67, 186–87
Incest AWARE, 38, 46, 165, 186, 190, 228
Indiana, 135–39
International Criminal Court (ICC), 220–21
internationalism, 220–22, 233–34, 243
Iorg, Jeff, 88
Iowa, 4–11, 70–75, 86, 113, 135, 206
Isaza, Suzanne, 38, 189–90, 228
Isley, Peter, 211
Iwu, Adama, 120

J

Jehovah's Witnesses, 143, 180–81
Jervis, Lisa, 61
Jesse, David, 214
Jessup-Anger, Jody, 110
Jones, Judy, 140
Jordan, June, 170
Joyful Heart Foundation, 187

K

Kantor, Jodi, 144, 147, 153
Kavanaugh, Brett, 53–55, 80
Keep Kids Safe (KKS), 196–97
Kelly, Michael Father, 161–62
Kelly, R., 34–35
Kempe, C. Henry, 102
Kessler, Brandie, 211
King, Martin Luther Jr., 204, 225
Klein, Ezra, 54–55
Klein, Sarah, 30–32, 39, 116–17
Ko, Mary P., 110
Koedt, Anne, 106
Kulwicki, Cara, 63
Kuran, Timur, 61
Kwiatkowski, Marisa, 144
Kwiatkowski, Ronan Farrow, 144

L

Lanning, Ken, 114
Latinx victims, 46, 65, 110
Law, Bernard Francis Cardinal, 21–22, 31, 161
lawsuits, 13, 21, 28, 56–60, 73, 81–86, 104–5, 112, 117, 123–30, 152–53, 158–59, 205–6, 225
Leila Grace Foundation, 187–88
LGBTQ+ population, 46, 64, 109, 141, 174, 227, 231
Light, Terri, 6
Ligiero, Daniela, 201
Lopez, Elise, 110
Louisiana, 23, 132, 166, 217–18

M

Machcinski, Anthony J., 115
MacKay, Sarah, 121–22
Madigan, Lisa, 209
Maestra, 181
Mahony, Roger, 56
male supremacy. *See* patriarchy
Male Survivor, 185
male victims, 51, 128–29, 185. *See also* molestation
Malone, Richard J. Bishop, 75
Manly, John, 30, 56, 89, 137, 159–62, 213
Maroney, McKayla, 30, 138–39
Martinez, Lizzette, 34–35
Marx, Reinhard, 75–76
Maryland, 206–7, 210
Massachusetts. *See* Boston Globe exposé
Masse, Sarah Ann, 181
matriarchy, 98–100
McDougal, Karen, 152
McFadden, George B. Father, 2
McGowan, Rose, 147
McGuire, Danielle, 106, 109, 130–31
McKiernan, Terry, 167, 207–8
McSally, Martha, 50
Me Too Movement, 18, 23, 28–38, 54, 61, 135, 145–57, 164, 172–73, 195–200, 226, 243

media exposure, 22–39, 54–60, 75, 92–93, 116–17, 121, 126–55, 188, 196, 209–12, vi. *See also* Me Too Movement
Mennonite Abuse Prevention (MAP), 180
Mennonites, 167, 180
Michigan, 29, 76, 116–17, 126, 137–38, 209–10, 214. *See also* gymnastics; Larry Nassar
Milano, Alyssa, 147–48
military, 50–51, 185–86
Miller, Chanel, 56
Minnesota, 142, 159, 184
Minnesota Indian Women's Sexual Assault Coalition (MIWSAC), 184
Mintz, Steven, 101
Missing and Murdered Indigenous Women USA, 184
Missouri, 210
Mitchell, Rachel, 53
Mohammed, Farahnaz, 115
molestation: effects of, 4, 9, 11–13, 18, 33, 42–52, 61, 68–70, 103; history of, 40, 100–104, 130–31; widespread occurrences of, 24, 27, 39–42, 51–52, 120, 217
Moonves, Les, 152
Moore Center for the Prevention of Child Sexual Abuse, 188
Mormon church, 88–89, 123–24
Mothers of Adult Survivors of Incest and Sexual Abuse (M*OASIS), 187
Mouton, Ray, 165–66
Mueller, Joseph M. Bishop, 3, 8, 12–13
Mukhopadhyay, Samhita, 109, 130
Murphy, Peter B. Father, 1–7, 67, 77, 135, 168; arrival at parish, 4; death of, 8; and parish transfers, 3–5, 71
music/musicians, 32–35, 181, 202–3
Myer, John, 102

N

Nassar, Larry, 29–31, 49, 116–17, 126, 135–39, 159, 196, 213–14
National Alliance to End Sexual Violence (NAESV), 198
National Catholic Worker Movement, 20
National Center for Missing & Exploited Children (NCMEC), 178
National Center on Sexual Exploitation (NCOSE), 199
National Coalition Against Sexual Assault, 108
National Coalition for Child + Family Well-Being, 192
National Coalition to Prevent Child Sexual Abuse and Exploitation, 192
National Organization of Asians and Pacific Islanders Ending Sexual Violence, 184, 195
National Sexual Violence Resource Center (NSVRC), 64–65, 109–10, 136, 189
Native Americans, 64–65, 98–99, 110, 122–24, 143, 184–85, 194
Nebraska, 135
New York, 121–22, 152
Nickless, Ralph W. Bishop, 10–11, 71, 86
non-disclosure agreements (NDAs), 21, 59–60, 74, 85–89, 127, 153
North Dakota, 206

O

O'Brien, Susan, 74–75
O'Connor, Lauren, 121
O'Connor, Siobhan, 75
O'Reilly, Bill, 59, 85, 89–90, 153
Oak Foundation, 188
Ohio, 49, 116
Olivine, Ashley, 62
Online Sexual Exploitation and Abuse of Children (OSEAC), 192–93
Out of the Shadows, 224–25

P

Parks, Rosa, 129–31, 234
Paterno, Joe, 137
patriarchy, 41, 52–57, 64–65, 89, 95–114, 120–21, 154, 227; and chauvinism, 47, 52–54, 95–96, 105–7
Patterson, Paige, 92
Pecker, David, 151–52
Pennsylvania, 23–28, 68, 72, 76, 85, 115–16, 136–40, 196, 207–12, 215
people of color, 46, 58, 64–65, 108–10, 122, 128–31, 183–84, 194–95, 200, 241
Perry, Tyler, 128–29
Persky, Michael, 56–57
Peterson, Michael R. Rev., 165–66
Piercy, Marge, 236, 240
Pittman, Dave, 93
Polaris, 182–83
police negligence, 64, 126, 138–39, 213–15
politics, 41–42, 50, 53, 95–96, 156, 197, 206, 215–16, 230–33
predators: characteristics of, 3–4, 24, 113–20, 125; and data bases, 71, 75, 118–19
Promoting Awareness Victim Empowerment (PAVE), 165, 178
Protect All Children from Trafficking (PACT), 182
Protect Our Defenders (POD), 185–86
Pucci, Francis, 115
Punk Rock Therapist, 34

R

race privilege, 57–65, 104–5, 109, 125, 129–31
race/racism, 46, 48, 57, 64–65, 96, 104–5, 108–11, 122, 129, 130–31
Racketeer Influenced and Corrupt Organizations (RICO), 214
Raisman, Aly, 138
Raoul, Kwame, 209

rape, 27–72, 99, 104, 107–12, 122–25, 140, 152, 163–64, 170–77, 222
Rape Prevention and Education (RPE), 108
Rape, Abuse, Incest National Network (RAINN), 37–38, 41, 43–44, 58, 63, 68, 164, 172–73, 176, 218–19, 232
Reade, Tara, 80
Reed, Evelyn, 99
reporting. See stigma of reporting
Representation Project, 34
resources, 71, 75, 163–201, 216–17, 243–44
Respect for Child Survivors Act, 217
Rezendes, Mike, 22
Rights4Girls, 177–78
Riley, Miles O'Brien Father, 80–81
Russell, Diana, 120

S

Sakoda, Melanie, 118
Sanar Institute, 188
Sandusky, Jerry, 49, 68, 115–16, 136–37
Saviano, Phil, 5, 21–22
Schmidt, Michael, 153
Service Women Action Network (SWAN), 186
sexual abuse. See incest; molestation; rape
Sexual Assault Advocacy Network (SAAN), 178–79
Shapiro, Josh, 208
Shulman, Alix Kates, 107
Silence Breakers, 39, 151–54
Silent Lambs, 180–81
Simpson, Alan, 95
Sisters of Color Ending Sexual Assault (SCESA), 183
slavery, 130
Sommers, Kirby, 144
South Dakota, 122–23
Southern Baptist Conference (SBC), 26–27, 87–94, 213

SouthWest Indigenous Women's Coalition (SWIWC), 184
Speak Out Act, 60, 89, 215–16
Speak Out to Stop Child Sex Abuse (SOSCSA), 177
Specter, Arlen, 64
Spees, Pamela C., 215, 220–22
sports, 29–30, 48–49, 68, 108, 115–17, 135–38, 162, 232
StandUpSpeakUp.org, 14, 189
Stankorb, Sarah, 91–92, 212
Starr, Kenneth, 125
statistics, 13, 24, 40–59, 63–69, 109–10, 115, 120, 126, 142, 176
statute of limitations (SOL), 121, 174, 188, 201–7, 214–16, 229–30
Steel, Emily, 153
Stemple, Lara, 51
stigma of reporting, 42–46, 53–70, 90–91, 108, 121, 131, 140–42
Stockholm Syndrome, 62
Stop Educator Sexual Abuse (SESAME), 182
Strauss, Richard, 49, 116
Strong Hearts Native Helpline, 185
Sullivan, Elizabeth, 177
Sunstein, Cass, 61
survivor support: and emerging activism, 22–26, 100–13, 132, 145, 154–56, 164; and organizations, 26–27, 108, 141, 163–65, 171–205
Survivors Network of those Abused by Priests (SNAP), 5–18, 75, 87, 114, 119, 133–34, 172, 175, 195, 204, 208–26; and network, 20, 123, 132–34, 139–40, 164–65, 175–76, 204, 234; origins of, 19–20, 132–34, 164–65, 175
Survivors of Incest Anonymous (SIA), 186
Survivors' Agenda, 173, 197–98

T

Tails, Toni, 68–69
Take Back the Night (TBTN), 108, 170–71
Taylor, Chellee, 93
Taylor, Recy, 129–31
terminology, 140–43, 146, 230–31
Texas, 26, 126, 140, 210
The National Native American Boarding School Healing Coalition (NABS), 194–95
therapy, 11–12, 36–37, 43, 180
Thomas, Clarence, 53, 64, 95
Thorn, 177
To Zero, 202
Toback, James, 121–22, 152
Together for Girls, 176–77, 201
Trump, Donald, 54–55, 57, 125, 151–52
Turner, Brock, 56–57, 125
Twohey, Megan, 144, 147, 153
Tyndall, George, 159, 162

U

UBUNTU, 39
Ujima, 183–84
UNICEF, 201
United Nations (UN), 163, 197, 201, 211, 221–22, 228–29, 233–34, 243
Utah, 143

V

Valenti, Jessica, 39
Vance, Cyrus Jr., 152
Victims of Crime Act (1984), 108
Violence Against Women Act (VAWA) (1994), 108, 216

W

Wahl, David W., 77
Warren, Chet Rev., 19–20
Weinstein, Harvey, 59, 84–85, 121, 135, 147–55. *See also* Me Too Movement
Welliver, Sarah, 143
Wetterling, Jacob, 179
Whyatt, Robin, 123
WhyIDidntReport, 54–62, 69
Wiehl, Lis, 153
Winfrey, Oprah, 128–29, 133, 136
Wolk, Robert, 115
women predators, 51–52
women/women's rights, 46–49, 57–59, 95–12, 120–21, 129–31, 147–51, 163–94, 204, 216, 228, 234
Woodall, Candy, 211
World Health Organization (WHO), 201
World War II era, 100–101

Z

Zero Abuse Project, 179, 185
Zirwas, George, 115
Zula, Richard, 115

Tim Lennon, a survivor of childhood sexual abuse by a Catholic priest, has been an activist and advocate, supporting survivors for over three decades. He has volunteered with SNAP, one of the largest survivor support organizations in the world, since 1995. Tim worked as a volunteer at the national office from 2010 to 2018, during which time he corresponded with thousands of victims. He has served on the SNAP Board of Directors for twelve years and as president for three years.

He twice traveled to Rome as the leader of the SNAP delegation to challenge the Vatican on its failure to protect the vulnerable and remove accused predators from ministry. Tim continues his volunteer work as co-leader of the Arizona SNAP peer support group, which he has led for the past nine years, meeting twice a month.

His book, *Stand Up Speak Up—How Survivors Created a Movement to End Sexual Violence,* documents the emerging movement of survivors, who have created hundreds of national organizations in the past twenty-five years, forming the core of the Survivors Movement. His book celebrates the courage of survivors who bravely step forward to support others, challenge the powerful, and build a movement based on justice, respect, and dignity. His book offers a comprehensive account of the history, challenges, and successes of this new social movement, providing affirmation, validation, and support. He continues to fight for a safer world for all survivors.

www.ingramcontent.com/pod-product-compliance
Lightning Source LLC
Chambersburg PA
CBHW020533030426
42337CB00013B/829